EATING RIGHT TO LIVE SOBER

EATING RIGHT TO LIVE SOBER

KATHERINE KETCHAM

L. ANN MUELLER, M.D.

Madrona Publishers Seattle 1983

Published by Madrona Publishers, Inc.
P.O. Box 22667
Seattle, Washington 98122

10 9 8 7 6 5 4 3

Library of Congress Cataloging in Publication Data
Ketcham, Katherine, 1949-
Eating right to live sober.
Bibliography: p.
Includes index.
1. Alcoholism—Nutritional aspects. 2. Alcoholism—Diet therapy—Recipes.
I. Mueller, L. Ann, 1942- . II. Title.
RC565.K43 1983 616.86'1 83-16274
ISBN 0-914842-97-8

To our husbands,

DWIGHT MUELLER
and
PATRICK SPENCER

Foreword

WHEN Dorris Hutchinson and I founded the Alcenas Hospital program in 1970, we were aware that a great number of recovering alcoholics suffer the effects of severe and widespread nutritional deficiencies and imbalances. A.A. often refers to them as "dry but not sober," or as having a "white-knuckle" sobriety. There was an extensive and rapidly-expanding literature on the special functions and health benefits of all of the known vitamins and minerals. However, there were only scattered references to the special nutritional needs of alcoholics, and little evidence of clinical validation. Megavitamin therapy was in vogue during that time, but there was disturbing evidence that massive doses of any one or a few vitamins could aggravate or even cause serious deficiencies in others. Clearly, scientific knowledge and medical skill were needed to guide diagnosis and nutritional therapy with alcoholic patients.

Unfortunately, the medical profession had misclassified alcoholism as a psychiatric disorder, and very few physicians in the other branches of medicine had had any opportunity to learn either to diagnose or to treat alcoholism as a disease. Furthermore, then as now the nutritional education of most physicians was limited to the importance of some of the B vitamins in alleviating the more advanced pathologies of alcoholism, such as Wernicke's disease. It was clear that popular need and enthusiasm had far outrun professional competence or interest in either alcoholism or nutrition.

Meanwhile, as Executive Director of Alcenas, Mrs. Hutchison had created a treatment milieu that implied nutritional therapy, and we had sick alcoholics to care for. We felt we had to act in their behalf. But how? We were indeed fortunate to find Dr. L. Ann Mueller, who had formerly worked with heroin addicts and who had an open mind, a keen interest in working with alcoholics, and, with some reservations and a measure of skepticism, a willingness to learn to do nutritional therapy with our alcoholic patients. In April of 1973 she accepted the assignment of Medical Director of Alcenas Hospital. Lacking formal training in nutritional therapy, she first made a critical, discriminating review of the relevant literature on both alcoholism and nutrition, and then set about her clinical task. Within months her skepticism disappeared as she saw dramatic improvement in some patients and significant improvement in the patient population as a whole. They recovered faster and to a higher level of well-being. Even alcoholics with long-standing, severe psychological problems, who had been misdiagnosed as manic depressives or schizophrenics, normalized and stablized under her enlightened therapy.

As a pioneer in the field, Dr. Mueller has kept a watchful eye on both the alcoholism and the nutrition literatures, winnowing the wheat from the chaff and further validating the sounder portions in her practice. More recently, as Medical Director of the Milam Recovery Centers, Dr. Mueller, after a decade of this specialized practice, is now sharing her disciplined fund of knowledge with the public in *Eating Right to Live Sober.*

Katherine Ketcham has once again demonstrated her extraordinary ability to assimilate and organize an enormous amount of complicated information and to present it to the reader in clear, uncomplicated language. Everyone who understands alcoholism as a disease, as fully explained in *Under the Influence* (Milam and Ketcham), also needs to know what to do about it. Here is a valid core material to build on . How fortunate that now the reading public can acquire this basic information so painlessly, even pleasurably!

The most urgent need is to get the book into the hands of alcoholics, their family members, their physicians, their therapists, their employers, their attorneys, their insurance carriers, their nutritionists, and everyone else who is directly concerned. Physicians and other therapists in the field will find this book an essential reference and guide to alcoholism diagnosis and treatment. Alcoholism educators will find it a vital companion to *Under the Influence* in their core curriculum. For researchers it will provide a much-needed territorial map.

In short, *Eating Right to Live Sober* will be quickly recognized as a pivotal book at this turning point in the history of alcoholism.

James R. Milam, Ph.D.
Author, Lecturer
Cofounder, Professional Director of
Milam Recovery Centers, Inc.

Acknowledgments

THIS book could not have been conceived or written without the firm theoretical foundation established by James R. Milam, Ph.D., our friend and mentor. Dr. Milam's research and brilliant insight was first set forth in his book *The Emergent Comprehensive Concept of Alcoholism* and later expanded in *Under the Influence: A Guide to the Myths and Realities of Alcoholism.* His work has literally revolutionized the field of alcoholism, changing the way we think about alcoholics and the way we treat them.

Most theories gather dust on textbook shelves; Milam's concept of alcoholism was fortunate to find a convert in Dorris Hutchison, whose astounding energy and unshakable optimism led to the founding of Alcenas Hospital in Kirkland, Washington. More than anyone else, she is responsible for proving that the concept worked.

Several friends and colleagues, all of whom have made outstanding contributions to the fields of nutrition and alcoholism, gave us valuable comments and criticism on the manuscript of this book. Our thanks and gratitude to Sandra Counts, M.D., Robert Morgan, M.S.W., Carol Sinape, C.R.N.-Nurse Practitioner, and Mildred Price, R.N. Nutritionist Edward Chang helped develop the actual structure and content of the diet, and we gratefully acknowledge his work as a foundation for the meal and diet plans in Chapter 7.

Finally, we owe a debt of thanks to our families who have listened, counseled, commiserated, endured, and in countless other ways contributed to this book.

TO THE READER

The case histories in this book are based on the experiences of real people, but names and some distinguishing details have been changed.

When discussing alcoholics in general terms, we've used the word "they" whenever possible. At times, however, we've used the pronoun *he*. This is for simplicity and ease of reading: alcoholism, like most diseases, has no sexual preferences.

Contents

PART THREE
The Diet

PART ONE

The Disorders

1

The Dry Drunk: An Introduction

"WHITE-knuckle sobriety" some people call it; others call it "dry but not sober." Whatever the label, it is a painful and dangerous sobriety. The dry drunk is like an itch that can't be scratched, a wound that won't heal, a craving that can't be satisfied, a misery without a cure. Periods of despair and depression alternate with feelings of guilt and shame; and the craving to drink builds until it becomes an agony that seems to top even the miseries of drinking.

Any recovering alcoholic who is having that much trouble hanging on might at any time let go and seek relief. Alcohol provides exquisite relief, and every alcoholic knows it. But for a terrible price; alcoholics know that, too. For some—for too many—living the continuing agonies of the dry drunk seems worse than the remembered misery of drinking, and the battle to stay sober is lost. Others struggle through sobriety, believing that nothing can be done to relieve the persistent and nagging headaches, mood swings, anxiety, irritability, and insomnia. While they may never consider drinking again, their daily lives are often difficult and uncomfortable, and sometimes almost unbearable.

Sobriety does not need to be torture. A recovering alcoholic should not have to suffer continually. The dry drunk need not be waged like a never-ending battle against the urge to drink. The craving for alcohol, the mood swings, the fatigue, anxiety, depression, and irritability that so many thousands of recovering alcoholics suffer to one degree or another can be eliminated—wiped out—through careful attention to nutrition: eating the right foods in the right amounts and avoiding those foods that upset the body's chemistry, weakening mental and physical health.

Most recovering alcoholics have no idea that their diet can contribute to a relapse. The most common mistake they make is to load up on sweets, which work quickly and effectively to get rid of fatigue, depression, the mid-morning blahs, and even the craving for alcohol; but sweets contain a hidden time bomb that can transform the immediate relief into long-term discomfort and even agony. For alcoholics, sweets can actually be deadly, weakening sobriety to the point where the alcoholic is no longer able to fight the urge to drink—no matter how much he may want to stay sober. A recovering alcoholic who frequently skips meals, gives in to a craving for candy bars, glazed doughnuts, and root beers when he needs a lift, and drinks four or five cups of coffee spiked with sugar every day, is playing fast and loose—however ignorantly—not only with his sobriety but with his life.

THE CASE OF NANCY S.

Nancy S. had been sober for one year, seven months, and three days. That was a long time, longer than she had ever thought she could make it. She went to Alcoholics Anonymous meetings twice a week and, although a shy person, she forced herself to be an active participant and soon became known as one of the most steadfast members of the group.

Nancy's husband and three daughters were delighted with her recovery and made a point of telling her how proud they were of her. Not everything was perfect, though, and sometimes Nancy complained of depression, headaches, nervousness, or exhaustion. Her husband recognized these symptoms from the drinking days and anxiously held his breath for a few days until she felt better. Afterward, the family talked about the bad days, coming to the conclusion that Nancy would always have rough times and that they must all try hard to help her through them. One solution, they believed, was to keep the refrigerator packed with Nancy's favorite food, chocolate-chip ice cream. She was crazy about ice cream, eating it for dessert after lunch and dinner and claiming that it did wonders for her tension and depression and gave her a temporary lift.

Just before her two-year "birthday" party at A.A., the day marking her second year of sobriety, Nancy started drinking again. Her husband had stayed up late that night to finish some pressing business, and when he came to bed he found her passed out on the floor with an empty vodka bottle. He rushed her to the hospital and several days later she was transferred to a private treatment center. The counselor in charge spent hours with Nancy, helping her to analyze and understand the tensions and anxieties that apparently contributed to her relapse. "Why," Nancy wondered during and after these sessions, "do I always have to ruin everything? Why am I so weak?"

When Nancy returned home after treatment, she told her husband that something had just snapped inside her, and she wasn't able to fight the urge to drink. She repeatedly told him how sorry she was and begged his forgiveness; he assured her that he loved her and wanted only to see her happy and healthy. Together they went through the weeks leading up to the drinking episode, trying to uncover the hidden tensions that might have caused her to start drinking again. Her daughter was living with a man they had never met; the A.A. birthday party might have proved too big a strain. They'd been invited to several cocktail parties during the upcoming holiday season; perhaps she was nervous and depressed about not being able to join in and drink like everyone else. After discussing all the possibilities, they agreed to cut down on their social life to see if that would help.

It worked for almost a year. But the tensions built, the headaches got worse, the moodiness increased. She'd been through it before, but this was the last time. Nancy swallowed a bottle of sleeping pills along with the next bottle of vodka. She was in a coma for eight days before she died.

DRY BUT NOT SOBER

Nancy and her family thought they had tried everything. What went wrong? Was Nancy too weak; did she lack the will power to stay away from alcohol? Was the addiction too strong, the depression too persistent? Was the accumulation of tensions and stresses simply too much for her?

What finally defeated Nancy? One of the answers is, simply and astonishingly, her diet: her ice cream habit, the doughnuts and coffee she gulped down at every A.A. meeting, the periodic fasts she went on when she feared she was gaining weight. Although two years sober, Nancy was still sick, still under the influence of her addiction to alcohol. She wasn't drinking, but her poor eating habits prevented her body's cells from getting the help they needed to repair themselves and strengthen their defenses. Heavy loads of sugar and caffeine kept her blood sugar unstable, and she wasn't eating enough good, nutritious foods to make up for the damage that had been done during the many years of heavy drinking. Her diet, in other words, muddled her brain, fed her depression, increased her desire for alcohol, and made her sobriety hell.

Nancy's attendance at A.A. meetings was the one steady foundation in her desire and ability to stay sober as long as she did. But even A.A. couldn't help her fight the persistent depression and anxiety that seemed to come from nowhere and had no relationship to the events in her life, or the craving for alcohol that never seemed to leave her alone. She was dry, but she never stopped thirsting for alcohol because the heavy doses of sugar she ate every day upset her body chemistry, causing her to feel tense, anxious, depressed, and moody. The quick rise in blood sugar followed by the inevitable steep drop worked to increase her desire for more sugar. And more sugar, while giving her some immediate relief, increasingly caused mental and physical agony, producing a net result that felt eerily like withdrawal from alcohol.

In fact, the blood-sugar roller coaster that held Nancy captive caused symptoms that were startlingly like those she had experienced during alcohol withdrawal. And alcohol, of course, provided the perfect remedy for these symptoms because it immediately raised Nancy's blood sugar and temporarily relieved her depression, anxiety, and mood swings. Sugar, then, held Nancy prisoner to her addiction to alcohol, and she never stopped craving the one substance that had always worked to make her feel better fast—alcohol.

Nancy never suspected her eating habits were actually making her feel worse, not better. She thought that abstinence was the only requirement for sobriety. Not one of her physicians or therapists had ever mentioned the word *nutrition* or suggested that she watch her intake of sweets or caffeine. Her continuing craving for alcohol was, she believed, her cross to bear, part of the disease that would always plague her. She attributed it to personal weakness, and to her inability to live without a chemical crutch.

But Nancy had completed only part of her recovery. She had stopped drinking, the essential first step, and she became involved in A.A., which introduced her to a deeper sense of spirituality, meaningful relationships, and a forum for enriching her life, all of which fueled her desire and motivation to stay sober. But she had not taken care of another, crucial part of getting well: making sure that she ate nutritious foods. This neglect was from ignorance, for she did not understand the biochemical nature of her addiction, and she had never been taught how to protect herself against it.

Many recovering alcoholics are suffering, like Nancy, and many are in danger of relapse—not because they are weak or fooling themselves about their disease, but because their eating habits contribute to their mental and physical complaints. These alcoholics can be spared much mental and physical suffering if they avoid those foods that play havoc with their blood-sugar chemistry and concentrate instead on eating the right foods. Proper nutrition might, in fact, save their lives.

RESEARCH AND CLINICAL EXPERIENCE

The power of nutritious food and vitamin and mineral supplements to promote healing and health in recovering alcoholics is supported both by research and clinical experience. The research solidly links diet to mental as well as physical health, and the ever-growing evidence points clearly to the connection that what we eat directly influences how we think and feel. (The highlights of nutrition and alcoholism research are discussed throughout this book, but for a more comprehensive look at nutritional theory and research, we encourage the reader to consult the suggested reading list.)

While research in nutrition has provided invaluable

information about how specific nutrients work in the body, contributing to health and fighting disease, real-life experiences visibly demonstrate that when good nutrition is conscientiously practiced, recovering alcoholics can benefit enormously. Many alcoholics have recovered without it, as evidenced by thousands whose sole guidance has come through A.A. or other nonmedical support systems. But many others who have not received nutritional therapy have suffered needless agonies of prolonged biochemical and nutritional disturbances. And many continue to seek counseling for symptoms that are simply nutritional in origin, often endangering themselves by taking prescription pills such as tranquilizers, sedatives, and antidepressants. Nutritional therapy, on the other hand, strengthens the groundwork for recovery upon which a sane and sound sobriety can be built.

The clinical experiences related throughout this book paint a dramatic picture of the power of nutritional therapy to stabilize and change alcoholics' lives, to transform sick, confused, and suicidally depressed alcoholics into people who are confident, healthy, and strong in spirit. This is such a dramatic experience for some people that they describe it as a "miracle"—doctors, nurses, and the alcoholic's family can see the transformation, but the alcoholic himself actually witnesses the miracle of having his life restored, its meaning renewed.

The scientific literature regarding nutritional therapy for alcoholics and the clinical experiences and observations described in the remaining chapters provide a direct challenge to professionals to learn more about the physiological processes at work. That the great majority of alcoholics suffer from varying degrees of both malnutrition and unstable blood-sugar chemistry is not hypothesis but fact, and the dramatic improvement in physical and mental health when nutritional therapy is applied confirms the growing scientific evidence. But more work needs to be done to increase our understanding of the precise mechanisms underlying addiction to alcohol and alcohol's effect on blood-sugar levels and the nutritional status of the alcoholic. The potential effect of such research on how alcoholics are treated—and how they recover—is enormous.

While the professionals who work with recovering alcoholics and the researchers who are studying the disease of alcoholism may be enlightened and challenged by the information presented in this book, the primary goal is to provide a foundation of knowledge and give nutritional guidance to the recovering alcoholic—that is, the alcoholic who is not drinking and who is committed to staying sober. This guidance can increase the alcoholic's chances of staying sober and greatly enhance the quality of his sobriety.

THE SEQUENCE OF CARE

Nutrition cannot work miracles all by itself, however. No one claims that all a recovering alcoholic has to do is eat nutritious foods and take vitamin pills so that, within a few days or weeks, happiness and health will be forever his. Recovery from alcoholism must involve a sequence of care of which nutritional therapy is only a part—although an essential and crucial part. While this sequence of care is not as easy as A, B, and C, it is as orderly: A must come first, B second, and C third.

A. ABSTINENCE: Alcohol is the primary enemy and as long as the alcoholic continues to drink, *nothing* can restore him to health.

B. BODY HEALING: After the alcoholic stops drinking, his body requires time to heal. This is where nutritional therapy goes to work, helping the ravaged organs—the brain, liver, stomach, and other internal organs—to stabilize and strengthen their defenses. While the need for good nutrition is particularly strong in the first days and weeks of recovery, alcoholics must continue to watch their diet throughout their lives. Good nutrition will enhance the quality of sobriety and greatly reduce the risk of relapse.

C. COUNSELING: Alcoholics need to understand their disease, and they need help putting their disordered lives together—help in reconstructing marriages, jobs, and living successful, sober lives. This is where counseling is so valuable in treatment, but it must come at the right time. Counselors can talk their hearts out to a drinking alcoholic or an alcoholic still sick and shaky from withdrawal, but the words will get lost in the haze of his brain. Not until the alcoholic is able to think clearly and rationally—somewhere between the second and third week of sobriety, depending on how sick he is—can he begin to understand the nature of his disease and learn what he must do to return his life to normal and maintain his health and sobriety.

Recovery from alcoholism must involve *every* aspect of the alcoholic's mental and physical being. Alcoholism is a fierce and tenacious disease, devious in its methods, insidious in its onset, and pervasive in its effects on the body, mind, and even the soul. But its hold on the alcoholic can be broken, cleanly and forever. The goal throughout this book is to give the recovering alcoholic the information and knowledge he needs to protect himself against his disease and free himself from its power.

2
Alcoholism

Who has woe? Who has sorrow?
Who has contentions? Who has complaining?
Who has wounds without cause?
Who has redness of eyes?
Those who linger long over wine,
Those who go to taste mixed . . . . . wine.
Do not look on the wine when it is red.
When it sparkles in the cup.
When it goes down smoothly;
At the last it bites like a serpent,
And stings like a viper.
Your eyes will see strange things,
And your mind will utter perverse things.
And you will be like one who lies down in the middle of the sea,
Or like one who lies down on the top of the mast.
"They struck me, but I did not become ill;
They beat me, but I did not know it.
When shall I awake?
I will seek another drink."

Proverbs 23:29–35
New American Standard Bible

WHY ME?

Alcoholics, finally forced to recognize and admit that alcohol is destroying them and that they'll never be able to drink in control, often ask "Why me?" "Why," they wonder, "do I have this reaction to alcohol when just about everyone else can drink as much and as often as they please?"

Every alcoholic asks himself this question at some point during recovery, and every alcoholic comes up with a slightly different answer. One alcoholic may believe that the answer lies in his unhappy childhood; another may fix the blame on his difficult and demanding children; others single out feelings of frustration or depression, career pressures, unhappy marriages, repressive social climates, or insensitive political systems. Some alcoholics believe the answer is physiological: an allergy, perhaps, or a genetic weakness.

"Why me?" is a question that has also haunted researchers and social theorists trying to make sense of the bewildering array of physical and psychological symptoms evident in alcoholism. In times past, alcoholism has been seen as a weakness of will—alcoholics, it was assumed, have the same appetite for alcohol as other people, but they lack the will power to stop drinking. Research conducted in the last twenty years strongly indicates, however, that alcoholics have the same will power as everyone else, but their appetite is somehow different; and this appetite for alcohol is determined by physical factors over which the alcoholic has no control. Alcoholism is caused not by social, environmental, or psychological pressures or by a weak personality, but by a weakness in the physical makeup of the drinker. In other words, alcoholics don't abuse alcohol—alcohol abuses them.

This concept of alcoholism is directly at odds with the traditionally accepted theory that alcoholism is caused by psychological and/or social factors. The evidence supporting this concept of alcoholism as a physiological disease is summarized below, but for a more comprehensive and detailed look at the facts and the specific controversies involved in alcoholism theory and treatment, we refer the reader to *Under the Influence* by James Milam and Katherine Ketcham.

THE HIDDEN STAGE

Like all chronic illnesses, alcoholism begins in a hidden stage when the victim is unaware that anything unusual is going on inside him. During this stage alcohol works certain changes in the cells, laying down the groundwork for the massive damage that occurs later. Despite these cellular changes, the alcoholic does not yet act like an alcoholic. He does not necessarily drink heavily or even regularly and does not suffer from withdrawal symptoms such as shakiness, nervousness, anxiety, nausea or depression. The hidden-stage alcoholic is, to all outward appearances, normal. His doctor would probably give him a clean bill of health. He has no reason to complain and no cause to believe he should quit drinking.

A person in the first stages of heart disease suffers the same illusion of good health. He doesn't feel sick, his yearly check-ups show nothing abnormal, he has no clue that the cells in his heart are weakening. As the damage progresses, his blood pressure may rise or his cholesterol count may be high, but he does not appear to have a degenerative disease —until the day he suffers a heart attack. But, of course, his disease didn't begin with the massive eruption of damage; it began months or years before, when his cells were undergoing changes that could not be detected but that nevertheless initiated a lethal disease process.

Like the victim of heart disease, the alcoholic in the early stage of his disease experiences undetectable changes in his cells, changes that will eventually cause his body to adapt to alcohol. The cells are actually adjusting themselves to the presence of alcohol and becoming more efficient at using it as an energy source. These adjustments, or adaptations, gradually allow the cells to work smoothly and efficiently even when alcohol is present in the body in large quantities. Thus, as the alcoholic's body adapts, he will drink more and more often and suffer both mentally and physically when he stops drinking.

THE TELL-TALE MITOCHONDRIA

This adaptation process can be seen in the liver mitochondria of alcoholics. The mitochondria are tiny, pod-shaped structures within each cell whose primary responsibility is to release energy from food. In alcoholics and, significantly, even in early-stage alcoholics, the liver mitochondria are noticeably altered: While normal mitochondria are round with clearly defined outer walls and inner structures, in alcoholics the walls stretch, becoming enlarged and misshapen, and the inner structurcs arc visibly distorted.

With these changes in cell structure, the liver is able to process alcohol more efficiently, and the alcoholic is able to drink increasingly large amounts of alcohol and still function normally. His tolerance, in other words, is increasing, and he is able to "handle" a lot of alcohol without becoming noticeably intoxicated. This ability to drink a lot without getting obviously drunk works against early recognition of the disease, for the alcoholic will think to himself, and be able to convince others, that "I'll never be an alcoholic; look how I can hold my liquor—I can drink everyone else under the table!"

But after a while—it could be several months or several years—other symptoms become obvious. The alcoholic may be unable to stop once he starts drinking, and he may experience the morning-after shakes or a queasy stomach, or wake up in a sweat after a restless night. These problems get worse as the drinking continues. He may begin to suffer from blackouts, when he loses all or parts of his memory of what happened during a drinking bout; his personality may change as he becomes easily irritated or angered, and withdraws into himself; or he may become paranoid and hypersensitive to common noises such as a ringing telephone or doorbell.

These increasingly uncomfortable and odd reactions are actually withdrawal symptoms, and they indicate that something has gone wrong inside the body. A look at the mitochondria graphically confirms the damage inside the cells. Electron micrographs of chronic alcoholics' liver cells show a devastating battleground: the mitochondria are scattered haphazardly, some grotesquely misshapen, others with gaping holes in their membranes. Some cells are white and vacant, bled dry of everything inside. The adaptations that occurred in the early stage of alcoholism, allowing the alcoholic to drink large amounts of alcohol, have sabotaged the health of the liver, as well as that of the entire body; and the damage gets worse as the alcoholic continues to drink.

AN INVOLUNTARY SUICIDE

Why do the mitochondria, which like every living thing are geared to survival, allow themselves to embark on an essentially suicidal course by accepting alcohol in increasingly large amounts? It appears that they have no choice. Charles Lieber, M. D., chief of the research program on liver disease and nutrition at the Bronx Veterans Administration Hospital, discovered that the liver mitochondria in alcoholics are unable to process alcohol normally, even in the early stages of alcoholism. This foul-up in processing allows the poisonous byproduct of alcohol—acetaldehyde—to build up in the cell, causing a great deal of damage.

Comparison of Mitochondria in a Control Baboon and an Alcohol-fed Baboon

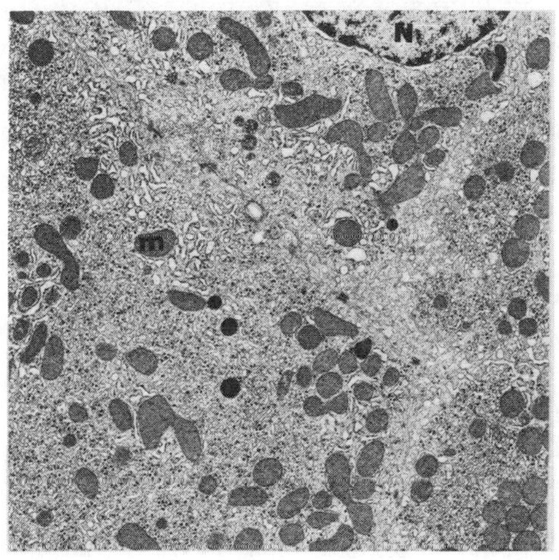

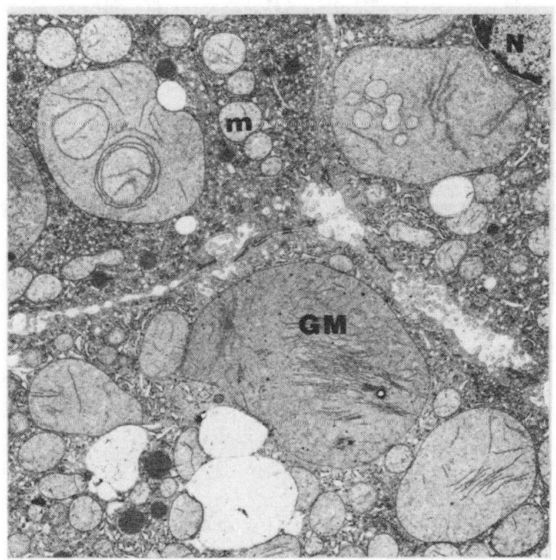

These electromicrographs provide dramatic evidence of the difference between the mitochondria of a control baboon (top) and an alcohol-fed baboon (bottom). N = nucleus; m = normal-size mitochondria; GM = giant mitochondria. Magnification: 11,600 times.

The electromicrographs were obtained by M.A. Leo, Assistant Professor of Medicine, Mount Sinai School of Medicine, in a study of alcohol-fed baboons directed by Dr. C.S. Lieber, Professor of Medicine and Pathology at the school and Director, Alcohol Research & Treatment Center, Bronx VA Medical Center. Photos courtesy Dr. Lieber.

In the liver, Lieber believes, a vicious cycle may be created: the high levels of acetaldehyde disturb the intricate activities of the cell, making it even more difficult for the cells to get rid of the poisonous acetaldehyde which, in turn, results in further damage to the cells. The more the alcoholic drinks and the more often he drinks, the worse the damage becomes.

In the brain, alcohol and acetaldehyde disrupt electrical and chemical signals, in part by competing with normal chemical substances that organize brain messages and regulate brain activity. Some of these normal brain chemicals (*neurotransmitters*) keep the brain from being too excited and hyperactive, while others are stimulators, giving the brain the "kick" it needs to keep functioning. A person whose brain is getting the wrong chemical signals may feel depressed, moody, hyperactive, or anxious. The chemical state of the brain, then, helps control our thoughts, feelings, and emotions.

Alcohol—and its byproducts—has the power to interfere with these controls, transforming grief to joy, depression to elation, and rationality to irrationality. Loneliness may be lifted by a few drinks but greatly intensified by many drinks; the euphoria experienced after a few beers may slowly change with continued drinking to moodiness and eventually to deep depression. Long and hard drinking invariably leads to emotional upsets, erratic behavior and personality deterioration, all caused by the action of alcohol on the body and brain.

WHY KEEP DRINKING?

Why does the alcoholic keep drinking if alcohol is so devastating to all the body's cells? This is the central question of the entire debate about the causes of alcoholism. Some experts emphasize social and psychological pressures driving alcoholics to drink; others point to the early physical changes that keep the alcoholic drinking.

The confusion about the causes of heavy drinking persists for one major reason: The physical changes that occur during the early stage of alcoholism are hidden and have no obvious effect on the alcoholic's behavior. The disease is difficult to recognize or diagnose in its early stages because the symptoms are so subtle and so easily confused with normal reactions to alcohol. No pain or visible malfunction is involved. The early alcoholic does not complain, has no reason to visit a doctor because of his drinking, and does not suffer abnormally when he drinks or after he stops drinking. Indeed, he appears to be just like all other drinkers. He has hangovers when he overdrinks, but so do his nonalcoholic friends. He enjoys drinking and looks forward to his evening cocktails, but so do his friends.

Because the early-stage alcoholic shows no sign of disease, the logical but wholly mistaken idea persists that alcoholism begins only when the drinker does suffer from drinking and does show some deterioration in physical functioning, such as severe withdrawal symptoms, personality changes, or inability to control his intake. But until these visible symptoms appear, most people assume that alcoholics and nonalcoholics experience precisely the same physical reaction to alcohol.

In fact, they do not. The alcoholic reacts physically in an abnormal way to alcohol, and his disease begins long before he behaves or thinks like an alcoholic. The reactions or adaptations of the body's cells to alcohol remain hidden in the early stages of the disease, but they are nevertheless happening. In months or years, the cells will have been so altered by alcohol that the alcoholic's behavior and thought processes will be affected. Then the disease will no longer be hidden, and the alcoholic will clearly be in trouble with alcohol.

By now the disease has progressed and the alcoholic starts drinking heavily and continuously, despite warnings from his doctors and loved ones, because he is physically addicted. The addiction and the physical need for alcohol, in other words, cause him to drink heavily and progressively. The alcoholic may have emotional and psychological problems that predated his heavy drinking, but those problems do not cause him to drink addictively—his early, abnormal physical reaction to alcohol is responsible for his later addictive drinking and his inability to stop drinking. As he starts drinking more and more often, any psychological problems he might have are increased and new ones are added.

THE CASE OF BOB D.

Bob D. was a capable and successful realtor who lived in a small Connecticut town with his wife and four children. Bob served as a member of the Rotary Club and the board of education and was president of the town's Y.M.C.A. He kept himself in top physical shape by swimming every day and playing tennis or golf on weekends.

Bob enjoyed drinking and was known as a great party man. One Saturday night after a golf tournament and dinner party where he drank five martinis and a bottle of wine, Bob drove his Mercedes at seventy m.p.h. into a telephone pole. He was hospitalized for six weeks with a broken leg, a fractured collarbone, and a ruptured spleen. After his accident, Bob seemed to lose interest in everything, and weeks went by when he didn't even go to work. He was deeply depressed, apparently because of his failing business and because he had to walk on crutches and couldn't participate in the sports he loved so much.

A year after his accident, Bob was driving home from work around 6 P.M. and was stopped by a policeman for weaving on the road. A blood-alcohol test showed a .15 B.A.L. (blood alcohol level)—the equivalent of approximately eight beers drunk within an hour and a half. Because the policeman was a friend, he drove Bob home without writing a ticket. But a month later, Bob was stopped and charged with Driving While Intoxicated; this time he lost his license for two months and was fined $500.

After his arrest, Bob started taking long walks, leaving home in the morning and returning in the afternoon. When he returned, his wife could tell he'd been drinking, but she was too frightened of his reaction to say anything. He was becoming more and more belligerent and had threatened to leave her if she didn't stop nagging him all the time. Then, one day Bob didn't come home for dinner; at 10 P.M. the police called to tell his wife that he'd been in a fight at the tavern downtown and was hospitalized with a broken jaw. This time his blood alcohol level was .20. He was charged with criminal assault, but the judge suspended his sentence on condition that he admit himself to an alcoholism-treatment program. This was the first time anyone had mentioned the word *alcoholism* in connection with Bob's drinking.

THE APPEARANCE AND THE REALITY

Most of his friends were shocked when they learned that Bob was an alcoholic. But, for anyone looking back at the events surrounding Bob's descent into chronic alcoholism, it becomes obvious that he was in big trouble with alcohol long before the judge labelled him an alcoholic. His work began to go downhill at about the same time his liquor intake increased—the housing market was doing just fine, but Bob was drinking too much to put any effort into selling houses. His relationship with his wife and family deteriorated as he drank more and more often. Again, the drinking was directly responsible. Bob's personality changed when he drank, and any attempt by his wife to talk was met with rage and hostility. "Quit nagging me," he would yell at her, "you're making my life miserable—no wonder I drink!" Bob's wife began to believe that part of the problem might be her fault; she even wondered if her "nagging" might be driving him to drink, as he kept insisting. Because she rarely saw Bob obviously drunk, she never made the connection that his drinking might be causing all the other problems. "He drinks too much sometimes," she thought, "but it's just because he's had a hard day." When she did begin to wonder if he might be an alcoholic, she was too embarrassed and confused to confide in anyone.

Bob suffered mood and personality changes when drinking because his brain cells were soaked in alcohol. And he was depressed, nervous, and anxious when he stopped drinking because these same cells were suffering from the withdrawal of alcohol. He lied about his drinking, rationalized and covered it up, blaming any number of people or events, not because he was a deceitful or devious man, but because he was already addicted to alcohol and needed it to continue functioning. When he stopped drinking, he felt so mentally and physically miserable that he couldn't even think straight, so his first priority was to drink and to make sure that he had enough alcohol to get him through the day. He began to hide bottles in the glove compartment of his car and beneath the tomato patch in his garden in order to make sure that he always had a reserve supply.

Not until Bob started drinking in the morning, was arrested for driving while intoxicated, and was involved in a tavern brawl, did his wife and friends believe he might be an alcoholic. Because the early symptoms had been ignored, however, it seemed to everyone that Bob was an "instant" alcoholic and therefore that his problems were related to his failures at work, his car accident, his arguments with his wife, and his severe depression. Bob believed this, too, and hoped that he could resolve his problems and then be able to drink like everyone else.

What Bob, his friends, and his family didn't know was that his addiction to alcohol was well established long before anyone bothered to call it alcoholism, and the addiction itself was responsible for causing Bob's increasingly serious social and psychological problems. Bob began to drink too much because his cells were unable to process alcohol normally, and he continued to drink because these same cells became addicted to alcohol, needing increasingly larger amounts to continue functioning. His abnormal metabolism thus paved the way for the heavier drinking that occurred in the later stages of his disease and the physical damage that resulted from this heavier drinking.

Bob had fallen victim to the double-edged sword of alcoholism: the "medicinal" value of alcohol, which he needed to keep going, and the poisonous effects of alcohol on the cells, causing progressive deterioration. At some point, he would reach the stage where he would be sick with it and sick without it. At that point, he would either get help and begin recovery or deteriorate and eventually die of his disease.

THE ROLE OF HEREDITY

The physical basis of alcoholism has been supported by studies of heredity. The susceptibility to alcoholism, like the susceptibility to diabetes, heart disease, and strokes, is inherited, passed on from parent to child. The child of one alcoholic parent has approximately a 25 percent chance of developing alcoholism while the child of two alcoholic parents has about a 50 percent chance.

Research conducted by psychiatrist Donald Goodwin, author of *Is Alcoholism Inherited?*, confirms the role of hered ity in susceptibility to alcoholism. In a series of experiments conducted in Denmark, Goodwin was able to separate hereditary influences from environmental influences by studying the children of alcoholics who were taken away from their parents at birth and adopted by nonrelatives. He theorized that if alcoholism were indeed inherited, these children would have a high rate of alcoholism even though they were not living with their biological alcoholic parents. If environmental influences were more important, the adopted children would be no more likely to become alcoholic than the children of nonalcoholics.

Goodwin found that the children of alcoholics do have a much higher risk of becoming alcoholics themselves—four times that of the children of nonalcoholics—despite having no exposure to their alcoholic parents after the first weeks of life. They were also likely to develop the disease earlier in life, usually in their twenties. The children of nonalcoholic parents, on the other hand, showed relatively low rates of alcoholism even if reared by alcoholic foster parents.

In a second study, Goodwin compared the sons of alcoholics who were adopted and raised by an unrelated family with their brothers who had been raised by the alcoholic parent. He found that the children raised by the biological alcoholic parent were no more likely to become alcoholic than their brothers who were raised by nonrelatives.

These studies provide compelling evidence that the susceptibility to alcoholism is, indeed, inherited. As Goodwin summarized his results in *Is Alcoholism Inherited?*:

> Our findings tend to contradict the oft-repeated assertion that alcoholism results from the interaction of multiple causes—social, psychological, biological . . . The "father's sins" may be visited on the sons even in the father's absence.

THE PSYCHOLOGICAL INFLUENCE

Goodwin's work demonstrates that the genes passed

down from fathers and mothers to their sons and daughters do not require any social, psychological, or behavioral problems to do their work. That is not to say that social and psychological factors don't *influence* the progression of alcoholism, for they do. Where and when a person drinks and how much and how often he drinks are all determined, in part, by the drinker's social and financial situation, career obligations, and psychological state of mind. Businessmen tend to drink in bars, loggers in taverns; Italians drink wine with their meals, the Irish traditionally drink whiskey and ale at local pubs. The death of a loved one may cause someone to drink more and more often; grief, loneliness, guilt, remorse, shame, and any number of emotions can contribute to a person's increased exposure to and use of alcohol. People have many reasons for starting to drink, and these reasons are the same for both alcoholic and nonalcoholic.

These psychological, social, financial, ethnic, and career factors do not, however, *cause* a person to start drinking addictively. The addiction is physical, and the alcoholic's body must be somehow physically capable of accepting the large amounts of alcohol necessary to feed the addiction. A widow, for example, may start drinking in the morning because she is bored and lonely and because alcohol takes away some of her grief and pain. But unless she has the *physical susceptibility* to become addicted, she will be able to control her drinking and when time has healed her psychological wounds and she is better able to deal with her emotions, she will probably cut down to a more socially acceptable level. The important point is that the nonalcoholic's drinking does not progress into an addictive disease—nonalcoholics do not experience a physical *need* to drink more and more often, and they don't experience withdrawal symptoms that increase in severity as they continue to drink. Nonalcoholics never experience the need to drink to relieve the physical and mental anguish of *not* drinking. *Not* drinking, in other words, is the more comfortable choice for the nonalcoholic, but the more agonizing choice for the alcoholic.

THE CASE OF MARTHA T.

PSYCHIATRIST'S REPORT

(General Hospital)

IDENTIFICATION: Martha T. is a forty-three-year-old Caucasian, married, a secretary, and the mother of two teen-age boys, ages thirteen and sixteen.

PRESENT PROBLEM: Patient admitted to hospital for an overdose of pills and alcohol. She states that for the past four months she has been somewhat out of control; she blames her problems on her inability to assert herself in her marriage. She finds it difficult to say no and finds herself taking care of everyone else, especially her husband (twenty years her senior), who wants to retire and have her support him. They've been married twenty-two years. She also has some difficulty with her sons, particularly the older boy, who she suspects is experimenting with drugs.

She feels put down in her marriage—that she has been more or less a servant. Feels that she has little power in the marriage, that her husband is totally in control. Wants to reverse this. There are recurring sexual conflicts.

She has had difficulty sleeping, although lately she's been mixing Valium or Empirin with codeine and alcohol, and then may sleep for ten to fourteen hours. She has overdosed about four times in the last four months; last week she took some of her husband's medicine, some of which was a heart medication. She denies that she was actively suicidal, and said she simply wanted to take something to block out consciousness for a while. However, this may be an unconscious death wish and should be considered dangerous behavior.

Patient apparently had some problems as a teen-ager with rather antisocial behavior such as drinking and mixing pills at the same time. However, she was able to settle down and marry and have a stable relationship until the present trouble.

FAMILY HISTORY: Patient is the youngest of four children, has three older brothers. She was raised in the Chicago area and grew up in a male-dominated environment. At age twelve, she was sexually abused by her oldest brother. Her father operated a riverboat and was gone from home much of the time. Her mother was a near-invalid with multiple sclerosis, and the patient was responsible for managing the household from age ten until she left home at eighteen.

MENTAL STATUS: Patient is oriented to person, place, and time, but underneath she appears to have some sadness of mood. However, she finds it very difficult to show or express sad feelings and resists them. She is of above average intelligence. Her recall and memory are intact. I see no evidence of any serious thought disorder nor any confusion of thought and no hallucinatory or delusional material. I feel that it's difficult to judge yet about her use of alcohol and pills. She admits that she has been blotting out clear thinking with the mixture of narcotic drugs and alcohol. Patient indicates that she mainly needs to get her mind clear and does not wish to take any type of mind-clouding medication.

IMPRESSIONS: (1) Adjustment disorder with depressive features; (2) Rule out affective disorder of manic/depressive type.

RECOMMENDATIONS: Admit to psychiatric unit. Possibility of marital therapy should be considered. She should be placed on vitamin therapy, particularly vitamin B1 because of her recent drinking history.

PHYSICIAN'S REPORT

(Alcoholism treatment center)

Admission History

Forty-three-year-old female transferred from local general hospital psychiatric ward for evaluation and treatment of alcohol/drug problem.

ALCOHOL/DRUG HISTORY

Patient admits to alcohol use in recent months but insists that it's only been a problem for the last four months, when she was drinking to relieve tensions and frustrations from personal and marital problems. She doesn't feel she's an alcoholic as she's been, essentially, a teetotaler most of her adult life. Her admission to the psychiatric unit of the general hospital three weeks ago was prompted by progressive depression and a drug-alcohol overdose (see psychiatric report).

PAST ALCOHOL USE

Patient began drinking in her early teens, developing an extremely high tolerance and a regular pattern of heavy drinking from ages fourteen to seventeen; started with beer, progressed to mixed drinks, then to hard liquor with a tolerance of two fifths of whiskey per day by age seventeen. Despite her heavy drinking she maintained school attendance enough to graduate. She drank a pint before school, left school during recess for more to control her shakes, nausea, and headaches. On test days when she couldn't as easily sneak out of class she hid liquor in her locker.

At seventeen she realized that alcohol was interfering with her life and sought treatment at a community health clinic—despite protests from her father that "no kid of mine needs help from a shrink." She was regularly hypnotized and negatively conditioned to the sight, smell, and taste of alcohol. This broke the cycle of excessive use and for the next twenty years she drank intermittently with only two binges of losing control.

Five years ago the patient experienced a religious conversion and completely abstained from alcohol until four months ago, when she began having increasing problems and stresses in her life. She started drinking with friends in an effort to help relieve some of the pressures, but her drinking urges seemed to quickly take over and she found herself drinking alone, staying at bars after her friends left or until the doors closed. She began mixing Valium and antidepressants with alcohol, and an unintentional overdose required hospitalization three weeks ago at the general hospital; she was subsequently referred here for observation and possible treatment.

Physical Exam

As per transfer records: essentially no active medical problems at this time. Blood pressure 140/70, pulse 78/min.

Mental status: alert, oriented, cooperative. No suicide tendencies, but generally bland attitude with little expression as she gave her history.

Impressions

1) Alcoholism, revived from earlier established addiction in teen years; 2) Alcoholism complicated by other central nervous system drugs—Valium, antidepressants, codeine; 3) Depression, likely resulting from central nervous system addictions.

Recommendations

1) Active alcoholism treatment and educational sequence; 2) *No* central nervous system drugs; 3) Mental/

emotional status to be determined during and following alcoholism treatment.

A SICK BRAIN

Alcoholism is a physiological, inherited disease caused in part by an inability to process alcohol normally. But one of the ironies of this disease is that the first obvious symptoms are psychological. The reason for this is that one of alcohol's primary targets is the brain. The brain is usually protected from chemicals and drugs by an electrical-chemical filter system known as the blood/brain barrier, which makes sure that only very simple (and essential) molecules such as those of oxygen and water can pass through. The simple molecular structure of alcohol allows it to penetrate this selective screen and gain easy access to the brain and its extension, the spinal cord. The brain is also continually hungry for glucose, which alcohol can readily supply.

A brain chronically affected by alcohol is a sick brain, incapable of normal functioning. Although the brain tissue doesn't actually feel pain, its agony is expressed in distorted, exaggerated, and sometimes irrational emotions, thoughts, and behavior. Alcoholics often think and behave in strange and uncharacteristic ways. They may become belligerent or weepy, hostile or affectionate, euphoric or severely depressed. These signs and symptoms* are too often misinterpreted as the *causes* of the alcoholic's heavy drinking, rather than the *consequences* of alcohol's profound effect on the brain and nervous system. It must be remembered that a drinking alcoholic is not acting in ways that are true to

**Signs* and *symptoms* are medical terms. Signs are what the observer—the physician, for example—sees, while symptoms are what the patient feels. Symptoms, in other words, are subjective, while signs are objective. A patient who complains of a sore belly is experiencing a *symptom* of some disorder; when the physician feels the belly and finds a tumor or an enlarged liver, that's an observed *sign* of disease.

himself—he is actually a caricature of his true self, his emotions and behavior being the expressions of a sick and deeply disturbed brain.

Brain abnormalities are even further exaggerated when

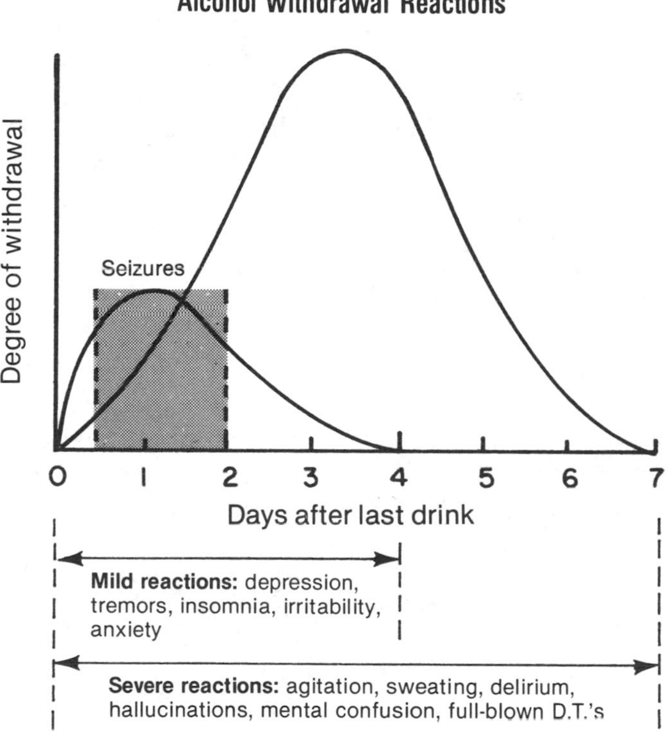

Typical alcohol withdrawal sequence. Some patients, however, may have a withdrawal seizure seven to ten days after their last drink. Others experience "protracted withdrawal symptoms," which can include sleep disturbances and cycles of anxiety and depression in the first few weeks or even months after treatment. This is more likely to occur in patients with dual addition, both to alcohol and to central-nervous system drugs.

alcoholics stop drinking and experience withdrawal. The brain is so profoundly affected that even after a few days or, in some cases, weeks of sobriety, alcoholics are still anxious, nervous, paranoid, or just generally befuddled. The first hours of withdrawal are the most obviously distressing, but any alcoholic who has stayed sober for more than a few days can attest to the enduring anguish of withdrawal. (Medical treatment greatly alleviates the anguish of this protracted withdrawal. See pages 38 to 39 of this chapter.)

During withdrawal the brain cells, which have become addicted to alcohol and need it to function, are in extreme distress. This distress may cause the withdrawing alcoholic to feel nervous, frightened, depressed, agitated, and paranoid. Chemical imbalances in the brain may cause him to hallucinate or go into convulsions. Severe headaches, irrational thoughts, and memory lapses are all expressions of a brain in torment. Such a brain distorts the alcoholic's every thought and emotion, making it impossible for him to think, feel, or react normally. And, tragically, even the best and most sincere efforts to stay sober can be defeated by the terrible and enduring power of the withdrawal syndrome.

THE CASE OF DONNA

After waking up with a particularly vicious hangover and surveying the junk heap of her apartment, Donna decided to quit cold turkey. She drained all her liquor bottles into the sink, and then proceeded to clean up. By midafternoon, she got the shakes so badly she couldn't hold a dishtowel without it flapping around "like a flag in the wind." She began to sweat, feeling dizzy and sick to her stomach. She couldn't think straight, her head pounded, and she began to panic at the thought that someone might ring the doorbell or call her on the phone. Cursing herself for throwing out all her liquor, she finally called a taxi and was dropped off at the nearest tavern. In a shaky voice she ordered a double scotch. She could barely lift the glass to her lips without spilling it, but after a few drinks she felt almost "normal" again.

Donna's brief experiment taught her an important lesson. "Alcohol isn't the problem," she concluded. "Being without it is!" And she swore that she would never be without it again.

NEEDING ALCOHOL TO KEEP GOING

The nature of an addiction is such that when the addicted person is under the influence of the addictive drug, he is able to function somewhat normally. His body has, in other words, developed a tolerance for the drug and become physically dependent on it. Tolerance indicates changes in the cell structure that allow the body to function normally even with large amounts of alcohol in the system. Patrick, for example, proudly told his treatment counselor that he could drink a fifth of bourbon a day, "and the only way anyone could tell was if they smelled it on my breath!" Patrick, along with many middle-stage alcoholics, was able to drink such staggering amounts because his cells had adjusted—developed a tolerance—to the presence of alcohol so that they actually needed it to function. When he stopped drinking, however, Patrick was a mess: shaky, fearful, sick to his stomach, and plagued by irrational fears. In withdrawal, his cells were thrown into an acute state of distress and he could no longer walk, talk, or think like a normal person.

Early- to mid-stage alcoholics are the most sick not when they drink, but when they *stop* drinking; and most learn, like Patrick and Donna, to keep a bottle or flask hidden in a glove compartment, purse, briefcase, or desk drawer. The bottle is there *just in case:* just in case the all too familiar withdrawal symptoms become too painful and debilitating. An alcoholic cannot drive a car if his hands are shaking uncontrollably, his head is throbbing, and he feels nauseous, dizzy, and mentally confused. Alcohol clears up these symptoms, and allows him to carry on. Every alcoholic knows the agony of withdrawal and not one will willingly endure it in the company of others. It may seem to these others that the alcoholic is being sneaky or devious as he excuses himself to go to the bathroom or out to his car for a hit off the hidden bottle. But in reality, he is protecting himself, at least for a little while, against the physical and mental anguish of withdrawal.

Of course, alcoholics aren't able to reason out why they continue to drink or behave in strange ways when they do drink. They are as confused by their actions as everyone else, and they, too, believe that psychological problems may have caused them to start drinking heavily. When trying to figure out why they drink so much, they often point a finger of blame at psychological problems or pressures:

- "My job was too demanding"
- "I never felt I could measure up to everyone's expectations."
- "My marriage was coming apart at the seams."
- "I was depressed because my mother died."
- "I've always been a nervous person and drinking seemed to calm me down."
- "My son was killed in Vietnam."
- "My dog got hit by a car."

and on and on and on.

Drinking alcoholics will also latch on to psychological explanations as a means of rationalizing their drinking. They drink, they say, because the wife nags, the baby whines, the boss demands, the job demands, the society devalues, the finances dwindle. Their depression, anxiety, and irritability can be defused, they believe, only when they drink. Again, the drinking alcoholic's brain is a sick brain. The one absolutely rational thought every drinking alcoholic's brain can register, however, is that it needs alcohol if it is to function at all—for withdrawal is much worse than drunkenness.

THE LIMITS OF TOLERANCE

The trick, of course, is to drink to one's tolerance—that is, to drink enough to stave off withdrawal and yet not drink so much as to get drunk, sick, and pass out. The early-stage alcoholic doesn't have too much trouble with this balancing act and drinking within his tolerance, but the late-stage alcoholic has an extremely difficult time because his tolerance level is decreasing (because of cell damage in the liver and central nervous system) at the same time his withdrawal symptoms are intensifying. The late-stage alcoholic will feel an overwhelming urge to drink to deaden the agony of withdrawal, but because the brain is so sick, he will be a poor judge of how much is too much. The margin of safety has narrowed to the point where drinking to his tolerance level is just a hair away from overdrinking. As a result, obvious drunkenness and periods of unconsciousness are not uncommon for later-stage alcoholics—not because they become more irresponsible and degenerate, but because they become sicker and their bodies are no longer able to tolerate or handle large amounts of alcohol.

TRYING TO ENDURE

Another problem all alcoholics eventually face is that no matter how hard they might try, they cannot drink all the time. An alcoholic has to sleep, buy groceries (the most important of which is alcohol), and carry on some semblance of normal behavior, and he must therefore endure withdrawal. The stronger his addiction, the worse the withdrawal syndrome. The early-stage alcoholic may suffer from symptoms similar to those a nonalcoholic might experience after a particularly heavy night of drinking: a headache, queasy stomach, the morning-after hangover. But as he drinks more and more often—which he will as the disease and its underlying addiction progress—the symptoms will get worse. He may suffer from chills or fever, shaky hands, insomnia, a general feeling of nervousness and anxiety. Tremors in his hands may become so noticeable that he is afraid to drink a cup of coffee for fear of spilling it all over himself. He may have increasingly severe and frequent episodes of blackouts, when he cannot remember the events that occurred in a certain time period—it could be a minute, hour, or days.

The late-stage alcoholic's emotions also become hopelessly confused. Guilt, depression, self-loathing, and a pervasive sense of despair return again and again, in ever stronger doses, to plague him. These emotions are understandable reactions to his inability to control his own drinking behavior and to the people around him who react to his drinking in disgust. The alcoholic, not knowing that he is addicted to alcohol, or knowing and hoping to overcome his addiction by force of will, comes to believe he is pathetic and weak. He repeatedly fails in his efforts to stop drinking or control his intake, and this failure feeds his guilt and his shame. "Why am I so weak?" he asks himself after getting drunk again. "Why can't I drink like everyone else? Why me?" The more he drinks, of course, the more tormented his emotions will become because of alcohol's toxic effect on his brain—a sick brain produces sick thoughts and sick emotions: "stinkin' thinkin'" as A.A. members say.

The withdrawal syndrome would be agony enough if it lasted for just a day or two; but gnawing symptoms can linger for weeks or even months of sobriety. And the longer they continue, the harder it is for the alcoholic to stay away from alcohol. Like a shipwrecked sailor trying desperately to hold onto an overturned boat in a stormy sea, the alcoholic finds himself slipping inch by inch into the substance that will destroy him. He tries to hang on with all his effort and every ounce of his will power. Too often he is defeated by the persistent and overwhelming desire for alcohol, for no matter how much he wants to quit, he begins to believe that he was better off when he was drinking—for at least then he had the exquisite relief of alcohol.

Getting Well

INTERVENTION

Without help, most alcoholics cannot stay sober on their own. Some have no difficulty stopping for a while, but weeks or months later they find themselves staring again into the face of an alive, compelling need to drink.* Others simply slide back into drinking, feeling complacent and sure about their ability to drink like everyone else. And there are those for whom the withdrawal syndrome is too painful and too frightening to endure without immediately returning to alcohol to end the torment. All these people are under the influence of an addiction and as long as that addiction is active and alive, they cannot make the decisions necessary for continued sobriety. The alcoholic is essentially chained to his addiction, for he does not have the insight to understand his problem or the rationality to seek a solution.

To break those chains, the alcoholic needs treatment, but to get into treatment, he needs help. It's not good enough to wait until the alcoholic himself is willing to ask for help, for most alcoholics cannot make it into treatment

*This need to drink, or craving for alcohol, is often personified by alcoholics as if "it" were, in fact, alive and growing. The force of the addiction is so powerful that it seems to be outside the alcoholic, a thing of terror and unpredictability.

by themselves. *Without help and outside intervention, most alcoholics will die of their disease or its complications.*

Help can come from any number of people; family and friends, physicians, policemen, judges, and attorneys are all in a position to step in and help the alcoholic into treatment. The procedures involved in intervention and what are called "confrontation strategies" can be tricky and complex, however, and anyone who wishes to know more about these techniques should read Vernon Johnson's excellent book, *I'll Quit Tomorrow.*

ABSTINENCE: THE FIRST PRIORITY OF TREATMENT

Once the alcoholic is in treatment, the first and foremost priority is to get alcohol out of his system. Without abstinence from alcohol, all treatment methods are doomed to failure. But withdrawal from alcohol is not as easy as taking the bottle away and, for many alcoholics, the withdrawal syndrome can be an extremely frightening and painful—even life-threatening—experience. Alcoholics can and do stop drinking by themselves, independent of any help—but only a very few can make it through the withdrawal process without drinking again to numb the physical and mental agony.

Early- and mid-stage alcoholics do not always suffer such agonizing withdrawal symptoms, and many can stop drinking for several weeks or months without outside help. But even "mild" withdrawal symptoms—vague feelings of anxiety, nervousness, irritability—can gnaw at the alcoholic and undermine his sobriety; and even early- or mid-stage alcoholics will tell you that they feel better when they're drinking than when they're not.

Ironically, the fact that an early- or mid-stage alcoholic isn't yet in terrible shape from drinking actually works against his getting effective treatment. He can talk himself out of staying sober for, after all, *he* doesn't get convulsions or hallucinations; *his* personality doesn't change when he drinks; *he* doesn't drink in the morning; *he* doesn't get paranoid or shaky—and if he can go on the wagon for a week or two, what better proof is there that he's *not* an alcoholic? Or so he thinks.

Withdrawal symptoms are withdrawal symptoms, however, and even mild withdrawal symptoms indicate addiction to alcohol. Early- and mid-stage alcoholics as well as late-stage alcoholics should go through a detoxification process, during which withdrawal symptoms are carefully monitored and any complications immediately spotted and treated. Acute withdrawal usually lasts between one and five days, depending on medical complications and the stage of illness (late-stage alcoholics typically have longer and more severe withdrawals).

After a thorough medical examination, effective treatment should include rest, adequate fluids, medication to prevent the more serious withdrawal reactions (convulsions or delirium tremens, for example), and a balanced diet with vitamin and mineral supplements adjusted to the patient's needs. Often special attention must be given to alcohol-related physical complications such as liver problems, gastritis, ulcers, bleeding, head injuries, broken bones, and burns. With this intensive medical care during the first days of withdrawal, the majority of alcoholics have no serious problems.

After a few days of abstinence, good food, nutritional supplements, rest, and medical attention, most patients experience a noticeable transformation. Clouded eyes clear, hands stop shaking, posture straightens, thinking becomes more rational, and depression, insomnia, and paranoia begin to fade. At this point, most patients are ready to begin the second phase of treatment—learning about their disease and what they must do to cope with it. In actual treatment, a strict sequence of care must be followed (briefly outlined at the end of Chapter 1). The following discussion highlights the most important aspects that must be introduced during this crucial sequence.

THE CRUCIAL TASK OF RE-EDUCATION

Educating the alcoholic about his illness is an important but difficult part of treatment because most people do not understand the disease or the reasons why certain people cannot drink "normally." Misunderstandings abound, and the alcoholic himself is often confused and bewildered by his disease. He must be re-educated—told why he is an alcoholic, what he must do to get well, and how he can protect himself against his own body chemistry and the social pressures to drink after he leaves treatment. Information and education alone cannot keep an alcoholic sober, but they are essential to his motivation and ability to learn the lifestyle that will protect his sobriety. The three basic elements of this protective system are: understanding the nature of the disease, nutritional therapy, and A.A. participation.

UNDERSTANDING THE NATURE OF THE DISEASE

The alcoholic, through intensive counseling and education, must come to fully and completely understand his disease—how it occurs; how it has affected his brain, personality, and behavior; why he is depressed when he stops drinking; why alcohol makes him feel better; why he experiences the urge to drink; why he cannot ever safely take a drink; why he will return to drinking if his disease is not treated. In short, all the basic questions must be confronted and answered.

Once he understands his disease, he can learn how to live with it. This is not as easy as it sounds. Alcoholics' lives are typically in chaos with broken marriages, estranged children, and confused coworkers. But effective counseling can help the alcoholic sort through the mess and begin the repair job necessary to build a new life. Once the alcoholic accepts the fact that he is an alcoholic, and commits himself to using the tools necessary to protect himself against his disease, he will have an excellent chance of recovery.

NUTRITIONAL THERAPY

A sound nutritional program is essential to successful treatment. Given vitamins and minerals in correct amounts and proportions, the cells will be able to generate new cells, repair injured cells, and strengthen their defenses against other diseases. Also crucial is a dietary plan to control blood-sugar problems, restore chemical balance, and prevent such symptoms as depression, irritability, shakiness, headaches, and mental confusion. With nutritional therapy, the alcoholic's addiction will remain in control, and he will not be threatened by the craving for alcohol that plagues so many alcoholics for months and even years after their last drink.

ALCOHOLICS ANONYMOUS

A.A. is far and away the most tried and proven program in the world for helping alcoholics to stay sober. Helping alcoholics to stay sober is the primary purpose of A.A., and its members are dedicated to supporting each other in this task. A.A. helps the alcoholic to recognize that he's licked by his disease and powerless to fight it on his own, and A.A. provides a fellowship and association of other sober alcoholics to support the alcoholic as he pieces together a new life-style. Belonging to such a fellowship helps the alcoholic acquire those living skills that were thwarted by years of drinking: "simple" skills such as listening, cooperating, relating to others, and dealing with failures. Most alcoholics readily take to the A.A. climate, although others require twenty or thirty meetings or more before they feel comfortable with A.A. activities. A good rule is to "go anyway, because it works." Millions of alcoholics can attest that it does.

THE BATTLE OF WILLS

About the second week of recovery the battle of wills occurs: the will to stay in control and retain the choice of drinking versus the will to give in and accept an outside system of protection. During early treatment, this outside system consists of the physician, counselor, dietitian, and other treatment staff, all of whom make decisions for the alcoholic until he is rationally able to make them for himself. If the alcoholic refuses to give in, if he continues to believe that he can make the decisions, including whether or not he will continue drinking—if, in other words, he refuses to give in to the better judgment of the treatment staff—he will almost certainly drink again. The alcoholic may appear to be stubborn and wilfull, but his addiction is masterminding his actions and overruling his ability to make sane and rational decisions.

One of the best signs of treatment success is when the alcoholic voluntarily gives up control. This actually shows on the face of an alcoholic, as he appears serene and at peace; the battle is over. When the alcoholic finally gives up control, he is recognizing and admitting that the inner physical drive to drink operates independently of and overrides his will to stay sober. He sees, at last, that he can no more control his drinking urge by will power than the diabetic can think down his blood sugar or the heart patient can drum up enough stamina to run a marathon. A body process is at work that is well beyond the spirit of will. Once the alcoholic acknowledges that process and gives up control to those who can guide him, he's begun the process of firmly cementing his sobriety.

THE BATTLE OF PILLS

In the early days of recovery, many alcoholics continue to feel depressed, anxious, and unable to sleep. These are symptoms of brain and nerve damage, and are particularly noticeable in those who receive no nutritional therapy. In fact, it's not unusual for recovering alcoholics to experience these lingering symptoms for weeks or even months after getting sober. Too often, alcoholics are given prescription drugs—tranquilizers, sedatives, pain killers, sleeping pills, and/or anti-depressants—to temporarily relieve their complaints.

Alcoholics must learn about the dangers and hazards of these drugs. They also need to know what to do about unexpected and unplanned drug exposure during major surgery and injury. They need to be aware of which medications are safe and which contain hidden drug substances that are dangerous to sobriety (see Appendix 1). Many alcoholics would never think of popping a pill for a good night's sleep or taking Valium to relieve anxiety; but unknowingly and innocently they take or are prescribed drugs that can undermine their sobriety by reawakening their addiction. Codeine, for example, is present in Empirin 3 and in most prescription cough medicines; Percodan, a potent pain killer, is often used following tooth extractions; and anyone who undergoes major surgery is given powerful anesthesia.

In whatever shape, size, or form, central nervous system (CNS) drugs *must not* be used in the treatment of recovering alcoholics.* This lifetime ban on drugs that affect the brain and nervous system is essential for several reasons. First, the use of these drugs can reinforce the alcoholic's belief that he is somehow unable to direct his own life without a chemical crutch. He comes to rely on drugs, believing that without them he is doomed to depression, anger, hostility,

*There are only three exceptions to this ban on CNS drugs. First, tranquilizers or sedatives are often used in the first days of recovery to lessen the severity of the more dangerous and life-threatening withdrawal symptoms. Second, CNS drugs must sometimes be used for surgery or major trauma (see Appendix 2 for suggestions on how to manage drug effects in temporary crises). And third, CNS drugs may be necessary in the rare cases of psychotic patients. These people frequently require intensive psychiatric care and typically cannot function without chemical help.

and nervousness. Drugs, in other words, promote the myth that alcoholism is a psychological illness and that alcoholics are somehow lacking in character or will power and can't survive without chemical help.

A second and more dangerous effect of these drugs occurs because they work on the same brain pathways, in similar ways, that alcohol (also a central nervous system drug) worked on, and alcoholics will quickly develop a tolerance (called *cross-tolerance*) to them, needing more than normal doses to achieve the desired effect. They will also become addicted (*cross-addiction*) to central nervous system drugs if they take them for any length of time, actually needing them to function normally and experiencing severe withdrawal symptoms when the drug effects wear off. This is what happened to Betty Ford, who apparently started to drink addictively only when she began to regularly take pills that her doctor prescribed for pain.

Substituting one drug for another is obviously not the way to a sane and steady sobriety; in fact, the use of such drugs can destroy sobriety by causing a new addiction to the substitute drug and reawakening the old addiction to alcohol. Once the alcoholic is hooked on pills, and suffering from withdrawal whenever he stops taking the pills, he's going to eventually turn to the substance that works better than any other to stop the distress: alcohol. This can happen even after years of sobriety.

THE CASE OF DORIS

Doris, sober for fifteen years, was hospitalized for acute back spasms. She actively resisted using any Valium but eventually had to be medicated because of continuous pain and spasms. Her friend Anne visited Doris in the hospital and saw the nurse give her Valium. Anne worked in an alcoholism treatment program and knew about the dangers of drugs for alcoholics. She gently asked Doris what she was going to do about continuing the drug, and how she planned to deal with a possible withdrawal syndrome once she stopped taking them. Doris's face became red, she clenched her fist, and pounded it on the bed. "I'm not here to be lectured to," she said, her voice near a scream. "And who are you to tell me about drugs? I'm the alcoholic, and I'm the one who had to go through treatment! I didn't ask to be in this hospital! I didn't ask for these pills!" And she settled back in bed and refused to discuss the subject.

Anne passed the incident off, believing that Doris was just having a bad day. But the next day she again asked about the pills, and again Doris was hostile, defensive, and full of rationalizations. Anne knew, then, that she was seeing Doris's addiction resurface; just a few Valium pills had completely changed her outlook and temperament. Anne called Doris's husband, who agreed to watch Doris's pill-taking after she left the hospital.

A few weeks after Doris was released from the hospital, she called Anne to apologize for her behavior. She told Anne that she'd been given a prescription for Valium when she was released, and her husband had to drag her away from the pharmacy where she was going to get more pills. The ride home was a nightmare, and she didn't know how her husband had put up with her tantrums and crying spells the last few weeks. But she'd made it; she'd thrown away all her pills, and she wanted to thank Anne for being a good and true friend. "You probably saved my life," she told her.

OTHER ESSENTIALS

Education, counseling, nutritional therapy, introduction to Alcoholics Anonymous, and avoidance of all mind- and mood-altering drugs are basic and crucial to starting the alcoholic on the road to recovery and must be included in any treatment program. Other essential elements of treatment can help cement and smooth out this road to recovery, and should be offered as part of the treatment sequence of care. These include *exercise* to build up and maintain physical health and mental alertness; *family counseling* to help the family learn about alcoholism, its causes and progression, and ways of contributing to the recovery process; and an *out-patient counseling program* to help the recovering alcoholic after in-patient treatment is finished.

Treatment of alcoholism is obviously not simple, and recovery takes time and enormous effort. Alcoholism is not a disease of one body part; it literally affects its victims from head to toe. And while the disease itself is deadly, its profound impact on the body's nutritional and chemical balance makes the alcoholic's suffering more severe and recovery more difficult.

3
The Malnourished Alcoholic

The body is a cell state in which every cell is a citizen.

Rudolf von Virchow
German pathologist, 1858

MANY alcoholics go into treatment expecting to get well within a few days. "I'm sick—treat me," is a common attitude, as if the alcoholic has a broken leg and needs only a cast to make it well, or his appendix is in danger of rupturing, requiring some quick and fancy surgery. Detoxification centers, which keep the alcoholic for only a few days until the worst of the withdrawal symptoms are over, help promote the myth that alcoholism can be treated in a few days.

But alcoholism does not do its damage cleanly, nor does it concentrate its attack in one, easy-to-reach part of the body. Instead, it requires a messy, complex clean-up job that takes time, patience, and a considerable amount of effort for the healing to be complete. The alcoholic who expects to get up after three days and walk away healthy and steady is going to be sorely disappointed when his feet hit the ground.

Recovery from the disease is never hopeless, however,

even for the skid-roader who has had more than one terrifying encounter with the D.T.'s and who is so weak he can barely lift the bottle to his lips. With the right kind of help, even sick and destitute alcoholics can get well again. But to get well, to become healty, the alcoholic must come to appreciate the full extent of his injuries. Knowing the extent of his illness, what organs and systems it has affected, how long he can expect recovery to take, and what lingering symptoms he will experience helps him to understand and then accept his disease. Knowing the facts, the alcoholic also knows how to protect and maintain his sobriety.

ALCOHOL: A NUTRITIONAL VACUUM CLEANER

Most alcoholics don't realize that alcohol, in addition to its direct, poisonous effects on organs such as the liver, heart, brain, and stomach, works indirectly as a sort of nutritional vacuum cleaner, sucking up vitamins and minerals and leaving the body with numerous deficiencies. Nutritional disorders are a devastating consequence of chronic alcoholism, for they literally affect every cell in the body, causing a wide array of mental and physical symptoms. Every drinking alcoholic is malnourished, meaning that many of his body's cells are weakened, sick, or dying. The longer the alcoholic drinks and the more he drinks, the sicker his cells will get. As Richard Bozian, M.D., said in *Patient Care* magazine:*

> There's no such thing as alcoholism as an isolated condition. It is virtually impossible for an alcoholic to get an adequate diet. For one thing, alcohol contains a lot of calories. Second, it interferes with nutrient absorption and increases excretion, thus increasing requirements. A social drinker—or even someone whose diet includes alcohol as 10 percent of calories—may suffer only from increased weight, but a person who takes 25–30 percent of his calories in alcohol, as alcoholics do, cannot be properly nourished.

*March 15, 1978, page 169.

THE UNSEEN GOES UNNOTICED

Nutritional disease in alcoholics is often hidden deep within the cell structure of the body. That is, it can't be seen with the naked eye, and in many cases the standard laboratory tests, which are designed to detect clear-cut malnutrition, don't pick up marginal but nevertheless disabling deficiencies. The unseen goes unnoticed—and untreated. Even the obvious and visible nutritional maladies of the stumbling, drunk skid-roader—wasted muscles, cracked lips, bleeding gums, skin sores, and anemia—are often overshadowed by life-threatening crises that demand immediate attention such as hemorrhaging, cirrhosis, or the D.T.'s. And not many physicians are trained or educated to uncover the more hidden and obscure nutritional problems of the well-dressed, seemingly healthy alcoholic.

But nutritional deficiencies do exist in alcoholics, even in alcoholics who look perfectly healthy and don't show any obvious signs of malnutrition. Given enough time, alcohol eventually disrupts the workings of various organs and entire body systems. But its devastating impact begins with the most basic of life's structures, the cell.

It is difficult to visualize a cell or imagine the way in which sickness in the cells adds up to sickness throughout the body. That's why it's important to understand how cells function, and how alcohol disrupts their inner workings, leading to cell injury and death.

COMMUNITIES OF CELLS

The body is composed of an estimated quadrillion—that's a million billion—cells. Like the organisms they compose, cells need certain essentials to stay alive and healthy. They need oxygen, for example, in constant and continual supply; even a few minutes without oxygen can cause widespread cell death. In addition to oxygen, the cells cannot survive without forty essential nutrients, which are used to energize the cells and keep them functioning normally. Cells cannot create these essential nutrients but must rely on food to supply them.

Cells live in groups, or communities composed of similar cells, and these communities form tissues, a group or layer of similarly specialized cells that together perform certain specialized functions. Tissues of different kinds form organs, those structural units such as the liver, heart, and spleen that also serve specific functions. And organs of different kinds work together to make a system, which performs a particular function for the body. The digestive system, for example, is a working composite of cells, tissues, and organs that take the food we eat and transform it into usable nutrients.

RELATIONSHIP AMONG CELLS, TISSUES, ORGANS, AND A SYSTEM

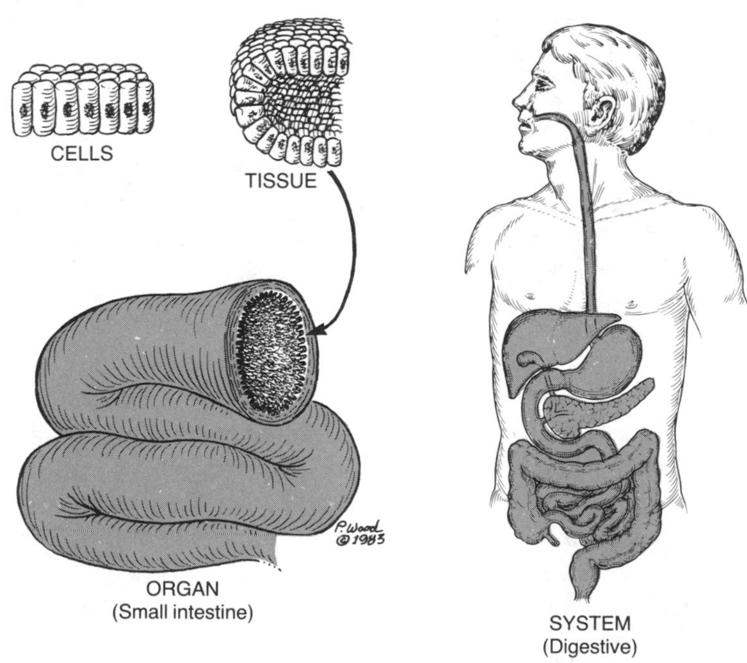

To understand how cells work and how they relate to tissues and organs, imagine a group of individuals that comprise a community that is part of a county that is part of a state and finally a nation. Each individual is dependent on certain basics to live: oxygen and water, which must be supplied continuously, and the forty essential nutrients, which can be circulated around every cellular community or kept in storage to be used later. Every day, on a regular schedule, the forty "packages" of nutrients are delivered to each community and divided up among the various individuals. When everyone has had enough, the surplus is either discarded or kept in the communities' storage tanks.

Suppose, however, that this delivery system is not working properly, and the nutrient packages consistently arrive late. The people in the communities may get hungry and feel tired, but as long as some packages are still circulating, community members can at least continue to carry on their every-day duties. Further suppose, though, that one day only thirty-eight of the forty packages are delivered; a week goes by, then a month, and two of the valuable packages are still missing.

At first, the people in the communities can get by, drawing on their storage tanks. Since they are still getting oxygen, water and the other thirty-eight packages, they will only slowly begin to feel the effects of the deprivation. But after a while the people will weaken, for they need every one of the forty packages if they are to stay healthy.

As the people begin to get sick and die, the individual communities weaken, and the entire state wobbles. And, of course, as the communities and states depend on their smaller parts, so does the nation. If the packages of nutrients are withheld for too long, sickness and death will become widespread, and the nation will not be able to hold up long under the stress.

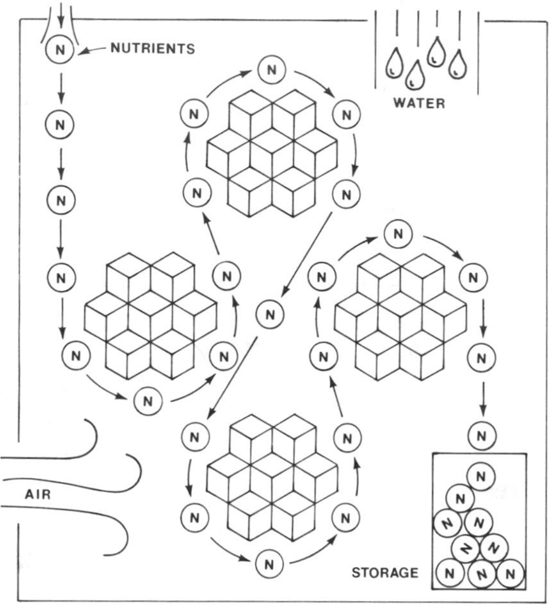

COMMUNITY OF CELLS

This simple structure of individuals, communities, states, and nations can be used to describe how cells, tissues, and organs work together to make a healthy body. While they have a life of their own, cells belong to communities (tissues) which form counties (organs) and states (systems), all of which comprise the entire nation (organism). The cells depend on a delivery system (circulation) for water and the forty packages of essential nutrients. These nutrients are only available through food—the body cannot make them itself. When the wrong kinds of food or not enough of the right foods are eaten, the cells get sick. This sickness does not happen all of a sudden, spreading like a flash fire, but develops and progresses slowly until eventually whole

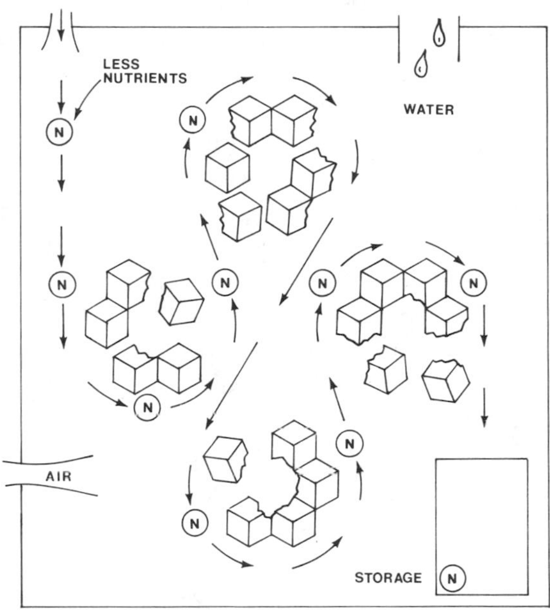

COMMUNITY OF SICK CELLS

communities of cells get sick and the entire body is weakened.

Alcohol is capable of causing widespread cell sickness and contributing to the potential collapse of the entire body. It acts directly as a poison to the cells, and indirectly by cutting off the flow and supply of nutrients to the cells. Alcohol can and does affect every cell in the body by interfering with nutrients and thus eating away at the core of the body's health and integrity.

ALCOHOL: THE FOOD THAT KILLS

Alcohol is considered a food because it contains calories, the units used for measuring the energy produced by food when burned up in the body. And in terms of calories, alcohol is one of the richest foods known to man: Every ounce of alcohol delivers about 70 calories when broken down in the body, or the equivalent of fourteen spears of asparagus, twelve almonds, one orange, one and a half slices of whole-grain bread, an egg, or two large tomatoes. Unfortunately, alcohol has only calories in common with these other foods, for it is almost totally devoid of nutrients: the amino acids (the building blocks of proteins), vitamins, and minerals that sustain life. Alcoholics can, and in the later stages of their disease often do, meet two-thirds of their bodies' caloric requirements just by drinking alcohol; but alcohol cannot meet their nutritional requirements. As an example, an alcoholic would have to drink about 40 quarts of beer or 200 quarts of wine every day just to meet his requirements for vitamin B-1!

Yet despite its nutritional inadequacies, alcohol is still an attractive source of fuel for the body; just a small amount of alcohol provides a big jolt of energy in the form of calories, and because of alcohol's simple molecular structure, the body does not have to work very hard to unlock this energy. Furthermore, unlike most foods, alcohol requires essentially no digestion and can rush quickly into the blood stream. An orange or a sweet roll may require an hour of soaking in the digestive acids secreted by the mouth, stomach, and small intestine before being absorbed into (and then used by) the body, and an eight-ounce steak may soak for three or four hours before all its nutrients and calories can be distributed to the body's cells. But alcohol quickly slides through all the normal channels of digestion, and within minutes is present in the blood stream, rushing directly to the liver, where enzymes immediately start breaking down the alcohol molecules. A few minutes after ingestion, then, alcohol's calories are available to the body's cells.

Of course, feeding the cells with alcohol alone is not a good idea, just as it is not efficient or wise to run an automobile on high-octane gas while neglecting to change the oil or lubricate the engine parts; the car may have plenty of high-energy fuel, but soon enough the engine parts will burn themselves out. Cells, too, need continual and careful maintenance if they are to stay healthy and carry on their normal every-day functions—but they won't get any help from alcohol, which provides only energy. Without the proper nutrients, damaged cell parts cannot be replaced, new cell materials cannot be created, and the cells cannot build or replenish tissues and organs. If the cells are continually denied nutrients for too long—if they are denied even just one nutrient—they will weaken, become sick, and eventually die.

Of course, most nonalcoholics don't use alcohol as their only or primary food source and, for these drinkers, alcohol's effects are usually minor and temporary. A few gin-and-tonics or a glass or two of wine won't necessarily do their bodies any good, but neither will this amount of alcohol cause any recognizable harm. Alcohol does begin to cause recognizable problems, however, when it is used frequently and in large amounts, and when the drinker neglects other, more nutritious foods. This perfectly describes the alcoholic. The alcoholic, it must be remembered, neglects food not because he is irresponsible, but because his addiction to alcohol overrides all his other needs. When your car is on fire, you don't worry about whether the oil is low—you do something to put out the fire. And when alcoholics are in withdrawal, they don't stop to eat a hamburger—they get a drink, the one, sure-fire way to relieve their misery, at least for a little while.

Because the continued, excessive use of alcohol affects just about every cell in the body, it necessarily disrupts the ability of the cells to process, use, and store nutrients. The digestive tract, liver, pancreas, adrenals, brain, and nervous system are among those organs hit hardest by alcoholism, and all of these organs are intricately involved in the processing, use, and storage of nutrients for other systems. No wonder so many alcoholics suffer from erratic blood-sugar levels; no wonder a reduced ability to fight infections is so common among drinking alcoholics; no wonder alcoholics have nutritional disturbances and display the early and progressive symptoms of vitamin and mineral deficiencies, including depression, mood swings, and mental confusion. All these disorders are related to alcohol's powerful impact on the body's nutritional equilibrium.

THE CASE OF FRANK

Frank had been sober for four and a half months, completely swearing off all alcohol and drugs. (He'd been taking Valium for five years under the supervision of his physician.) Alcohol did "weird" things to him, messing up his mind, as he put it, and changing his personality. The last time he drank he ran over a tricycle with his car. He had nightmares for months, dreaming that a child was riding the tricycle when he hit it. In other nightmares, he dreamt that he had started drinking again, and he would wake up in a drenching sweat. The nightmares and the fears they created propelled him into Alcoholics Anonymous. Because the meetings confirmed his desire not to drink and helped him come to terms with his alcoholism, Frank attended at least one meeting every night and sometimes two a day. In his four months of sobriety he'd been to over two hundred meetings.

Frank didn't want to drink, he didn't even crave alcohol like so many of the other A.A. members, but he couldn't seem to shake the depression that sometimes seemed to engulf him. He worked on a psychiatric ward of a state hospital, and he was beginning to see himself in some of the patients—perhaps he, too, was manic-depressive, or even schizophrenic? His moods would shoot up to uncomfortable highs that lasted a day or two and then, with no warning, plummet to the depths of depression. Sometimes he went from a high to a low in the same day. His sleep patterns were erratic; sometimes he just lay in bed, unable to sleep; other times he would wake up and not be able to get back to sleep. He had no energy in the morning and by noon he was exhausted. He suffered from severe headaches, and he was irritable and easily provoked to anger. Sometimes he even thought about suicide.

All these problems made working extremely difficult. His coworkers were becoming annoyed with his angry outbursts and bleak depressions. After his supervisor talked with him and insisted he take a rest, Frank knew he had to get help. One of his best friends worked at an in-patient alcoholism treatment center, and Frank decided to admit himself there.

The doctor at the treatment center told Frank that she suspected physical causes were "inciting a biochemical imbalance"—in other words, his depressions and mood swings were not really mental, but caused by certain physical abnormalities. Since Frank had been sober for four months, the doctor knew that alcohol was not the direct cause of his problems, and she suspected nutritional disorders, aggravated by Frank's long years of chronic drinking and poor nutrition.

After gathering a dietary history, her suspicions were confirmed. Frank tended to go long intervals without food, and much of the food he ate was sweet, sugary, and low in protein. On work days Frank usually got up at 5:30 or 6 A.M. and rushed off to the hospital without breakfast. About 8:30, he'd have a glass of milk or juice and throughout the morning he'd pump himself up with three or four cups of coffee mixed with hot chocolate. At noon he grabbed a salad and sandwich, the most substantial meal of his day. In midafternoon he'd drink more coffee mixed with cocoa, which carried him to his 5 o'clock A.A. meeting where he drank a few more cups of coffee loaded with sugar. He usually picked up the 8 o'clock A.A. meeting as well and treated himself afterward to a big piece of pie or cake.

Frank was surprised at the questions about his diet, and at first he thought the doctor might be some kind of a quack. His problems were much more severe, he thought, than the doctor realized and for a while he even considered dropping out of treatment. But he knew he'd lose his job if he didn't get help, so he reluctantly continued on in treatment and followed the staff's recommendations.

The doctor and staff nutritionist put Frank on a well-balanced diet of regular meals and between-meal snacks and prescribed multivitamin and mineral supplements. He was also required to participate in a series of lectures and discussions about the nature of addiction and the specific biochemical problems of the alcoholic. Despite his doubts, Frank soon began to feel better. After the first two or three days of treatment, his depression and suicidal thoughts diminished. His "foggy" head, as he described it, started to clear in the first week, his thoughts becoming more rational and orderly; his mood swings were less abrupt and severe, and he began to sleep as peacefully as he did before his drinking problems.

The week before his discharge, Frank went out on a weekend pass to visit friends and family. He got caught up visiting and talking, and after a few hours he was overcome by the all-too-familiar symptoms—the mood swings, foggy head, and feelings of panic. He realized he hadn't eaten anything in over six hours, and he immediately sat down and ate a good meal. After 45 minutes or so he felt refreshed, energetic, and clear-headed.

With that experience, Frank realized how closely linked were his psychological symptoms and his biological functions. He returned to the treatment center and rushed into the doctor's office. "You were right!" he exclaimed, giving the surprised doctor a big hug. "The diet really does work!" Frank has been sober for four years, continues to watch his diet, and claims he's never felt better in his life.

A MATTER OF DEGREE

Not every alcoholic has such obvious nutritional maladies as Frank. Many alcoholics have marginal vitamin and mineral deficiencies, which do not show up on laboratory tests designed to discover the full-blown nutritional disorders, but nevertheless these nutritional "gaps" have a profound effect on health and behavior.

Nutritional deficiencies are progressive, meaning that they start with no noticeable behavioral or physical symptoms, but get worse and worse until they do affect behavior and eventually show up on tests. The classic vitamin deficiency diseases such as pellagra, scurvy, and beri-beri are really only the end of the line, representing the worst possible damage a particular vitamin deficiency can cause. Today these deficiency diseases are rare, and because of their rarity many people believe that malnutrition has been done away with, especially in affluent countries like the U.S. But malnutrition develops in stages, literally working from the inside out, and the early stages are not rare at all, particularly in chronic alcoholism. The progressive stages of nutritional deficiencies are summarized in the following chart.

ALCOHOL AGAINST NUTRITION

Every alcoholic has nutritional problems, but those who drink heavily for years and who eat poorly are usually in the worst shape. However, even alcoholics who eat well during or between drinking bouts are malnourished because alcohol itself interferes with the body's ability to take in, use, and store nutrients.

Alcoholism *directly* causes or contributes to nutritional deficiencies in several ways.

Progressive Stages of Nutritional Deficiencies

Stage	Physical Signs	Patient's Symptoms
Stage 1: Hidden	Fewer nutrients in tissues; fewer nutrients excreted in urine.	No symptoms
Stage 2: Early chemical	Biochemical abnormalities: enzyme activity slows down, and can be picked up by sensitive tissue tests	"Minor" symptoms such as lack of energy, insomnia, and nervousness
Stage 3: Early physical	More severe and obvious biochemical findings; deficiencies that show up in standard lab tests.	Behavioral symptoms such as irritability, depression, anxiety, loss of appetite, weight loss, and decreased ability to fight infections
Stage 4: Visible	Classical deficiency diseases (scurvy, beriberi, pellagra)	Widespread physiological symptoms
Stage 5: Terminal	Severe tissue damage	Death

Adapted from Myron Brin, "Red Cell Transketolase as an Indicator of Nutritional Deficiency," *American Journal of Clinical Nutrition,* Vol. 33, February 1980, pp. 169–171.

FOOD INTAKE

Alcohol works in a number of ways to cut down on food intake. First, when someone drinks regularly and in large amounts, he doesn't feel like eating nutritious foods, for the empty calories of alcohol satisfy his hunger. A diet similar to the one below is not uncommon for chronic alcoholics. The alcoholic in this example was still working, but managed to squeeze in some heavy drinking at lunch as well as after work and well into the evening. Approximately 1,300 of his total 2,300 calories were supplied by alcohol alone, and the foods he did eat were not very nutritious.

Typical Daily Diet of a Chronic Alcoholic

Time	Place	Beverage or food	Amount	Description
8:30 A.M.	home	coffee	2 cups	black, with sugar
10:30	office	coffee & doughnut	2 cups 1½	black, with sugar glazed
1:30 P.M.	restaurant	salad, roll, & butter		
5:15	bar	gin	3	martinis
7:30	home	gin	2	martinis
8:30	home	spaghetti		
10:00	home	gin & tonic Doritos	1 30	

Alcoholics are also plagued with stomach and intestinal upsets that play havoc with their appetite for food. Nausea, vomiting, diarrhea, and stomach pain from gastritis, ulcers, swollen liver, or pancreatitis make the thought of eating extremely unpleasant, and any food that is eaten is usually promptly expelled in one way or another.

Finally, the alcoholic gets trapped in a vicious cycle in which regular and heavy drinking causes a loss of certain nutrients essential for a healthy appetite. Vitamins B-1, B-3, and B-6, for example, work as appetite stimulants; these vitamins are commonly deficient in drinking alcoholics. And alcoholics typically have low levels of zinc, which can cause a loss of taste and smell and therefore a lack of interest in food.

DIGESTION AND USE OF NUTRIENTS

Alcohol can produce changes in the *digestive system* that lead to interference in the absorption* and use of nutrients in

**Absorption* describes the passage of nutrients, liquids, and other substances through a surface of the body, such as the intestinal lining, into body fluids and tissues.

the body. In order to understand alcohol's devastating impact on this system, it's important to know something about how the various intestinal organs work.

The process of digestion begins in the mouth, where starches are partially broken down. Particles of food then travel down a tube (the esophagus) to the stomach where they are collected, churned and worked on by acids and enzymes.* After an hour or two, the partially digested food is emptied into the small intestine where more acids and enzymes (made by the liver and pancreas) go to work to break it down even further. Fingerlike cilia, which border the intestinal lining cells (endothelium), then sweep the digested foods through the cells into the neighboring blood stream. Only then can the nutrients circulate throughout the body and be used by the cells for repair and regeneration.

If any part of this complex system isn't working right, nutritional deficiencies will occur, and all the body's cells will feel the pinch. Alcohol attacks every organ in the digestive system and it hits them all hard, creating nutritional disaster for the alcoholic.

Alcohol's known and predictable impact on the digestive organs is illustrated and described in the following figure.

This brief look at the known and predictable impact of alcohol on the stomach, intestine, liver, and pancreas illustrates why the body's nutritional needs cannot be satisfied simply by eating the proper foods or even by proper absorption of essential nutrients. Only when the proper nutrients enter the cell and are properly used by the cell can nutritional requirements be met. Chronic consumption of alcohol prevents the proper entry and use of nutrients because alcohol sabotages every major organ involved in the processing and distribution of nutrients.

*Enzymes are substances, usually protein in nature, which, when coupled with a vitamin or mineral, start and speed up chemical reactions in the body.

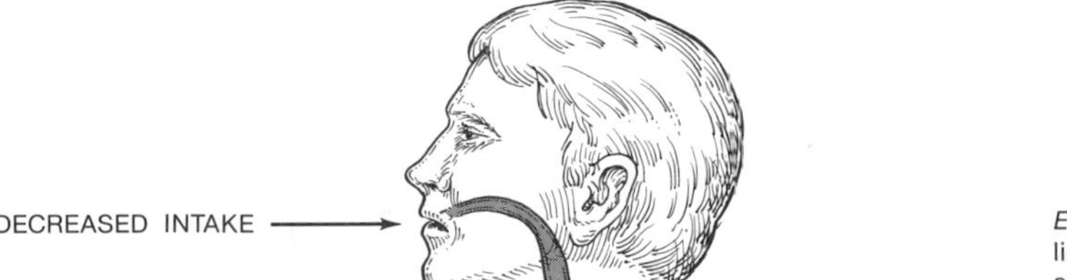

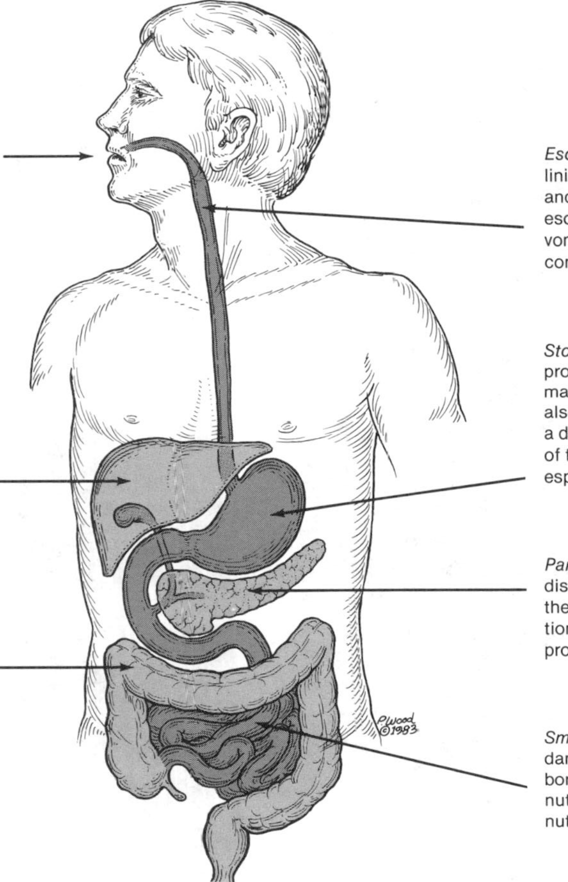
DECREASED INTAKE
Esophagus: Alcohol irritates and inflames the lining of the esophagus (causing esophagitis) and can interfere with swallowing. An inflamed esophagus will produce burning pain, nausea, vomiting, and loss of appetite—all of which contribute to nutritional problems.
Liver: When alcohol is in the body, the liver is forced to spend its time and energy getting rid of it, so the liver's normal nutritional chores go unattended. As a result, the manufacturing of proteins, carbohyrates, and fats slows down. The production of bile salts also decreases, resulting in a lowered ability to absorb fats, which in turn leads to diarrhea and poor absorption of fat-soluble vitamins (A, D, E, and K).
Stomach: Alcohol irritates stomach tissue, and prolonged, heavy drinking contributes to inflammation of this tissue (causing gastritis) and also contributes to ulcers. Alcohol also causes a decrease in digestive acids and enzymes. All of these effects lead to poor digestion, especially of proteins and minerals.
Pancreas: Excessive amounts of alcohol can disrupt the ability of the pancreas to produce the enzymes needed for protein and fat digestion. The pancreas may get plugged up with protein, leading to inflammation (pancreatitis).
Large intestine: Alcohol can either speed up or slow down the emptying rate of the large (and small) intestines. Speeding it up causes diarrhea and a loss of valuable nutrients; slowing it down can cause constipation, with reabsorption of toxins from the waste materials.
Small intestine: Excessive drinking causes damage to the lining cells and the cilia, which border them. This leads to poor absorption of nutrients as well as diarrhea and "flushing" of nutrients in the urine.
P. Wood ©1983

INDIRECT CAUSES OF NUTRITIONAL DISORDERS

The direct impact of alcohol on the cells is only one way in which alcoholism destroys the body's nutritional equilibrium. Indirect causes of nutritional disorders in alcoholics include other factors, including lifestyle, use of over-the-counter and prescription drugs, trauma, surgery, and infections.

LIFESTYLE FACTORS

Many alcoholics, particularly late-stage alcoholics, live alone. Having no one to cook for them and little money available for food, they eat poorly and are inevitably malnourished. When they do eat, their choice is generally snack-type foods such as potato chips, or fast foods like burgers and fries, all of which are high in calories but low in nutrients. The cost of nutritious foods, combined with low motivation and energy, all play a role in the alcoholic's nutritional deficiencies.

DRUGS

Alcoholics use over-the-counter drugs for a myriad of physical and mental complaints, including headaches, nausea, insomnia, and nervousness. And visits to the doctor frequently produce a prescription drug of one kind or another: tranquilizers, sedatives, sleeping pills, and/or antidepressants. While these drugs can be dangerous in and of themselves (see pages 42 to 43), they also interfere with the use and processing of nutrients in the body. See table on page 283 for a listing of which nutrients are depleted by commonly used drugs.

TRAUMA, SURGERY, AND INFECTIONS

Nutrients are quite literally the bodyguards of the body and, when assaulted by disease or subjected to great physical demands, the body needs extra nutritional protection. Trauma (bodily injury) surgery, and infections all put great stress on the body and deplete nutritional stores. Alcoholics, particularly late-stage alcoholics, are typically in and out of hospitals for accident-related injuries (head injuries from falling down stairs, broken jaws from barroom brawls, fractured legs and arms from car accidents) or for alcohol-induced illnesses such as gastritis, hepatitis, cirrhosis, pancreatitis, respiratory diseases, cardiovascular disease, and so on.

In summary, then, alcoholism causes malnutrition in a number of direct and indirect ways. Even the affluent alcoholic who eats every meal his cook prepares for him will suffer from malnutrition; the martinis he drinks will drain nutrients out of his body, as will the medications he takes for high blood pressure, and the two packs of cigarettes he may be smoking every day. Recurrent attacks of diarrhea wash away vitamins and other nutrients, and the stress of his job drains body reserves even further. The combination of all these nutrient "leaks" makes malnutrition inevitable, and the body cells, tissues, and organs will soon enough show their distress.

THE CONSEQUENCES OF MALNUTRITION

The undermining of the alcoholic's nutritional foundation, as discussed in the preceding section, eventually results in visible disease. This weakened condition, coupled with the direct toxic effects of alcohol on major organs, can lead to a wide path of destruction. Because so many different vitamins and minerals, organs and systems are involved, the symptoms are diverse and can mimic many diseases. Many alcoholics suffer from depression, for example, but the symptoms are usually dismissed as stress or tension or simply not connected at all with alcohol's effect on the brain's supply of vitamins and minerals.

Even obvious, nutritionally-induced maladies, such as skin infections, are often misdiagnosed. A woman with severe boils, for example, consulted three physicians, none of whom could find the cause of her infections. She took the antibiotics they prescribed, but the pills didn't get rid of her boils. She was finally diagnosed by a fourth doctor as an alcoholic, and her dietary history showed a very low protein consumption and obvious vitamin and mineral deficiencies. When she stopped drinking and started eating nutritious foods, the boils soon disappeared. Another alcoholic in his fifties had a compound fracture of the bones in his leg. An open wound developed that wouldn't heal despite constant visits to the doctor and eventually two surgeries. When he was finally treated for alcoholism and his diet supplemented with vitamins C, A, E, and zinc, all of which are essential for skin and wound healing, the leg ulcer cleared and soon disappeared.

The visible signs of malnutrition, then, are not always correctly diagnosed or even associated with alcoholism. Misdiagnosis results in a worsening of the condition, particularly if the alcoholic keeps drinking. Some known and established nutritionally-related disorders are briefly described below; some of these are common while others are rarely seen.*

Disorders of the Central Nervous System

The central nervous system (the brain, spinal cord, and branching nerves) is most profoundly affected by vitamin, mineral, and amino-acid deficiencies, particularly deficiencies in the B vitamin series, including B-1, B-3, B-6, B-12, and folic acid. When the brain is sick, it shows its agony in a wide spectrum of emotional, psychological, and behavioral symptoms.

Sometimes a severe deficiency in a particular vitamin or

* Anyone interested in a more in-depth discussion of the relationship between nutritional deficiencies and bodily disorders and disease should be sure to read Daphne Roe's excellent book *Alcohol and the Diet* and Charles Lieber's *Metabolic Aspects of Alcoholism.*

mineral will result in a specific disease that can be extremely painful and debilitating. Such is the case with a rather common nervous-system disorder among alcoholics known as polyneuropathy (literally, a disease of many nerves). More severe, but rarer, central nervous system (CNS) nutritional disorders include Wernicke's encephalopathy and Korsakoff's psychosis. Then there is a wide range of neuropsychiatric disorders that don't fit into any disease category.

POLYNEUROPATHY

Polyneuropathy is a nutritional disorder generally associated with deficiencies of the B-complex vitamins—including thiamine (B-1), pantothenic acid, nicotinic acid or niacin (B-3), and pyridoxine (B-6)—that weakens and eventually damages the nerves extending outside the brain and spinal cord. These nerves, which are similar to thin, elongated wires, carry electrical/chemical impulses that instruct the legs, arms, and torso to lift, move, run, and walk, and feel warmth, cold, pain, and pressure.

The first indications of polyneuropathy are numbness and tingling sensations ("pins and needles") in the extremities, usually the toes and fingers. These sensations are common in middle- and late-stage alcoholics. As the condition progresses, the sensations occur higher in the limbs, affecting hands and arms, feet and legs. Pain may be excruciating and muscle tone and coordination may be lost. Fortunately, polyneuropathy is reversible if arrested early enough. The nerves will heal themselves within several weeks or months once the alcoholic stops drinking and watches his diet, making sure to take in a rich supply of vitamins (particularly the B vitamins) and minerals.

WERNICKE'S ENCEPHALOPATHY

Named after a nineteenth-century German psychiatrist and brain specialist, Wernicke's encephalopathy is usually produced by a severe deficiency in thiamine (B-1). The disease is marked by rapid onset of headaches, double vision, abnormal eye movements, states of confusion, loss of balance, and brain hemorrhage. Until forty years ago, the prognosis invariably was death, but after the B vitamins were synthesized and became readily available, significant improvement in the condition became possible and the symptoms are now largely reversible if treated promptly. Immediate treatment is essential, however, because the condition swiftly progresses into the generally irreversible disorder known as Korsakoff's psychosis.

KORSAKOFF'S PSYCHOSIS

Korsakoff's psychosis, first described in 1890 by the Russian psychiatrist Sergeyevich Korsakoff, is caused, in part, by vitamin B-1 deficiencies, and generally results in irreversible brain damage. The disorder has several striking characteristics including hallucinations, the loss of short-term memory, and the consequent fabrication of stories to fill in the gaps (termed *confabulation*). The victim is often able to remember past events but is thoroughly confused as to present or recent events such as where he is, why he happens to be there, what he has just eaten, or who may be sitting next to him.

NEUROPSYCHIATRIC DISORDERS

The neuropsychiatric disorders associated with alcoholism are numerous, ranging from mild tremors and agitation to D.T.'s and psychosis. Some have names like Korsakoff's and Wernicke's and a few patients clearly match the clinical description of these diseases. Many alcoholics, however, show a complex array of nervous-system disorders that don't fit into any specific disease category. Sometimes alcoholics are diagnosed as schizophrenic, manic-depressive, neurotic, or psychotic—not because they are mentally ill, but because alcohol disrupts brain functioning and makes them *appear* mentally ill. Some brain disorders are clearly related to nutrient deficiencies while others are primarily caused by alcohol's direct toxic effects. The situation of Al is fairly typical of the neuropsychiatric disorders of many mid- to late-stage alcoholics.

THE CASE OF AL

Al, a sixty-four-year-old Norwegian truck driver, had a long and hard drinking history of heavy binges with prolonged periods of not eating. Through the years he became more confused and hostile when he was drinking, and in the intervals between drinking bouts he had trouble bouncing back. His memory seemed to be fading away, and driving a truck was becoming impossible because he couldn't read road maps or remember directions.

His family finally succeeded in getting him into treatment. On admission, the staff physician noted that Al was generally malnourished-looking, thin and scrawny. Although his thinking processes were obviously affected by alcohol, Al was generally clear-headed and cooperative. On the second day of withdrawal, his brain functioning began to deteriorate despite large doses of vitamins and proper sedation. While generally alert and able and willing to follow directions, Al had no idea what day, month, or year it was. He thought he was at his cousin's house and mistook the staff for family members, calling them by name. He was clear on past events, remembering the name of his first-grade teacher and keeping the staff amused with his off-color jokes, but when asked who the president of the United States was, he knitted his brow, sighed a few times, and finally gave up. On the fourth day of treatment, his mental state worsened and he was less alert, more combative, and generally very confused.

The staff agreed that Al needed further neurological testing and transferred him to a general hospital. In the next week he was in very bad shape: confused, delusional, and paranoid. X-rays and brain scans showed no tumors or hemorrhage—although his brain had shrunk, its tissues partly destroyed by alcohol. A physician finally told Al's family that his brain might have been permanently and severely damaged by alcohol and that they should consider nursing-home care. However, in the next few weeks, with continued good nutrition and B-vitamin replacement, Al slowly improved, regaining his sanity and rationality; the treatment staff believe that, with the help and support of his family, he will be able to care for himself and live a productive life.

OTHER AFFECTED AREAS

While the central nervous system is perhaps the part of the body most visibly affected by alcohol's disruption of the nutritional equilibrium, other organs and systems are also profoundly affected.

LIVER

The mighty liver, an organ responsible for hundreds of processes essential for life, can be reduced by excessive drinking to a decrepit structure clogged with poisons, wastes, and dead cells, and incapable of sustaining life. Alcohol and its byproduct acetaldehyde will destroy liver cells all by themselves, but nutritional deficiencies prevent the sickly cells from regaining their strength and producing new cells to fight off the lethal assault.

SKIN

Skin infections are common among alcoholics, for the body's immune system relies, in part, on an adequate store of proteins. Since the chronic alcoholic's diet is frequently low in protein and his liver may be damaged and unable to make sufficient protein, his body has a very low resistance to infection; once infection sets in, the cells are unable to adequately repair themselves. Protein deficiency also interferes with wound healing which, like infections, places great demands on the body's metabolism, requiring extra nutrients. Deficiencies in vitamins A, C, and E, and zinc, all of which are important in keeping the skin healthy and resistant to disease, are also common in alcoholics.

LUNGS

Susceptibility to respiratory infections (colds, bronchitis, pneumonia) are not only common among alcoholics but are much more severe than usual, destroying more tissue and penetrating deeper than they do in nonalcoholics. Deep penetration of the infection is a characteristic result of malnutrition, and antibiotics often don't work to heal the wound or stop the infection until the patient's nutritional problems are reversed. This is generally true of all infection in the body, including colds, bronchitis, kidney infections, and infected eyes—alcohol destroys the body's ability to defend itself.

HEART AND BLOOD VESSELS

Potassium, calcium, and magnesium deficiencies can cause arrhythmias (irregularities of the heartbeat). Thiamine (B-1) deficiencies can cause the heart to get flabby and eventually lead to heart failure. Alcohol also disrupts fat metabolism and increases triglycerides and cholesterol in the blood, setting the stage for hardening of the arteries. Alcoholics are generally at much greater risk for high blood pressure, heart attacks, and strokes.

BONES AND MUSCLES

When alcohol is in the blood, calcium and magnesium are rapidly excreted. In one study, researchers gave one ounce of alcohol to both alcoholics and nonalcoholics and twenty minutes later found that calcium losses in the urine increased by 100 percent and magnesium losses by 167 percent!* Because these minerals are crucial for strong, healthy bones, alcoholics typically have softer bones than nonalcoholics of the same age, making them more susceptible to fractures. In one group of alcoholics studied—all under age forty-five—bone density was about the same as in nonalcoholic men and women over seventy.† Low levels of calcium and magnesium, along with B-vitamin deficiencies, can also interfere with normal muscle contraction, leading to muscle soreness, leg cramps, and an irregular heart rate.

BLOOD CELLS

Distortions in the size and shape of red blood cells are found in somewhere between 80 and 90 percent of alcoholics. Anemia, the end result of sick and dying red blood cells, results from poor intake, absorption, and use of iron,** protein, vitamins B-6 and B-12, and/or folic acid. The anemic alcoholic may appear pale and washed-out, with symptoms of fatigue, headache, and loss of appetite. In progressive states of anemia, alcoholics may have heart palpitations, shortness of breath, slightly enlarged hearts, and swollen ankles.

The following table lists the major body systems affected by alcohol-induced nutritional disorders and the symptoms associated with these disorders.

Getting Help

The first priority of treatment is to cut off completely the primary cause of the trouble—alcohol. But abstinence alone

*J. M. Kalbfleisch et al., "Effects of Ethanol Administration on Urinary Excretion of Magnesium and Other Electrolytes in Alcoholic and Normal Subjects," *Journal of Clinical Investigations,* Vol. 42, 1963, p. 1,471.

†P. D. Saville, "Changes in Bone Mass with Age and Alcoholism," *Journal of Bone Joint Surgery,* Vol. 47A, 1965, p. 492.

**Iron deficiencies also result from blood loss due to trauma, bleeding ulcers, and ruptured veins in the esophagus (esophagal varices).

Body Systems Affected by Alcohol-induced Nutritional Disorders

System	Associated nutrients	Symptoms
Central nervous	B vitamins Calcium Magnesium Zinc Cerebral amines and neurotransmitters	Depression, anxiety, irritability, mental confusion, insomnia, convulsions, personality disturbance
Respiratory	Vitamin C Vitamin A	Colds, respiratory infections, pneumonia
Cardio-vascular	B-1 Magnesium Potassium	High blood pressure, irregular heart rate, heart failure
Digestive	B vitamins Minerals	Diarrhea
Skeletal-muscle	Calcium Magnesium	Muscle inflammation (myositis), decreased bone density, propensity to fracture
Blood	Folic acid Iron B-12 B-6	Anemia, lowered white-blood-cell count, fewer platelets
Skin	Zinc Vitamin A Vitamin C Vitamin E	Infections, poor healing ability, skin diseases and disorders (eczema, rashes, etc.)
Endocrine	B vitamins Vitamin C Vitamin E Pantothenic acid	Reduced sexual function, pancreatic malfunction, adrenal malfunction, thyroid malfunction

won't make the sick cells healthy again. One of the great and continuing tragedies of alcoholism treatment is the two-to-three-day "dry-out" in which the alcoholic is brought into treatment extremely sick, is dried out, and then released when he's able to stand up and walk to the bathroom without assistance. But while the dried-out alcoholic may be able to function by himself, he is not restored to health—just as someone with a broken leg cannot be considered completely recovered once the cast has been fitted. People with broken legs don't go mountain climbing the week after treatment, and people treated for alcoholism in three days cannot jump out of bed feeling healthy, energetic, and ready for a new life. The healing process takes time—weeks, months, sometimes years—because the disease has encompassed the entire body and disrupted the normal workings of the cells.

Sick cells need help; they need to be saturated with nutrients so that they can heal themselves, strengthen their defenses, and go about the business of becoming normal, healthy cells again. And as the cells get stronger, the tissues, organs, and systems they comprise will also perk up and start functioning normally once more.

Some alcoholics, particularly late-stage alcoholics who have been drinking steadily for months and years and who have not been eating well, need extensive medical and nutritional therapy to speed up this healing process and help combat the more serious withdrawal symptoms such as convulsions and D.T.'s. Alcoholics often need vitamin and mineral injections to "prime the pump" and get the sickly digestive system back on its feet again. Even early- and middle-stage alcoholics should receive vitamin and mineral supplements from the very first day of treatment to establish a firm foundation for recovery.

TOOLS FOR DIAGNOSING MALNUTRITION

Nutritional therapy will lessen the alcoholic's mental and physical discomfort in the first days of treatment and will help his body get started on the long and difficult repair job necessary for continuing good health. Right at the beginning of treatment, it's important to determine exactly what the alcoholic's nutritional problems are. The diagnosis of nutritional deficiencies, as with other body disorders, depends on four diagnostic tools: the medical history, physical exam, laboratory tests, and analysis of the patient's response to treatment.

MEDICAL HISTORY

Getting information about what the patient has been eating and drinking helps the treatment staff diagnose nutritional deficiencies, isolate specific causes of these deficiencies, and predict the patient's response to nutritional therapy. A detailed history of previous and current illnesses, which can be obtained from the patient, his relatives, his physical and/or medical records, is important because malnutrition is caused not only by inadequate food consumption, impaired absorption, use and increased excretion of nutrients, but also by trauma, infections, surgery, and the use of certain medications (see pages 64 to 65).

The medical history should also include the standard questions relating to previous diseases and hospitalizations, use of prescription medications and over-the-counter drugs, and other "street" drugs that disturb the brain and nervous system, such as marijuana, cocaine, amphetamines, Quaaludes, hallucinogens, heroin, morphine, and so on. A careful history can help uncover the reasons for a puzzling relapse. Mary, for example, relapsed after three years of sobriety for no apparent reason. When the physician took her medical history, he discovered that during a recent chest cold she sent her husband out for some Nyquil. After the first teaspoon or two, she found herself acting rather strangely—she kept reaching over and taking little nips from the Nyquil bottle. Soon the whole bottle was gone, and she sent her husband after another one, and then another. Within a few days she was back on the real thing—80-proof bourbon. Mary didn't know Nyquil was 25 percent alcohol, and her body wasn't able to distinguish between beverage and medicinal alcohols. For these reasons, all alcoholics must be warned about the hidden alcohols that can and too often do cause relapses. (See Appendix 1 for a listing of common medications that contain alcohol.)

PHYSICAL EXAM

In assessing nutritional deficiencies, the person conducting the physical exam should include a general recording of the alcoholic's appearance and any behavioral signs of drunkenness, lack of responsiveness, anxiety, depression, delusion, or hallucinations. Also important for accurate diagnosis are height and weight measurements, both of which should be taken into account when prescribing a diet. A nutritional profile should also be made in order to pinpoint any physical disorders that might indicate nutritional deficiencies and/or alcohol-induced disorders contributing to or associated with nutritional disease. Skin rashes, flaky skin, nosebleeds, bleeding gums, bruises, sores in the mouth, a red or inflamed tongue, tooth decay, dry, dull or coarse hair, and brittle fingernails are some of the physical signs of nutritional problems.

LABORATORY TESTS

The physical examination and the medical history will suggest certain vitamin and mineral deficiencies that can then be tested in the laboratory. A basic survey of blood chemistry, for example, can tell a great deal about whether the liver is functioning adequately and give some information about protein and calcium levels and how well the digestive system is working. A basic blood count can tell a lot about anemia. For the tired and easily fatigued patient, a look at thyroid function, anemia, and blood-sugar levels is helpful.

From these basic tests, a physician knowledgeable in the nutritional sciences and in the predictable effects of alcohol can develop a dietary/nutritional treatment plan that works well for the majority of recovering alcoholics. Those alcoholics who do not respond well should be tested further. Nutritional tests such as hair analysis and blood tests for various vitamin and mineral deficiencies can pinpoint specific problem areas.

PATIENT'S RESPONSE TO TREATMENT

The patient's response to treatment may be the most important aspect of diagnosing nutritional deficiencies, but it is traditionally the least respected because it depends on observations that can't readily be tested. Again, lab tests and physical exams detect only the later stages of nutritional disease and the more marginal and hidden disorders frequently go unnoticed. Unless nutritional deficiencies show up on laboratory tests—unless they are, in other words, scientifically certifiable—most physicians and researchers will not accept a diagnosis of malnutrition. Clinicians and scientists like to see proof, verified in research laboratories, that something exists or doesn't exist before they will prescribe medication or start treatment.

The doctor's office, however, can be a valuable "laboratory" for observing the benefits of various therapies. What better proof of nutritional deficiencies can there be than the visible and profound transformation in an alcoholic who has been treated with nutritional therapy? Such alcoholics typically look better, feel better, and are able to commit themselves to lifelong sobriety without the depression, anxiety, and craving for alcohol that plague the many recovering alcoholics who receive no nutritional therapy.

To forgo nutritional therapy because the patient has no active illness and appears outwardly healthy, or because standard lab tests show nothing unusual, is a serious mistake frequently made in treating alcoholics. Depression, insomnia, fatigue, headaches, and any number of other mental and physical complaints can be greatly relieved and even eliminated if the alcoholic's diet and eating patterns are carefully evaluated and a therapeutic program geared to his individual needs is prescribed. Given the fact that so many recovering alcoholics suffer from symptoms associated with marginal nutritional deficiencies, and that these symptoms are often associated with a return to drinking, the continuing neglect of nutritional therapy in most treatment programs is unacceptable. For such neglect can undermine the alcoholic's most determined efforts to stay sober and make sobriety a hellish existence in which the urge to drink becomes overpowering.

Yet in most alcoholism treatment centers throughout this country, nutritional assessment is not practiced, clinical nutritionists or dietitians are not included on the staff, no laboratory facilities exist where biochemical tests can be carried out, and the staff are not encouraged to ask questions about diet or eating patterns. Alcoholism, in these treatment centers, is treated as if it had no effect at all on the alcoholic's nutritional health, and the attitude seems to be that any nutritional problems an alcoholic might have will be cleared up after a week or two of sobriety.

Neglect of the alcoholic's nutritional needs is spawned by, and feeds on, a basic misconception of the disease. Alcoholism may be an illness, these treatment programs seem to profess, but it's primarily a psychological illness with potential physical complications. Once the obvious complications —cirrhosis, heart disease, ulcers, and diarrhea—are treated, the alcoholic is expected to rely on will power and self-motivation to stay healthy and sober. His mind, in other words, is considered the basic battleground where sobriety will be won or lost; his body is just a willing listener to whatever the mind tells it to do. This separation of the mind and the body—as if they were ruled by entirely different mechanisms—paints a clear picture of alcoholism as a psychological illness and allows treatment personnel to overlook the primary neurochemical causes of "mental" problems such as depression, mood swings, anxiety, and confusion. And it propagates the myth of the alcoholic as a psychologically and emotionally impaired person.

A LETHAL CATCH 22

Lack of attention to nutritional needs will also do nothing to break the bad eating habits that can undermine sobriety. Without help and guidance, most alcoholics will revert to their old ways of eating, which usually include drinking lots of coffee and eating heavy loads of sugar and processed foods. These foods make the alcoholic feel better temporarily and may even relieve the craving for alcohol. But—and this is the Catch 22 of most recoveries—the relief is soon replaced with an even stronger desire for alcohol and even more severe feelings of depression, fatigue, nervousness, and despair.

Alcoholics who are given no training or guidance in nutritional therapy have no idea that their continuing "psychological" problems are very likely related to physical disturbances in the body. These physical disturbances are not easily or quickly gotten rid of—despite the prevailing myth that nutritional problems are minor and have no lasting impact. Drinking alcoholics, like many other people, believe that if they take a vitamin pill every day, they will be protected from nutritional diseases. "But I take multivitamin pills," was the explanation given to her doctor by an alcoholic who suffered from bleeding gums and sores around her mouth. "So this can't be a nutritional problem!"

Of course, human beings cannot live on just vitamin pills, which supply only a few of the approximately forty essential nutrients the body needs. Food must supply the other nutrients, including proteins, fats, and carbohydrates and the energy these foods supply. The intake of food must be balanced so that the body gets what it needs in the right proportions; too much food, of course, can be just as dangerous as too little, the most obvious example being obesity and the lethal stresses extra pounds put on the heart and other vital organs.

THE BASICS OF NUTRITIONAL THERAPY

The basic nutritional therapy for the alcoholic patient is a nutritious, appetizing diet based on the individual's specific deficiencies and requirements. Frequent meals and high-protein snacks between meals will help control unstable blood sugar and provide a source of slowly available glucose. Concentrated sweets such as candy, chocolates, ice cream, and cake must be strictly avoided since they are rapidly absorbed and cause a sudden surge in blood sugar, leading to peaks and valleys in the blood-sugar level and the distressing symptoms that accompany these peaks and valleys. A late-night, high-protein snack will help sustain the blood sugar through the night and prevent early-morning hypoglycemic symptoms.

Caffeine use should be eliminated or, at the very least, drastically cut back since caffeine can aggravate stomach disorders and disturb blood-sugar control, causing restlessness, irritability, insomnia, and headaches. The caffeine in coffee, tea, chocolate, and cola beverages can also irritate and stimulate the central nervous system, heart muscles, and respiration. Extensive liver damage can cause caffeine to accumulate to toxic levels.

The basic diet is described in Chapter 7, but it's important to remember that individual adjustments of the diet may be necessary in order to treat complications of alcoholism like cirrhosis, hepatitis, gastritis, and pancreatitis. Liver damage, for example, will lower the alcoholic's tolerance for proteins, and when liver damage is extensive, as in cirrhosis and, in some cases, hepatitis, the diet should be adjusted to limit protein intake.

Those people with specific problems such as diabetes, heart trouble, or cirrhosis should be sure to consult a physician before starting this diet. We want to emphasize, however, that nutritional therapy is a specialty just like surgery or obstetrics, and not all physicians have an interest or training in this area. One resource for the reader is the International College of Applied Nutrition, a society of physicians who have developed an interest and specialty in the areas of applied nutrition and preventive medicine. For a listing of health professionals in your own area, send a letter explaining what you want, along with a self-addressed, stamped envelope, to the college at P.O. Box 386, La Habra, California 90631.

4
Hypoglycemia: The Blood-Sugar Roller Coaster

Hypoglycemia is the most perplexing, mysterious, complicated, contradictory, as well as controversial and complex "disease. . ."

Paavo Airola, Ph.D.
Hypoglycemia: A Better Approach

A WORD ABOUT THE WORD

THE word *hypoglycemia* has generated enormous controversy, splitting the medical world in two: the "believers" and the "nonbelievers." The believers point to the fact that many people (some say as many as 20 million Americans) suffer, both mentally and physically, when their blood sugar drops below normal and that careful attention to diet can relieve their suffering and make them feel normal again. The nonbelievers insist that hypoglycemia is an extremely rare condition and that most people diagnosed as hypoglycemic actually have a perfectly normal reaction to sugar and are simply trying to find some convenient excuse for their psychological problems.

Much of the controversy and confusion centers around a precise definition of the word. Literally, hypoglycemia means *low-sugar blood,* or a low amount of sugar in the blood. But there is no agreement about how low the blood sugar must fall before it is considered abnormal and labelled hypoglycemia. Some people experience symptoms at a point just below normal, others suffer when their blood sugar drops quickly and steeply, and still others are most affected by wide swings between highs and lows—which of these is hypoglycemia? Can all of these conditions be called hypoglycemia? Again, there is no agreement.

In an attempt to clarify the confusion, hypoglycemia has been divided into two basic categories according to causes. (1) Low blood-sugar states caused by certain diseases such as disorders or tumors of the pancreas, intestinal tract, or liver. These conditions are rare, affecting less than 10 percent of the people diagnosed as hypoglycemic. (2) Hypoglycemia caused by the body's reaction to certain foods, specifically sugar; some even consider hypoglycemia an allergic reaction to certain foods, and not necessarily just sugary foods. Physicians generally label these hypoglycemic reactions to food as *functional* or *reactive* hypoglycemia. Ninety percent of the people diagnosed as hypoglycemic fall into this category.

Obviously, much work needs to be done to describe the complex of blood-sugar abnormalities that are lumped under the label of hypoglycemia, particularly the type considered to be functional hypoglycemia. But the existing inadequacies of the word, or uncertainties about the exact nature of the biochemical processes at work, do not change the fact that certain people—particularly alcoholics—suffer from abnormal swings in blood sugar which cause both mental and physical suffering.

THE CASE OF SANDRA

Sandra thought she might be going crazy. Her doctors told her she was fine physically, and yet she was an emotional and psychological wreck. She suffered from insomnia, often waking up in the middle of the night for no apparent reason. During the day she felt exhausted, irritable, and constantly on edge, as if she had to continually control herself just to stay together. She found herself crying or shouting at her husband for no reason at all.

She worried that maybe she had a brain tumor or some kind of cancer. She suffered from pounding headaches, sometimes three or four a day; other times she had a "pounder," as she called it, that lasted all day long. She was nervous and tense, and yet she never had any energy and just the slightest exertion wore her out. Doing the dishes had become a major event. Her daily walks, which she had always looked forward to, shortened and eventually stopped altogether. Her garden went to seed. She didn't care about much of anything.

The only time she felt somewhat normal was when she was drinking. Alcohol seemed to pep her up, give her motivation and energy and make her her old self again. In an effort to get some sound sleep, she began to drink a glass or two of wine just before bed. But she still couldn't relax or get to sleep and, in desperation, she asked her doctor for some sleeping pills. But the pills only worked for a little while, and she had to ask for something stronger. She also asked for something to calm her nerves during the day. "I'm jumpy and nervous," she told her doctor, "and yet I'm always tired. Just making breakfast exhausts me." He prescribed an antidepressant and suggested seeing a psychiatrist. "Midlife changes can be upsetting," he explained. "Maybe it would help if you could talk things out."

It did help to discuss her doubts and fears and have the psychiatrist assure her she was, in fact, sane, but her depression and insomnia didn't go away. She wondered again if she might be slowly dying of some dread but unrecognized disease, and she became so depressed that she stopped calling her friends and simply stayed home all day. Her only consolation was her drinking. "At least I have those few hours during the day when I feel normal again," she thought.

Sandra is an alcoholic. She is also suffering from unstable blood-sugar (glucose) levels. Drinking alcohol makes her blood-sugar lows worse, and the lows increase her desire to drink more alcohol—a deadly cycle that happens to many alcoholics. Chronic drinking has fouled up her body's ability to control the glucose level, and Sandra is caught on a roller coaster of blood-sugar highs and lows—with alcohol controlling the power switch. If Sandra stopped drinking, would she be able to jump off the roller coaster and feel normal again? Not necessarily. Alcohol is only one source of power capable of sending the blood sugar skyrocketing or plummeting; other sources, specifically heavy loads of sugar, can keep Sandra and others like her chained up, seemingly helpless victims of their own biochemistry.

THE SUGAR CONTROL SYSTEM: HOW IT *SHOULD* WORK

Glucose is the body's main source of fuel, and it's needed in constant and continual supply to provide every part of the body with energy to do its work. The body gets this fuel from the food we eat, but how slowly or quickly glucose is made available to the cells depends on the specific type of food.

Glucose is found in carbohydrate-rich foods (starches) like bread, grains, vegetables, fruit, beans, and corn, all of which are made up of long-chain, complex molecules that are slowly broken down and changed into the smaller, simple glucose molecule. But glucose is also found in "concentrated" carbohydrates as in alcohol, sugar, and sweets, which are made up of smaller molecules and are thus more quickly absorbed, causing a sudden rush of glucose into the blood stream. These concentrated carbohydrates are often the villains that disrupt the crucial blood-sugar regulating system.

Keeping the blood sugar in balance requires a complex chain of events involving the digestive tract, pancreas, brain, liver, and endocrine glands, including the adrenals, pituitary, and thyroid. In simplified form, this is how the sugar-control system should work:

• After we eat, the starches and sugars in the food are broken down during digestion into glucose.

• Glucose is passed through the intestine and then circulated in the blood stream, where it is available to the cells as an energy source.

• While glucose circulates throughout the body, the pancreas releases the hormone insulin to help the glucose enter the cells and be put to work.

• Other hormone responses stimulate the liver to convert unused glucose to glycogen, the stored form of glucose.

• Glycogen stores are in constant flux, being broken down to glucose and released by the liver when the body is low on glucose, or built back up by new supplies of excess glucose.

• When glycogen and glucose stores are used up, hormones secreted by the pituitary and adrenal glands tell the body to use fat and protein to make alternative energy supplies.

Since the body needs a regular and continuous flow of

THE SUGAR-REGULATING SYSTEM

Major organs involved in the absorption, production, regulation, and storage of glucose.

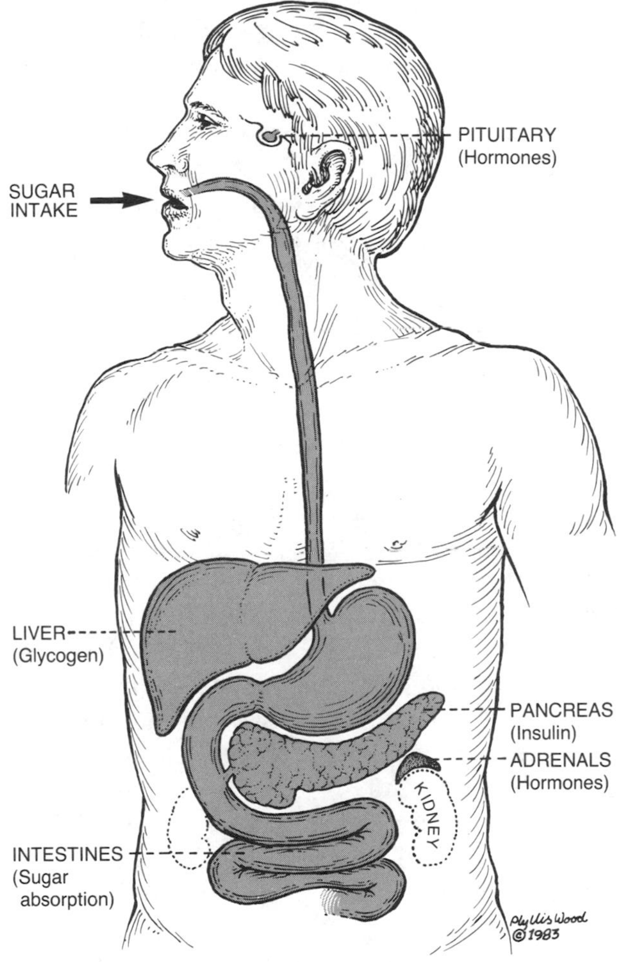

glucose to function, it will do all it can to make sure the supply is constant. When the blood sugar drops, either because of a poor diet or a foul-up in the sugar-control machinery, the body immediately signals an alarm by releasing adrenalin and other hormones to prevent a calamity—at the worst, coma and death. Adrenalin alerts the liver to begin breaking down glycogen into glucose, while other hormones signal the body to build up and store new glucose for future demands, and start converting stored fat to usable energy. If these methods fail, the body can even burn up its own muscles for fuel; this, in fact, is what happens in extreme states of starvation.

BUT IN ALCOHOLICS . . .

Something happens in alcoholics to disrupt this intricate sugar-control system and make the blood sugar fluctuate erratically. Why this happens is as yet unclear, although some obvious possibilities emerge. First, the sugar-rich alcohol hits the blood stream like a lightning bolt, short-circuiting the sugar-control system and causing the normally smooth flow of sugar to become rough and uneven. Second, continual and heavy drinking hits the liver, pancreas, intestinal tract, adrenal glands, and brain hard; and these are the primary organs responsible for controlling and monitoring the blood sugar. If these organs are sick and diseased, the blood-sugar levels become unstable. It's also possible that alcoholics have some kind of genetic weakness in their ability to regulate blood-sugar levels. Research on this is scanty, but many alcoholics tell of apparent blood-sugar problems that occurred before they started drinking heavily and regularly.

Alcohol, then, appears to have a combined effect by being a sugar-rich food as well as helping to damage and weaken the organs responsible for controlling blood sugar. But whatever the cause, alcoholics frequently have blood-

Five-Hour Glucose Tolerance Test of 135 Alcoholics Tested by L. Ann Mueller

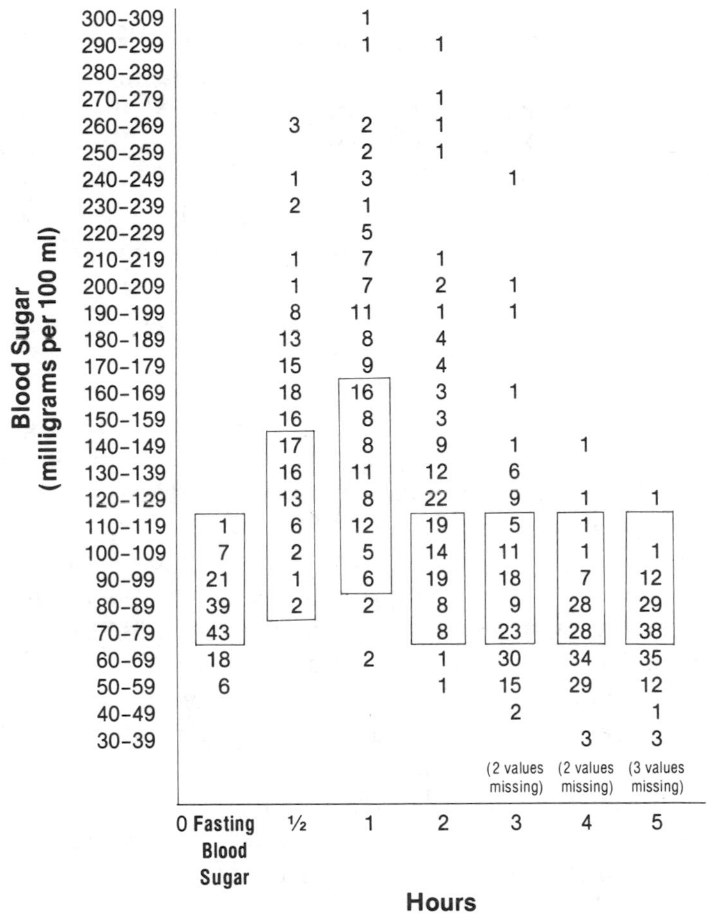

Numbers indicate number of patients at that level
Boxes indicate normal range

Blood Sugar (milligrams per 100 ml)	0 Fasting Blood Sugar	½	1	2	3	4	5
300–309			1				
290–299			1	1			
280–289							
270–279				1			
260–269		3	2	1			
250–259			2	1			
240–249		1	3		1		
230–239		2	1				
220–229			5				
210–219		1	7	1			
200–209		1	7	2	1		
190–199		8	11	1	1		
180–189		13	8	4			
170–179		15	9	4			
160–169		18	16	3	1		
150–159		16	8	3			
140–149		17	8	9	1	1	
130–139		16	11	12	6		
120–129		13	8	22	9	1	1
110–119	1	6	12	19	5	1	
100–109	7	2	5	14	11	1	1
90–99	21	1	6	19	18	7	12
80–89	39	2	2	8	9	28	29
70–79	43			8	23	28	38
60–69	18		2	1	30	34	35
50–59	6			1	15	29	12
40–49					2		1
30–39						3	3
					(2 values missing)	(2 values missing)	(3 values missing)

Hours

sugar problems that occur both when they're drinking and when they're sober. When he's drinking, the alcoholic's blood sugar tends to shoot up high only to drop steeply when he stops drinking. When he's sober, the cycle of ups and downs is often fueled by his getting too much sugar from other foods.

The net result is a body catapulted into distress. The sugar lows throw the adrenalin switch, causing nervousness, sweats, shakes, nausea, and unreasonable fears. Low blood-sugar levels also cause stress to the brain, which is dependent on a smooth flow of glucose, causing confusion, irritability, and depression. These are the same distressing symptoms and personality changes that Sandra, as well as many other alcoholics, experienced.

How many alcoholics suffer from these attacks of low blood sugar? In a 1981 survey conducted by L. Ann Mueller, 93 percent of alcoholics tested showed disturbances in blood-sugar regulation when given a five- or six-hour glucose tolerance test—GTT—(chart, page 89). These alcoholics had been sober for about two weeks before taking the test.

Approximately a third of the 93 percent who had an abnormal response experienced a cluster of symptoms when the blood sugar dropped to its lowest point—even though that low point may not have deviated too far from normal. The blood sugar of some alcoholics, for example, dropped to only ten points below the bottom range of normal, and yet they were so incapacitated they couldn't think straight or function normally. One subject, a nurse who was also a recovering alcoholic, decided to take the test while she was working her shift. Her blood sugar dropped to just below normal, yet she became so lethargic and confused that she had to lie down for several hours.

Another third of the patients with abnormal responses showed scattered symptoms throughout the test, some when their blood sugar peaked and some when it fell to its low point. And the final third reported few or no symptoms at all even though the test showed highs and lows bouncing out of the normal range of values. The treatment staff noted, however, that some of these patients were affected by the test, experiencing changes in mood or temperament or having trouble thinking or responding clearly.

In summary, of the group of 135 alcoholics tested, about 93 percent showed abnormal peaks and valleys in blood-sugar patterns. Two-thirds of these suffered both mental and physical symptoms, some at the lowest point of blood sugar and others throughout the test.

THE GLUCOSE TOLERANCE TEST

The GTT tries to answer the question of how well the body tolerates concentrated sweets, somewhat the way an exercise test shows how well the heart tolerates exercise. Its original use was to detect high blood sugar, or *hyper*glycemia as found in diabetes. But it is also a useful tool to detect *hypo*glycemia, or low blood sugar.

To take the test, a patient has no food or stimulants after 10 P.M. the night before. The next morning a blood sample is drawn, and the blood-sugar value in a relatively stable state, unaffected by food or stimulants, is recorded. The patient then drinks a measured amount of quick-energy sugar, usually of a corn-syrup base. (This sugary drink is equivalent to a piece of pie with a scoop of ice cream.) Following the sugar drink, more blood is drawn after a half hour, after another half hour, and then hourly for a total of five or six hours, and tested for blood-sugar levels. These recorded blood-sugar levels show how the body responds to a concentrated dose of glucose. As seen in the informal study just discussed, most alcoholics have an abnormal response to the GTT, with their blood sugar rising into peaks and then dropping into valleys. The graphs show some typical alcoholic curves from this study.

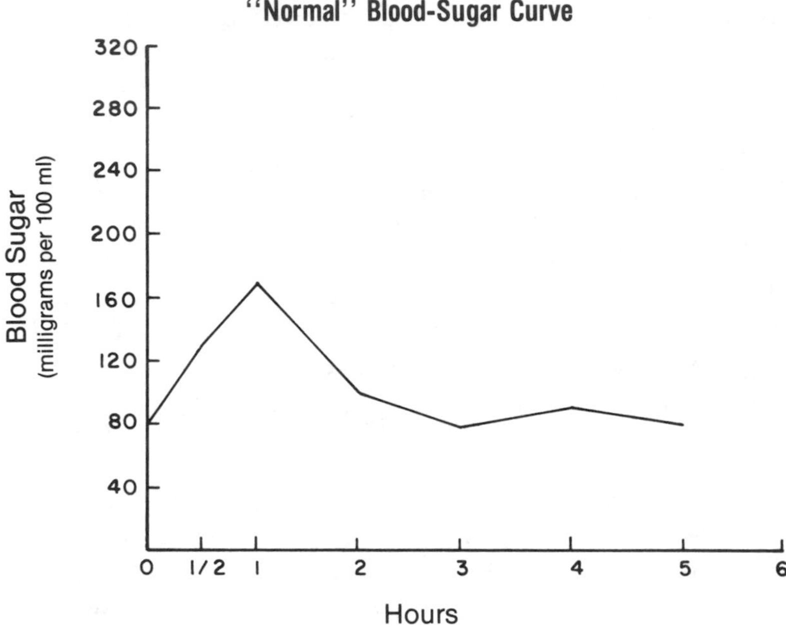

Normal blood-sugar response during a five-hour glucose tolerance test. The sugar rise in the first hour does not exceed 180 mg percent, and the blood sugar then stabilizes to levels near the fasting blood-sugar level.

INTERPRETING THE TEST

The physician's task is to determine how (or if) these ups and downs affect the patient's health and well-being. Since the definition and diagnosis of hypoglycemia are not uniformly agreed upon, the interpretation of the test graph often differs according to who reads it. Some physicians are not concerned, for example, unless the blood sugar drops below 50 milligrams percent (50 mg per 100 cc of blood); others argue that no abnormality exists unless the blood sugar falls below 50 milligrams percent *and* the patient experiences symptoms at the lowest point. Some physicians dismiss even obvious symptoms and fluctuations as insig-

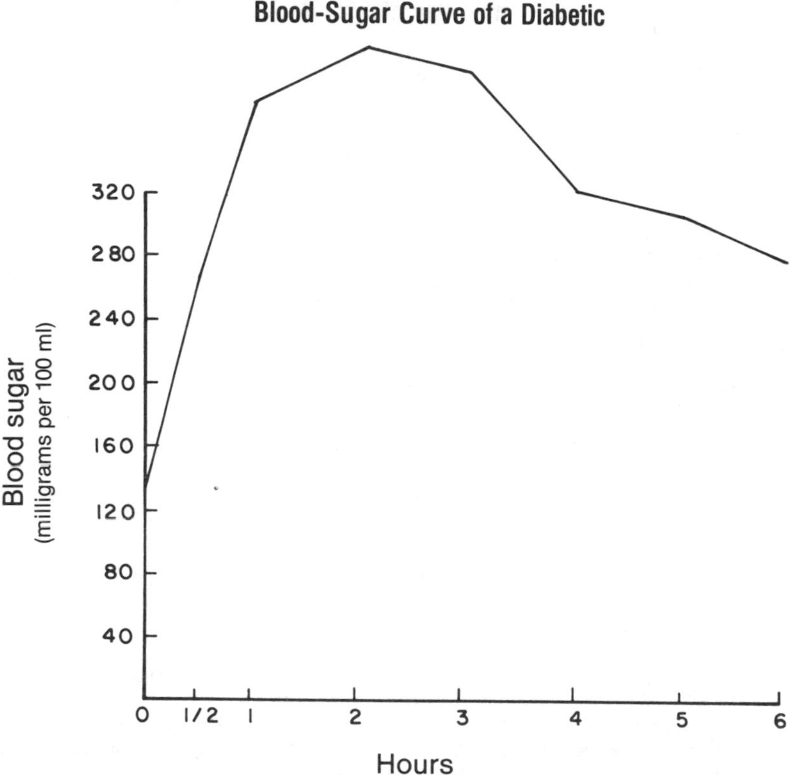

This patient, not previously diagnosed as a diabetic, demonstrated a highly abnormal blood-sugar response, with values off the chart at one hour, two hours, and three hours, and sustained high values throughout the test.

nificant and become concerned only if the values are in dangerous, precoma levels.

Some doctors, however, read these tests with a more sensitive eye and consider a ten-point fall from the beginning (first) blood sugar as hypoglycemia. The speed of the drop is of most concern to other experts, who argue that the symptoms are caused not by how *low* the blood sugar drops, but by how *fast* it drops.

Hypoglycemic Variations: Group 1

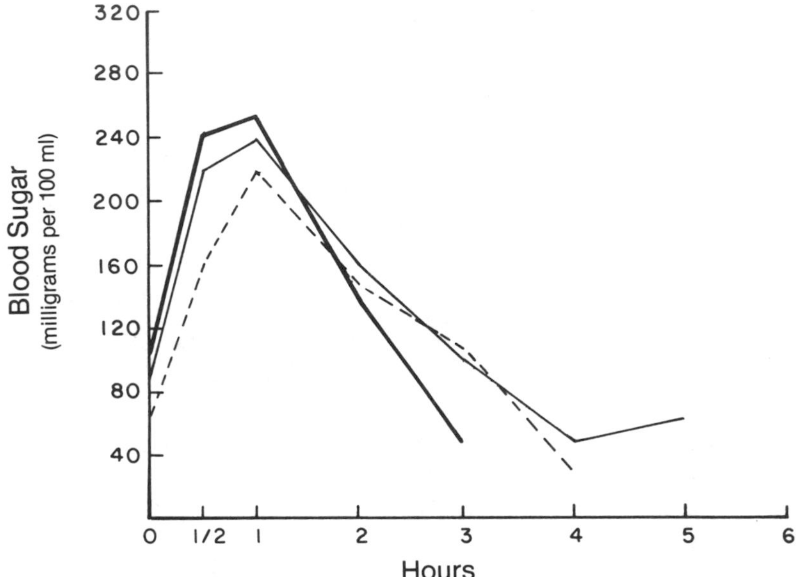

These patients show a sudden rise in blood sugar, then a steep drop to hypoglycemic levels, typically showing symptoms of hypoglycemia during the drop or at its lowest point. For two of these patients the test had to be stopped early due to marked symptoms of tremor, headaches, dizziness, and nausea. The symptoms disappeared after the patients had something to eat.

The experts' opinions are obviously in conflict, and it's no wonder that the term *hypoglycemia* has caused so much controversy and confusion. However, until some kind of agreement is reached on exactly what hypoglycemia is, why it affects certain people, and how a diagnosis can best be reached, patients and their doctors will have to put up with this confusion while trying to seek a solution for the problem. The best alternative is, obviously, not to throw up one's hands in frustration, but to try to relieve the symptoms—symptoms that, no matter what their cause, are distressing and disabling.

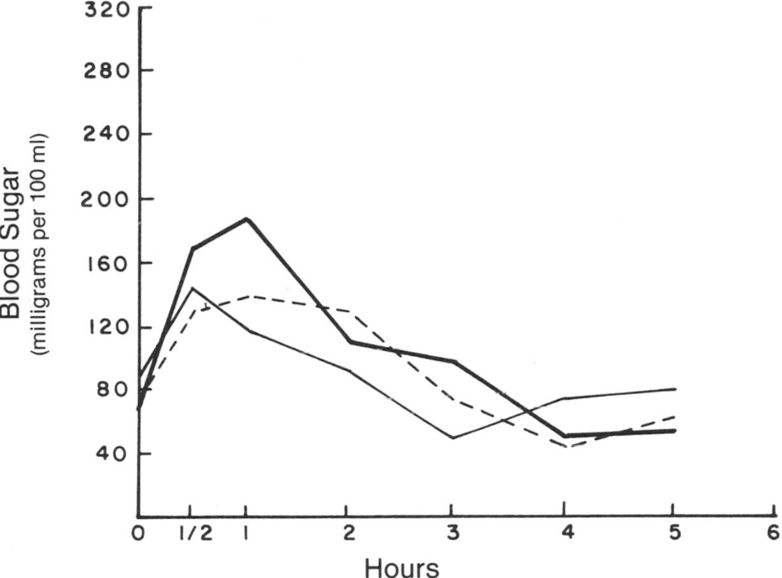

These patients show less blood-sugar fluctuations than the patients in Group 1. In this group, the patients have near normal values in the early part of the test, but around the third and fourth hours, the blood sugar drops mildly to moderately. Some of these patients, however, had as many symptoms of hypoglycemia as those who experienced more dramatic fluctuations.

THE SYMPTOMS

A listing of the most common symptoms associated with hypoglycemia gives an idea of exactly how debilitating this condition can be. Such a list, along with the percentage of patients complaining of them, was compiled by Harry M. Salzer, M.D., a psychiatrist at the University of Cincinnati College of Medicine. Most alcoholics are familiar with many of these unpleasant symptoms:

Paavo Airola, M.D., in his book *Hypoglycemia: A Better Approach* mentions twenty-four more symptoms he has encountered in his work with hypoglycemic patients.

Hypoglycemic Variations: Group 3

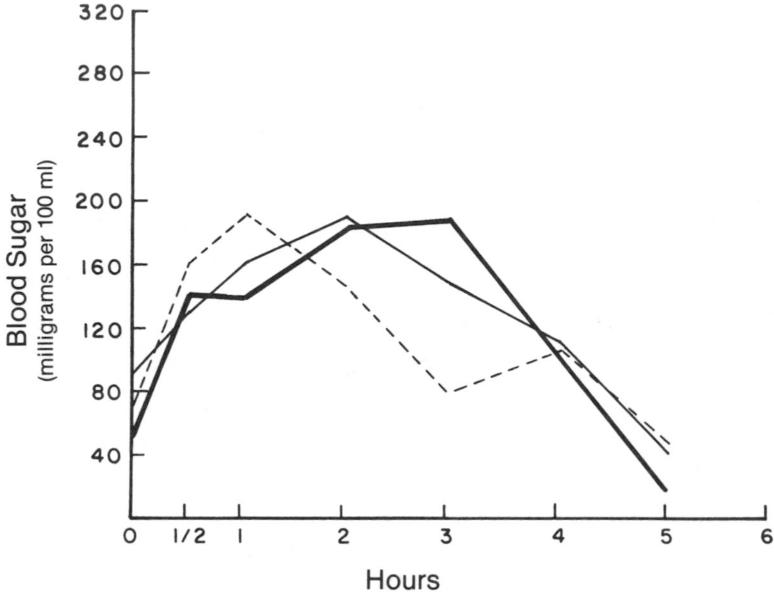

These patients showed a delayed hypoglycemic response at the fifth hour of the test. Occasionally, patients will not demonstrate hypoglycemia until the sixth hour.

WHERE THE SYMPTOMS COME FROM

These diverse symptoms arise from two different reactions. The first reaction involves the hormone adrenalin. When the blood sugar drops below a certain level, the adrenal glands release adrenalin in an attempt to correct a potentially life-threatening problem. Adrenalin is the "emergency" hormone that generates the flood of glucose, preparing the body with energy for the "fight or flight" response. The side effects of this response are extremely unpleasant: pounding of the heart, the shakes, sweats, feelings of great anxiety and fear, nervousness, nausea, and intense hunger. Everyone has experienced this reaction in one form or

Salzer's List of Symptoms of Hypoglycemia

Symptom	Percentage showing the symptom
Exhaustion	67%
Depression	60%
Insomnia	50%
Anxiety	50%
Irritability	45%
Headaches	45%
Vertigo	42%
Sweating	41%
Tremor (internal trembling)	38%
Tachycardia (palpitation of heart)	37%
Muscle pain and backache	33%
Anorexia (significant lack of appetite)	32%
Crying spells	32%
Phobias (unjustified fears)	31%
Difficulty in concentration	30%
Numbness	29%
Chronic indigestion	29%
Mental confusion	26%
Cold hands or feet	26%
Blurred vision	24%
Muscular twitching or cramps	23%
Joint pain	23%
Unsocial or anti-social behavior	22%
Restlessness	20%
Obesity	19%
Staggering	18%
Abdominal spasms	16%
Fainting or blackouts	14%
Convulsions	14%
Suicidal tendencies	10%

From Paavo Airola, Ph.D., *Hypoglycemia: A Better Approach,* Health Plus Publishers, P.O. Box 22001, Phoenix, AZ 85028. By permission of the publisher.

Airola's List of Symptoms of Hypoglycemia

Forgetfulness
Nervousness
Constant worrying
Ravenous hunger between meals
Indecisiveness
Lack of sex drive (females)
Craving for sweets
Impotence (males)
Moodiness
Allergies
Feeling of "going crazy"
Un-coordination
Itching and crawling sensations on skin
Gasping for breath
Smothering spells
Sighing and yawning
Unconsciousness
Night terrors, nightmares
Dry or burning mouth
Ringing in ears
Peculiar breath or perspiration odor
Temper tantrums
Hot flashes
Noise and light sensitivity

Ibid. By permission of the publisher.

another: having to suddenly swerve a car to avoid hitting an animal causes an adrenalin rush, as does, for some people, the fear of public speaking.

Other symptoms, such as headaches, insomnia, irritability, and mental confusion arise from a different source: the brain. The brain is very picky about the energy it uses and relies almost exclusively on glucose. During temporary shortages of glucose, the brain suffers mightily and registers its complaints in the form of headaches, confusion, irritability, nervousness, and/or depression. Severely deprived of

SOURCES OF SYMPTOMS
OF HYPOGLYCEMIA

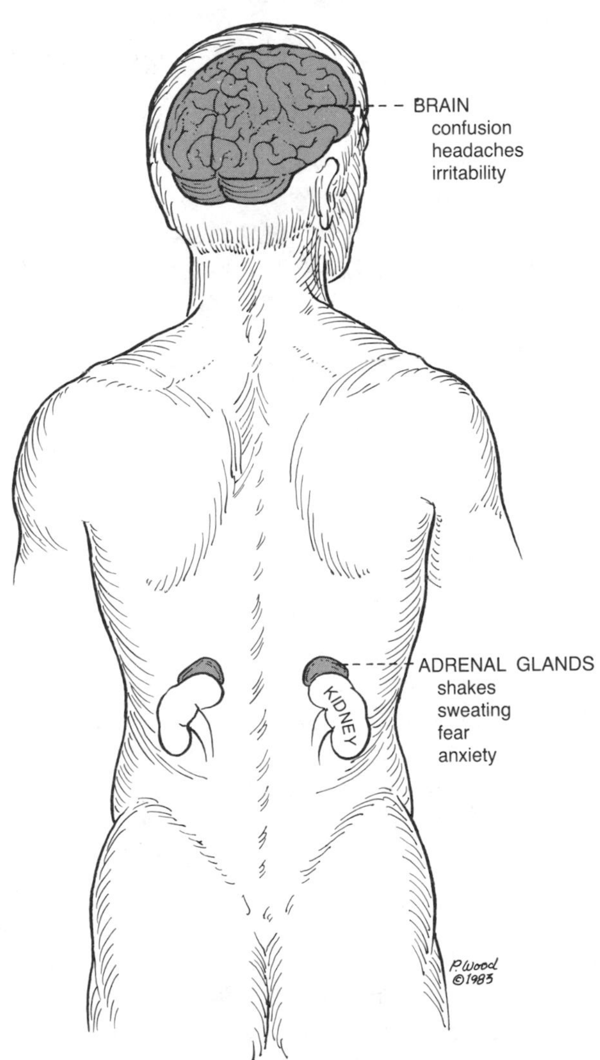

glucose for more than a few minutes, the brain is quite literally dying, and the sufferer may lapse into an irreversible coma.

Even with a slight drop in glucose, the brain can be seriously affected. During a GTT, when the brain is under stress because of the drop in blood sugar, it is not unusual for a normally tranquil alcoholic to become belligerent, drowsy, depressed, or uncooperative, and to continue to experience these unpleasant symptoms periodically for two or three days after the test. On rare occasions, a patient may faint or have a seizure during or after the test—further evidence of the brain's deep-seated dependence on glucose. The test, of course, simply exaggerates or brings out what happens in real-life situations when the hypoglycemic eats sugar or sweets.

THE CASE OF MONA

One morning Mona's children refused to eat breakfast. When she asked why, they replied, "You always get mad after breakfast." Mona knew she had a bad temper and she noticed that she was particularly irritable after eating her typical breakfast of two doughnuts and several cups of coffee. But she shrugged her kids' complaints off—until, as the months went by, her life became a constant misery of fatigue, fear, and depression.

It began to take all her energy just to get out of bed in the morning; when her husband and children finally left the house, she would lock all the doors, close the drapes, and "hide out," as she called it. She couldn't read, because she couldn't concentrate long enough on a subject to make any sense of the words. Even as a teen-ager she'd had trouble learning and retaining information, and she'd always thought she was slow and somewhat stupid. Now she was beginning to think she might be dangerous, for she sometimes thought about harming herself or her children. When her kids cried and she couldn't immediately comfort them, she wanted to shake or strike them—anything to shut them up.

Even simple activities like grocery shopping became impossible. One day Mona became so distraught trying to decide between two brands of ketchup that she left her cart full of food in the store and escaped to her house. Sometimes she was so drowsy and fatigued that she'd go to bed on a Friday night and not get out of bed until Monday morning.

One of Mona's doctors prescribed amphetamines to help her keep awake and functioning; another gave her antidepressants. She hoarded the pills, trying not to use them regularly but saving them for "special" occasions: cleaning the house for company, for example, or attending an evening P.T.A. meeting. Taking pills scared her; her mother had died of an overdose of alcohol and barbiturates. Besides, they didn't really work to get rid of her depressions. In fact, things just seemed to be getting worse, no matter what kind of pills she took. So, after a while, she stopped taking them, deciding that if she was going to suffer, she'd rather do it without the added fear of getting addicted to pills.

During one of her bad spells, when she locked herself in the bedroom and refused to come out, her husband sought advice from a university psychiatric service. After undergoing half a dozen psychological tests, Mona was diagnosed as a manic-depressive (a previous doctor had labelled her schizophrenic) and it was suggested that she be committed for treatment. But her husband couldn't bring himself to commit his obviously frightened wife.

One way or another, the family hung together as Mona learned to schedule her life around the predictable depressions. Finally, a good friend who had become deeply concerned about Mona's health and state of mind suggested that a change in eating patterns might help. The friend knew about a nutrition clinic that was close by and one morning she talked Mona into going over for a checkup. Mona was given a GTT, which showed a drop in blood sugar three hours after she drank the sugary solution. With the sudden drop in glucose, she felt confused, shaky, sick to her stomach, and scared to death. When she'd calmed down several hours later, the nutritionist carefully instructed her to eat regular meals and snacks and to stay away from sugar, alcohol, and other sugary foods.

Within a few weeks, her fears and depression began to fade, the indecisiveness was gone and, most impressive to her, she was able to read and retain information—she could learn! Six years later, Mona still follows the diet, and although she occasionally cheats, she's found that it's much more trouble than it's worth, for it always takes a few days until she feels right again.

THE PROBLEMS OF MISDIAGNOSIS

Most alcoholics have no idea that hypoglycemia may be causing them to feel depressed, tired, or anxious, and instead they fear a mental or emotional breakdown. Unfortunately, many physicians and counselors tend to confirm this diagnosis. The wide range of hypoglycemic symptoms, many of which appear to be psychological in nature, lead physicians to suspect hypochondria or to look for psychological upsets. Continuing depression and irritability seem to confirm the myth that alcoholics are basically depressed, lonely, confused, and unhappy people. The alcoholic who has fits of bad temper or is anxious and not thinking clearly is, in effect, written off with the conclusion, "Well, that's just the way alcoholics are."

Misdiagnosis has some potentially dangerous side effects. Believing the complaints to be psychological or emotional, doctors often prescribe a variety of pills to relieve the distress. Complaints of anxiety or nervousness will bring forth a prescription for tranquilizers; depression gets an antidepressant; insomnia is quickly fixed with sleeping pills. Both the doctor and the patient are relieved to have a treatment for the symptoms.

But for alcoholics, pills are ineffective, dangerous, and even deadly. Antidepressants, tranquilizers, and sedatives don't make the alcoholic's blood sugar normal again; and they only temporarily mask his most frequent complaints. In fact, the alcoholic's "psychological" problems of insomnia, anxiety, and depression will continue despite medication and are often dangerously increased.

THE CASE OF BEN

Ben was treated for alcoholism when he was thirty. He'd been a happy drunk—no brawls, fights, or belligerance marred his drinking days—but he knew he was dependent on alcohol and needed help. His family finally intervened, and he was admitted to an alcoholism treatment program. With the on-going support of Alcoholics Anonymous, Ben was sober for twelve years, with just one one-day relapse that only reinforced his desire to stay sober.

In 1976 Ben began to have stomach problems, diagnosed as duodenal ulcers with chronic gastro-intestinal problems involving abdominal cramping and heartburn. For three years his health went downhill. His stomach was constantly upset and even small amounts of food made him nauseous. He lost weight and looked pale and emaciated. In 1979 part of his stomach was surgically removed. He was given Percodan, a potent pain-killer, for three weeks following surgery, along with some Valium, a muscle relaxant and tranquilizer. He came home from the hospital quite depressed and couldn't seem to shake it.

The depression gradually got worse, and Ben became suicidal. His doctor diagnosed chronic depression and prescribed Elavil, an antidepressant, and Meprobomate, a tranquilizer. Two months later, Ben felt even worse, and his doctor recommended he see a psychiatrist. The psychiatrist switched his medications to Sinequan, another antidepressant; for the first few weeks of taking this new medication, Ben felt some relief. But his depression, lack of ambition, and suicidal thoughts gradually became even worse. The psychiatrist increased his dosage and Ben had another temporary period of relief. But the dosage had to be increased again and again, until he was taking 200 milligrams daily (he had started at 75). His life became unbearable, and fearing another alcoholic relapse, he admitted himself to an alcoholism treatment center.

On initial examination, Ben was in obvious emotional distress. He frequently broke down in tears, seemed on the edge of despair, and talked about suicide. His medications at this time were Sinequan (an antidepressant), Tranxene (a tranquilizer), and Tylenol with codeine for continuing abdominal discomforts. He had been on thyroid medications for a year and a half and had previously been treated with iron for anemia. His laboratory studies showed low calcium, low protein, and anemia, along with low thyroid function. His glucose tolerance test was highly abnormal, with a quick sugar rise and a sudden plummet to 35 mg percent (45 points below what is considered normal) during the second hour of the test, accompanied by symptoms of fatigue and severe depression.

Ben's treatment included withdrawal from all central-nervous-system pills, education about the physical nature of his addiction to alcohol and the effects of taking central-nervous-system drugs, and nutritional therapy to stabilize his blood sugar, correct his nutritional deficiencies, and begin the job of repairing and restoring his health. His thyroid medications were continued.

The first two weeks were touch-and-go, with his depression and emotional ups and downs only slowly decreasing. The addominal pain was a consistent problem, with cramps and diarrhea, but the treatment staff persisted with a nondrug approach and nutritional therapy until Ben was able to tolerate more and more food without discomfort. By the end of his fourth week in treatment, Ben couldn't believe the transformation in his mental and physical health. His appearance confirmed his statements of feeling like a new man, and laboratory tests continued to indicate improvement. He left treatment after five weeks feeling healthy, happy, and firmly committed to a chemical-free life.

THE PHYSICIAN'S DILEMMA

The consequences of misinterpreting the alcoholic's behavior as psychologically unbalanced are clearly disastrous, yet most physicians never even suspect nutritional and blood-sugar imbalances. Why? Generally, most physicians don't suspect that sober alcoholics have nutritional problems of any importance; specifically, they don't suspect that hypoglycemia poses a real and serious problem for many of their alcoholic patients.

Physicians tend to be disbelievers and skeptics for several reasons. The classic medical textbooks focus on only a few of the more obvious vitamin-deficiency states of the alcoholic. Little attention is paid to low-blood-sugar problems, and only those rare low-blood-sugar states caused by physical problems such as a tumor on the pancreas, an insulin overdose, or a liver-glycogen-storage disease are emphasized.

Physicians have also been put off by the hypoglycemia craze spawned over the last decade by several popular books promising an end to depression and fatigue, a new outlook on life, and greatly improved health just by changes in diet and eating habits. Physicians are naturally skeptical of these claims and equate hypoglycemic diets with other dietary fads that are unscientific and eventually ineffective. And, to traditionally schooled medical minds, all the talk about "sugar blues" and "white death" sounds like so much hocus pocus.

Blood-sugar disorders are also overlooked or misdiagnosed because physicians are oriented toward diseases with certain *specific* symptoms that can be treated by certain *specific* procedures. Doctors, in other words, are not likely to treat a condition until a diagnosis is made and a label is attached. Only when a patient's complaints add up to an identifiable illness is a specific treatment plan prescribed. Ulcers, for example, indicate some type of sore or crater in the stomach or intestinal tract for which antacids or acid blockers are typically prescribed. Pneumonia defines a deteriorative process in the lungs, usually infectious, for which antibiotics are appropriate. But the words *hypoglycemia* and *low blood sugar* leave most physicians cold because they don't really describe anything specific. The hypoglycemia label is inadequate, uncertain, ill-defined and confusing, leading most doctors to place no confidence in diagnostic techniques or treatments.

The majority of physicians find hypoglycemia a difficult diagnosis to make for three major reasons. First, low blood sugar is not specifically destructive to a particular organ or organs; second, the symptoms vary from person to person;

and third, the symptoms are diffuse and nonspecific and include many "psychological" complaints. Most doctors, plagued by busy schedules and an abiding belief that psychological problems are best treated with drugs or handled by a psychiatrist, find it easiest and most acceptable to simply write out a prescription or refer a patient to counseling. For most doctors, questioning patients about their diet seems like an unproductive way to spend their time.

ONE PHYSICIAN'S QUANDARY

One physician described the quandary she faced when she began to suspect that many of her patients were suffering from diet-related problems and she tried to switch from her orthodox drug-oriented training to a nutritional focus.

> It was foreign for me to use nutritional tools as a primary attack upon disease because that wasn't the emphasis in school—the only weapons I knew about were drugs, various medications, and surgery. Ten years ago, when I began to think about vitamins as "medicine," I had no idea what doses to prescribe, for how long, or what to expect as a result. I couldn't look up in the *Physician's Desk Reference* or drug manuals what doses of vitamins or minerals to use; I couldn't call a specialist and ask [because back then there were no respected nutritional "specialists"!]; and there were few if any laboratory indicators to "scientifically" follow the patient's progress and document a response or give guidance to therapy.
>
> When I first began to suspect blood-sugar problems and treated my patients' complaints with dietary changes and nutritional supplements, I felt like I was "flying by the seat of my pants"—the therapy just didn't seem very scientific, and my fellow doctors insisted it wasn't scientific. I remember the furor that erupted in the medical community when Linus Pauling had the nerve to suggest that vitamin C might be linked to colds and even to cancer! The intense and hostile nature of this controversy made me wonder if I really wanted to get involved in the nutrition field.
>
> But I knew that diet had to be related to health, and as I saw my patients respond to nutritional therapy with improved men-

> tal and physical well-being, I wanted to find out why the therapy worked. I read the medical textbooks again and researched the literature on nutrition and nutritional therapy. From my research I gained an entirely different perspective ón disease and the prevention of disease through nutrition. I learned again, but with greater understanding this time, that disease doesn't begin with a big trauma like a heart attack or stroke, but with invisible changes in the cells. And, I was slowly able to accept the fact that just because the effects of nutrients on the cells are *unseen* does not mean that they are *unscientific.*
>
> My uncertainties and unanswered questions as to how and why became less and less important. The important focus was that with nutritional therapy, my patients felt better, looked better, got well, and, in the case of alcoholics, stayed sober.

After several years of careful study and thought, this physician was able to move away from an exclusive drug-oriented treatment of disease to an understanding and appreciation of the effect of diet on health and disease. But most physicians have great difficulty pulling away from the traditional medical perspective and encompassing the nutritional point of view. Unfortunately, this makes it difficult for many recovering alcoholics to receive proper and effective therapy for their subtle but physically based problems. And without proper therapy, the problems and complications will inevitably get worse.

A CHRONIC AGGRAVATION

Hypoglycemia is not just a minor ailment that goes away after a few weeks like a cold or the flu, but a chronic aggravation that tends to get worse if left untreated. The body loses its "wisdom," as biochemist Roger Williams puts it, and seems to get stuck in a vicious cycle of foolish actions and reactions. Once the blood sugar drops below normal and remains unstable, the body needs glucose to bring it back to normal, and the fastest way to get a big dose of glucose into the blood stream is to consume foods with a high sugar content—sweets or alcohol. Thus, when the blood sugar drops, the body sends out an alert in the form of a craving for sweets or alcohol, both of which play havoc with blood-sugar stability and cause further cravings for more sweets or alcohol. These biochemical compulsions are often interchangeable, and many alcoholics are buffeted back and forth, craving alcohol, then sweets, then alcohol, and so on.

The body, in a sense, becomes more and more confused and less and less able to come up with the right food choices. Thus, an alcoholic suffering from low blood sugar often feels a craving for alcohol, which he can relieve for a little while by eating candy bars, ice cream, doughnuts, cake, and so on. But the spike in blood sugar is soon followed by a steep drop and with the drop comes an even greater desire for sweets, or alcohol.

The alcoholic becomes a helpless prisoner of this blood-sugar roller coaster, with his antidote becoming his poison. He doesn't know that he is making his problems worse by eating sweets, for they initially relieve his nervousness, anxiety, and depression. And the symptoms don't return until a few hours later, when the blood sugar again drops to a low level and the craving for sweets or alcohol begins to build all over.

SEIZURES, ARRHYTHMIAS, AND OTHER BODY REACTIONS

When the blood sugar drops too fast and too low, cells are starved of glucose, and the body chemistry is thrown out of balance. The repercussions can be felt throughout the body in many of the vital organs and systems—nervous, cardiovascular, reproductive, endocrine, and digestive.

Prolonged blood-sugar and nutritional problems can provoke these organs and systems to malfunction. The serious problems that result often appear to have nothing to do with blood-sugar control and nutritional imbalances, and only careful diagnosis can uncover the cause of the problem and suggest a proper course of treatment. Paul T., for example, is a teen-age alcoholic with a history of cardiac arrhythmia—irregularities in his heart rate—but when he stopped drinking and cut out sweets and caffeine, his arrhythmia simply disappeared. Or consider the case of Carol, who had a history of seizures for which her doctor prescribed Dilantin and phenobarbitol. Eventually she was diagnosed as an alcoholic and during treatment she was given a glucose tolerance test. During the test Carol had a grand mal seizure; her blood sugar was so abnormal that the lab technician thought he'd misread the chart. But after four weeks of sobriety and nutritional therapy, Carol stopped having seizures and no longer needed medication. She hasn't had a seizure in the two and a half years since her treatment.

Treatment

In alcoholics who have blood-sugar problems, two basic problems must be tackled. First, the major organs involved in the absorption, production, regulation, and storage of glucose—specifically, the liver, pancreas, adrenals, and digestive organs—have undoubtedly been weakened by long exposures to large doses of alcohol. These organs must be repaired and their functions put back into balance. Second, the typical alcoholic brought into treatment has lived for months or even years on a diet deficient in proteins, vitamins, and minerals. He's malnourished, and his blood-sugar levels are typically unstable.

To relieve these problems and help repair and heal injured organs, the recovering alcoholic must:

• *Avoid* sweets, stimulants, and stress (and, obviously, alcohol);

• *Add* nutritious foods to his diet and consume them on a regular and continuing basis;

• *Add* vitamins and minerals (particularly vitamin C, the B-complex vitamins, calcium, magnesium, and zinc) to help the body regain health and strength.

TO AVOID: THE THREE NEGATIVE S'S

SWEETS

Cutting way back on sweets or, better yet, avoiding them altogether, is essential for the alcoholic, because regular consumption of sweets disrupts nutritional balance, causing peaks and valleys in the blood-sugar level and leading to the unpleasant symptoms described in this chapter.

STIMULANTS

Sugar is not the only substance that triggers hypoglycemia. Stimulants like caffeine, which is found in coffee, tea, cola beverages, and chocolate, or nicotine can also have an adrenalin-like action, stirring up the blood sugar. For these reasons, alcoholics should avoid foods and beverages containing caffeine and will do best to stop smoking as well.

STRESS

Stress causes many alcoholics to have unstable blood-sugar levels. When a person is under stress, the body's response is to pump adrenalin into the blood stream, which may cause the blood sugar to fluctuate abnormally, causing even more stress.

In its most acute form, released adrenalin prepares the body to meet the demand of an urgent situation. This fight or flight response immediately floods the body with glucose energy, allowing us to perform incredible feats. The case of the woman who was able to lift the back end of a Volkswagen that had collapsed on her son as he was working beneath it is just one example of the extraordinary strength provided by this response. But while this adrenalin release has positive effects, it can also chronically upset glucose control and body chemistry in sensitive people like alcoholics.

Stress is, without a doubt, a biological experience that can have profound effects on the body's intricate biochemical balancing act. How well someone tolerates stress depends in part on how well his body responds to the release of adrenalin. The recovering alcoholic is less able to tolerate stress not because he is inherently tense or anxious but because his biological equipment for dealing with stress—the adrenal glands—has been damaged by long and heavy drinking. Autopsies on alcoholics show visible and measurable loss of adrenal gland tissue; in some alcoholics, the outer rim of the gland is almost nonexistent.

The alcoholic must be careful to protect himself against those situations which provoke on-going anxiety and tension. Traveling, disruptions in routine, social obligations, job pressures, and marriage difficulties are just a few of the common stresses that can unhinge the alcoholic's biological equilibrium in the early days of recovery and physical repair. The alcoholic must try to avoid stress whenever possible; when he can't avoid it, he can do a lot to help himself by understanding and accepting his body's limitations, particularly in the first weeks and months of recovery.

In summary, stress can aggravate hypoglycemia; eating well will strengthen the alcoholic's defenses and allow him to cope better with stress.

TO ADD: THE THREE POSITIVE S'S

SUITABLE DIET

In 1924 Searle Harris, M.D., devised a high-protein, low-carbohydrate diet to combat chronic low blood sugar. "The more protein the better," describes the general thrust of his diet, and the largest portion of this protein was to be supplied by meat and meat products. But nutritional science has undergone dramatic changes since 1924, and scientific research now shows that our daily need for protein is much less than previously thought. In fact, an excess of protein, particularly meat protein, can be harmful to health and contribute to many degenerative diseases, including cancer and heart disease.

The diet now recommended for controlling blood-sugar problems is higher in complex—or whole-food, high-quality—carbohydrates (fruits, vegetables, and whole grains); high in fiber (bran, wheat germ); and lower in protein, particularly meat protein. But consistent with both diets is strict avoidance of concentrated sweets.

SNACKS

Snacks help combat the drop in blood sugar that occurs two to four hours after meals and also help sustain the blood-sugar level between meals. Allowable snacks are not of the candy bar, coke, and milkshake variety, but are actually nutritious minimeals of fruit and protein foods like nuts, seeds, cheese, or celery sticks with peanut butter.

SUPPLEMENTS

Supplements are just that—supplements for a good diet, not replacements. Because of long years of heavy drinking, alcoholics have numerous vitamin and mineral deficiencies that daily supplements can help correct. But even after their bodies have fully recovered, many alcoholics need to continue taking supplements in order to maintain good health.

Nutritional therapy is an essential element of treatment for alcoholism and its two common companions, malnutrition and hypoglycemia. Yet its use is still hotly debated. Many treatment centers provide only limited nutritional guidance and therapy during the recovery period and some offer none at all. Treatment staffs and private practitioners often scoff at the idea that a change in diet can help alcoholics to a more comfortable and secure sobriety. Research investigating the link between alcoholism and nutritional deficiencies has been sporadic and sparse. Alcoholics themselves remain ignorant of the many benefits available from simple dietary changes.

The reasons for this continuing neglect and a look at the major controversies surrounding nutritional theory and therapy will be explored in Part 2.

PART TWO

The Controversies

5

Science or Sorcery?

We doctors are the most stubborn lot in the world! Many doctors are so stubborn as to think that a fact can't be true if they were not taught it in medical school.

W.C. Alvarez, M.D., *The Neuroses*

TWENTY-five-hundred years ago, Hippocrates, the Father of Medicine, exhorted his students to "Let thy food be thy medicine and thy medicine thy food." He left no doubt about his preference for food as medicine and his objection to strong drugs when he said, "Leave your drugs in the chemist's pot if you can heal the patient with food!"

Today's medical students get an entirely different message that can be summed up like this: food is food and medicine is something completely different. To rely solely on food for healing would be considered barbaric, nonsensical, and a waste of superb technology. Hippocrates relied on proper diet, fresh air, and close attention to habits and living conditions, but twentieth-century physicians have immediate access to amazing chemical products that can alter moods, induce sleep, fight infection, and halt the progress of malignant cancers. The modern doctor has an arsenal of healing and diasnostic devices such as machines that keep the patient's heart pumping and blood coursing, lasers that zap diseased body parts, and ultrasounds that paint a picture of the inner organs with sound waves.

WHAT FOOD CAN DO

How can the simple act of eating compare with this glittering parade of high technology? Can food cut out diseased tissue with the skill of a surgeon's knife? Can carbohydrates, proteins, and fats take the place of an artificial heart or kidney? Can vitamins and minerals halt the flow of blood from a severed artery. Of course not. Food is not a heroic healer, and once disease has erupted and the cells are visibly sick, food is relatively powerless to effect a quick cure. Food may be a necessity, but it can't perform miracles in a pinch.

But nutritious food is nonetheless a tool that the body uses to trigger its powerful healing properties—a fact that 2,500 years haven't changed. Unfortunately, medical students today spend the majority of their time learning about the heroics of healing a disease that has already erupted and little or no time at all learning about the powers of nutrition to *prevent* disease. The subject of nutrition has been considered peripheral to the modern-day physician's art, as if it had nothing to do with health and disease. As syndicated columnist Lester Coleman, M.D., explained in November 1982:

> For many years doctors have assiduously avoided discussions that centered around the relationship between food, diet, and illness. Many of us can recall that throughout the entire medical school curriculum there might have been half a dozen lectures on food, lectures that were considered to be a bore and a total waste of time. Even the instructors seemed to consider this a total waste of their valuable time.

This modern-day nutritional neglect is unfortunate because eating certain foods while avoiding others can do much to prevent disease from taking hold and can also help in healing once disease has begun. In our quest for miracle cures and a quick end to painful and uncomfortable symptoms, we've forgotten that disease is not just an end product but a long process of deterioration, and that nutrients are the most natural and time-proven weapons in preventing and then fighting disease. Why, we have to wonder, do we wait until a disease process takes firm hold, requiring expensive and heroic tests and treatments, when more natural, simpler, and less expensive measures can prevent the crisis from ever happening? What we've ended up with, according to the American Health Foundation, is "a legacy of a medical system that provides *too much too late.*"

A NEW DISCOVERY OF AN OLD DISCIPLINE

Those who proclaim the power of nutrients to halt and even reverse the process of degenerative disease are not sorcerers or charlatans. They do not call on mystical powers, brew strange and foul-smelling potions, or chant to mysterious gods. Instead, they use nature's own weapons—nutrients—to do battle with disease and promote optimum health.

This revived emphasis represents a radical shift in the philosophy and practice of modern-day medicine. Nutrition-oriented physicians emphasize health rather than disease, and prevention in addition to cure. They have observed that much mental and physical distress is the result of inadequate nutrition—the cells are sick because they are not being adequately provided with the nutrients necessary for proper metabolism and health. A healthy body and mind, in fact, depend on healthy cells.

NUTRIENTS AS WEAPONS

The nutritional weapons used by physicians to fight disease and promote health are the same used by the body in its own system of health and defense: vitamins, minerals, and the large molecules of the cell, including fats, proteins, and carbohydrates. These are the natural components of cells, the building materials that make the cells healthy and strong. When cells are sick or damaged, they use these same materials to repair themselves and shore up their own natural defenses against disease. Nutrients have added benefits in that they are not toxic,* do not promote physical dependence, and are inexpensive.

Drugs, on the other hand, can be toxic, often cause addiction, and are frequently very expensive. Worst of all, they treat the symptoms, not the causes, of disease. Physicians understand that these drugs are alien chemicals that can radically alter our biochemical makeup and cause numerous dangerous side effects. In *A Physician's Handbook on Orthomolecular Medicine,* Roger Williams, a biochemist and outspoken advocate of nutritional therapy, describes a major problem associated with using drugs:**

> Drugs at best are only a palliative form of treatment. . . . The basic fault of these weapons [drugs] is that they have no known connection with the disease process itself. . . . These drugs are wholly unlike nature's weapons [nutrients]. . . . They tend to mask the difficulty, not eliminate it. They contaminate the internal environment, create dependence on the part of the patient, and often complicate the physician's job by erasing valuable clues as to the real source of the trouble.

Williams is not suggesting that all drugs be thrown out and never used again; modern-day techniques and the host

*In extremely large doses, certain nutrients such as the fat-soluble vitamins, particularly A and D, can be toxic (see Chapter 8).

** Roger Williams and Dwight Kalita. *A Physician's Handbook on Orthomolecular Medicine*, Keats Publishing Inc., New Canaan, CT, 1979.

of chemicals now used to treat disease can be life-saving and are often necessary in acute situations when the patient is desperately ill or in severe pain. But Williams is concerned about the overuse and abuse of drugs that give only temporary relief, do nothing to help the body heal itself, and become substitutes for safer, more natural treatments.

And the body does have remarkable healing abilities. Consider the case of Larry, a sixty-five-year-old alcoholic with a liver half choked off by cirrhosis, a stomach lining in shreds from gastritis, and a brain soaked for so long in alcohol that it took him three weeks of intensive medical treatment to realize where he was. Larry had hit bottom hard and his physicians were afraid he had no reserves left to bounce back. But with continued abstinence, nutritional therapy, and education about his disease, Larry slowly recovered. After seven weeks of treatment, he was released and five years later he's still sober—and healthy.

A DIFFERENT VIEW OF THE PATIENT

Nutrition-focused physicians also view the patient in a different way from most disease-oriented physicians. In the usual, traditional medical approach, the patient is frequently seen as the cause of the problems. For the most part, counseling and psychiatric treatment proceed on the theory that neurotic and psychotic symptoms arise in people whose biological bodies are sound: the ethereal mind is disordered, the physical body is presumably healthy. The great majority of psychological problems, most counselors and psychiatrists believe, arise from an assortment of hostilities, dependencies, conflicts, inadequate coping mechanisms, guilt, self-loathing, and immaturity. Physicians prescribe tranquilizers for their nervous, anxious, irritable, and depressed patients, reasoning that the drugs will help them relax while they try to work out their problems. Physicians are careful, of course, to make sure that no obvious physical problem—a brain tumor, for example, or a hormone imbalance—is causing the psychological disturbances. But this is where most physicians stop; they would be venturing onto foreign ground if they looked at their patients' diets, tested for vitamin and mineral deficiencies, or prescribed nutritional supplements as a means of uncovering and then correcting the more hidden causes of physically-induced disease.

Physicians sensitive to nutritionally-induced disorders, on the other hand, immediately suspect and look for imbalances in their patients' biochemical makeup when they complain of psychological symptoms. Investigating the patient's dietary habits, suggesting supplementary vitamins and minerals, encouraging vigorous exercise to promote circulation and physical well-being, and counseling the avoidance of toxic substances like lead, mercury, aluminum, and nicotine are all considered by such doctors to be important therapies for "mental" problems. Not all psychological problems, of course, are physically based, but it's impossible to know the true cause of these problems until the possible physical and biochemical causes of disease are thoroughly explored. Only then can an accurate diagnosis of psychological problems be made and a course of treatment prescribed.

A RENEGADE BRANCH

Physicians who use nutritional tools sometimes get the cold shoulder from traditional medical practitioners; but a new discovery about "brain allergies" has caused some jaws to drop and breathing to become irregular. Allergies to common foods and chemicals,* some physicians insist, can alter brain and nervous-system functioning and cause a

*These chemicals include hair dyes, shampoos and conditioners; cosmetics; perfumes; gasoline; soaps; oil or gas from furnaces; moth balls; spray fresheners; flea and tick powders; paints; and a myriad of other common "conveniences."

wide assortment of mental and physical symptoms. Most neuroses and psychoses, these doctors observe, are at bottom physiological, and the primary cause of physical damage to the cells is faulty nutrition.

William Philpott, M. D., is an outspoken advocate of this concept of brain allergies. In his controversial book *Brain Allergies: The Psychonutrient Connection,* Philpott describes how frequently eaten foods and common chemicals are capable of adversely affecting brain and nervous-system functioning and creating "mental" illness. He cites several dramatic examples of neurotic and psychotic symptoms caused by exposure to common foods or chemicals:

> A fifty-two-year-old woman with a neurotic depression was tested for wheat. She developed a stiff neck and tightness in the chest and throat; even worse, she felt like hitting or punching someone. She was so frightened she might act on these compulsive urges that she went to a room by herself until the reaction subsided.
>
> Pineapple evoked irritability, blocking of thought, dizziness, and a severe headache in a thirty-six-year-old psychoneurotic woman. Oranges made her violently angry, and she fought with her son; her mind functioned so poorly she could hardly carry on a conversation. Rice brought on uncontrollable giggling followed by crying.
>
> A four-year-old boy diagnosed as hyperkinetic had a variety of reactions. String beans made him hyperactive, and he wanted to fight everyone. Celery gave him a severe stomach ache, after which he cried and became grouchy. Strawberries made him angry and hyperactive and caused a great deal of coughing. Unrefined cane sugar caused him to be irritable, after which he coughed and developed a stuffy nose.

PREPOSTEROUS AND HERETICAL?

Philpott's brain-allergy theory is as welcome to most orthodox medical practitioners as was Copernicus's theory of a round earth to people basing their whole sense of things on the belief that the earth was flat. Both theories raise questions that, to minds schooled differently, seem at once preposterous and heretical. For if the earth is round, people once thought, then won't we all fall off? Likewise, if food is addictive and capable of causing bizarre behavior, what is safe any more? We think we're standing on safe and secure ground regarding mental health and then Philpott pulls the rug out from underneath us, exposing all sorts of strange and unwelcome thoughts. Mental illness isn't mental, but physical, he proposes; don't treat mental complaints with drugs or psychotherapy, but with the right kinds of food.

People whose view of the world is shattered by such unorthodox theories are quick to point their fingers and cry "Quack! Fraud! Charlatan!" Philpott himself went through a similar disbelief and, in fact, outright rejection of allergy theories of psychological illness when he was in medical school and for twenty years more, while practicing traditional psychiatry. But, as he describes it in *Brain Allergies,* the evidence itself eventually overcame his bias: "After reading the overwhelming evidence, I developed the conviction that I, too, should take these [allergic] reactions into account in my diagnoses, and let the evidence, rather than prejudice, speak for itself."

Philpott's work with food allergies adds validity to the theory that man's internal biochemical makeup can be disturbed and severely disrupted by common substances like food. The obvious difference in people's reactions to alcohol seems to fit well with this theory—most people can drink alcohol with no serious long-term side effects, but others have uncomfortable, unpleasant, and even life-threatening reactions. Most people drink alcohol regularly without ever experiencing a need or desire to drink more and more often; but a minority of drinkers—namely alcoholics—react differently and eventually become addicted to alcohol. A dramatic example of alcohol's ability to evoke different reactions in different people is the typical response of the Native

American and Oriental: flushing, lightheadedness, and immediate intoxication with even a small amount of alcohol. Philpott concludes that the biochemical nature of alcoholism is related to the body's allergic reaction to alcohol.

HORIZONTAL AND VERTICAL DISEASES

While Philpott's brain-allergy concepts are a long way from being accepted by most members of the medical community, even the basic tenets of nutritional medicine challenge the ideas and practices of most physicians. One way to understand the basic theoretical and practical differences between the nutritional approach to health care and the common method of treating patients with drugs and medicine is to think in terms of "horizontal" versus "vertical" disease—a concept that Jeffrey Bland, Ph.D., carefully explains in his book *Your Health Under Siege: Using Nutrition to Fight Back.*

Barbara T., for example, is an alcoholic who was brought into the hospital emergency room on a stretcher obviously drunk and in excruciating pain. She complained of nausea, vomiting, and abdominal pain, and she was jaundiced and had a fever of 103 degrees. The examining doctor discovered a severe case of gastritis, or inflammation of the stomach lining, and pneumonia. Later, a liver biopsy revealed fatty deposits in the liver, and a diagnosis of alcoholic hepatitis was confirmed.

The doctors knew exactly what to do with this horizontal patient. They sent Barbara up to the medical ward where she lay flat on her back while nurses and physicians took her blood, set up I.V.'s, gave her pills, and ordered tests. At regular intervals they wrote down her blood pressure and temperature, keeping careful records of her progress. After a few hours the pills and I.V.'s started to work, her fever went down, and she began to feel a little better. Her recovery progressed and after two weeks in the hospital, she was released.

The horizontal patient is just that: flat on his back, knocked out by the intensity of an illness, no longer able to function normally. Like Barbara, the patient has such symptoms as nausea, fever, headaches, diarrhea, or stomach cramps, which could add up to any one of a number of diagnoses: flu, appendicitis, cancer, diabetes, or heart disease. For each of these diagnoses the doctors and nurses follow a specific plan of care, dispensing pills that do very specific things, ordering tests to determine the patient's progress and general state of health, and recording progress at specific times. When the patient begins to feel better, he makes a slow transition from being a horizontal patient to a vertical and presumably healthy patient, and when he is able to function on his own, he is released—usually with several bottles of pills to alleviate any continued pain or uncomfortable symptoms.

In contrast to this familiar treatment of horizontal patients, some physicians emphasize health-care treatment that can be prescribed for patients before they are acutely ill, treatment that may even prevent them from becoming ill and therefore horizontal. The vertical patient is thus as much a part of their practice as the more severely ill horizontal patient.

THE CASE OF CARL J.

Carl J. is a vertical patient suffering from a vertical illness. He goes to work every day. He has no specific symptoms, although he complains to his wife that he doesn't feel quite right. But he can't put his finger on what is wrong—he is just generally tired out, out of sorts, and intermittently depressed. He doesn't have much energy, particularly at the end of the day; he has trouble sleeping; and he can't seem to get himself motivated to do much of anything. His moods fluctuate dramatically, but that doesn't surprise him because his job is difficult and demanding, and he doesn't get along with his boss. He's having difficulties with his wife, too, but they both believe the arguments and constant bickering are just temporary.

Carl drinks a lot, but neither he nor his wife suspect he is an alcoholic—how could he be when he's still going to work and providing for his family? At his annual checkup his doctor casually asked about his drinking habits. Carl shrugged his shoulders and said, "Well, I like the stuff, and I drink almost every day, but I'm not an alcoholic, if that's what you're getting at. I can go days, even weeks, without drinking." He admitted that he had at least two or three drinks every day, and sometimes he drank much more than that, but no one could accuse him of being a lush, he insisted. After all, he could drink twice as much as most of his friends and still drive home!

Carl's eating habits are also normal, at least when compared with his friends'. He skips breakfast most days and eats a doughnut or sweet roll at midmorning if he's hungry. He drinks lots of coffee in the mornings, about five or six cups, and he has a few drinks with lunch—but he always soaks up the alcohol with a sandwich or taco salad. At the cocktail hour he has two or three double Scotches and slakes his appetite with peanuts or chips. If he's hungry enough, he eats a hamburger or a TV dinner sometime later in the evening.

Most physicians would agree that while Carl's may not be the optimal diet, it's probably adequate. Because Carl appears strong and robust, his weight is in the average range (although his blood pressure and blood fats are a little high) and all his other tests are normal, his physician declared him in good health and asked him to return in a year to have another routine checkup. Although Carl complained of fatigue, nervousness, and periods of moodiness and irritability, his physician suspected only job-related stress. He gave Carl some tranquilizers and the advice to take it easy and not push himself so hard.

Carl's complaints didn't add up to symptoms of any recognizable disease, but he continued to feel worse and his health deteriorated. Still, he didn't think anything was physically wrong with him. Then, "out of the blue" as Carl later described it, he had a heart attack. Doctors went to work on his problems with a vengeance: prescribing oxygen, diuretics, digitalis, and bed rest; counseling bypass surgery; and ordering a battery of lab tests. He was horizontal now, in acute distress, they could see what was wrong with him, and they knew exactly what to do.

But as dedicated and hard-working as his physicians were, they missed a crucial diagnosis: Carl *was* an alcoholic. He might have had a heart attack even if he hadn't been drinking almost a fifth of Scotch a day (the two or three drinks a day had increased in just a few years to ten or twelve), but there's no question that this heavy drinking put severe stresses on his body and particularly on the cells in his heart muscle. Thiamine, calcium, magnesium, potassium, and triglyceride and cholesterol imbalances caused by his drinking also contributed to his massive heart attack. Yet not one of Carl's half a dozen physicians ever mentioned the word *alcoholism* and not one considered nutrition as an important part of Carl's treatment. Carl was released with more tranquilizers and more advice to go slow, perhaps take a vacation.

Carl will be back. Next time it may be another heart attack, perhaps a fatal one, or a broken leg from running his car into a tree, or a head injury from falling down the stairs after drinking too much. Even then the chances are good that he will make the transition from vertical to horizontal and back to vertical (if he survives) without ever being forced to confront his underlying disease of alcoholism—the cause of most of his physical and mental problems.

THE PROBLEM WITH VERTICAL PATIENTS

Vertical patients pose a problem for physicians because nothing is obviously wrong with them and they have no nameable disease. They may drink too much and their eating habits may be less than optimal, but most physicians feel distinctly uncomfortable suggesting lifestyle changes for their patients—especially if they look healthy. The typical physician believes that his patients' lifestyles are outside his province and area of expertise; he has been trained, after all, to diagnose and treat *diseases.* If the patient isn't complaining, or if his complaints appear basically psychological, then the physician assumes that nothing is physically wrong. Physicians also resist prying into their patients' private affairs because they fear they will establish an adversary relationship, with the physician as patronizing lecturer and the patient as squirming student. "My patients are grown up," one physician explained. "I don't ask them what they eat, how much they drink, or who they sleep with because it's none of my business."

Many physicians feel uncomfortable suggesting lifestyle changes for patients when they themselves are pursuing many of the same bad habits. "How can I suggest that patients cut down on sweets when I have a sweet tooth myself?" a physician might ask himself. "Or stop smoking when I also smoke a pack a day? Or cut down on alcohol, when I drink two or three martinis every night before dinner?" It also takes time and energy to motivate vertical patients to change their lifestyles—time and energy that most doctors simply don't have.

A SILENCE OF IGNORANCE

Another reason physicians are silent about nutrition is that they have never received the knowledge or training necessary to give informed advice. In fact, most physicians have no more practical knowledge about nutrition than their patients. A study published in the *Journal of Medical Education* in 1975 found that practicing medical doctors and senior medical students did very poorly on standard nutritional questionnaires. Those questions that they did answer correctly were the same questions that the public at large answered correctly. The study concluded that most practicing physicians get their information about nutrition from the same sources their patients do: magazines such as *Time* and *Newsweek* and newspaper reports.

Most physicians now in practice have had no formal education or training in nutritional theory or therapy. They received what some critics wryly refer to as the one-line nutrition course, which can be summed up like this: "As long as your patients are eating three square meals a day, there's nothing to worry about." Although more medical schools are now offering courses in nutrition, these courses tend to be offered in the first two years; later on, the knowledge is not applied in actual patient health-care situations. In his first-year physiology courses, the medical student learns by rote the complex vitamin-dependent energy cycle of the cell—but by the fourth year of clinical training, he is not trained to think about specific nutritional deficiencies that might account for a patient's complaints of fatigue, depression, irritability, mental confusion, lack of motivation or general lack of well-being.

Even with recent discoveries linking diet to disease and pointing up serious deficiencies in the basic American diet, nutritional science is still considered outside the physician's area of expertise, a sort of expendable sideline. When programs are cut, courses in nutrition are the first to go. When

Governor Jerry Brown asked California medical schools to shave the costs of medical education, the schools immediately proposed cutting back programs on nutrition. In a similar situation, the University of Washington, forced to cut millions of dollars from its budget in 1982, proposed the elimination of the nutritional sciences program as one of its first cuts.

No wonder physicians who shift their emphasis to nutritional therapy are regarded with skepticism or treated as outcasts. Nutrition has been neglected and derided for so long by medical practitioners that, to many, it seems a foolish waste of time. Physicians have not been taught to think of illness in terms of prevention but have been taught to concentrate on relieving symptoms and trying to halt the disease process once it is already established. Many learn to instantly distrust anything outside their education and experience, if only for the reason that they are dealing with human lives and their responsibilities to their patients prevent any kind of "experimentation."

Nutritional therapy is not, however, a new or unproven method of treatment, nor is it dangerous in any way when practiced by a physician who has acquired a working knowledge of body metabolism, nutritional deficiencies, and the body's needs of various nutrients. Prejudice against nutritional therapy is often based on ignorance of its premise and methods rather than proof that it does not work.

OVERCOMING PREJUDICE AND IGNORANCE

Proof that nutritional therapy does work is the best way to overcome prejudice and ignorance. And this is coming: the McGovern Committee on Nutrition started the ball rolling with its report linking diet with disease and setting dietary goals for American citizens. Senator George McGovern set the no-nonsense tone of this report in his January 1977 statement to the press:

> The simple fact is that our diets have changed radically within the last fifty years, with great and often very harmful effects on our health. These dietary changes represent as great a threat to public health as smoking. Too much fat, too much sugar or salt, can be and are linked directly to heart disease, cancer, obesity, and stroke, among other killer diseases. In all, six of the ten leading causes of death in the United States have been linked to our diet.

In 1982, the National Research Council of the National Academy of Sciences reported new emphasis on dietary intervention for cancer, and the value of vitamins and minerals (specifically vitamins A and E, and the mineral selenium) for cancer protection. The September 1982 meeting of the International Cancer Congress repeatedly focussed attention on the link between diet and cancer and urged Americans to change their eating habits and dietary patterns. Newspapers and magazines continually report new evidence about the value of nutrition in fighting disease and growing concerns about marginal nutritional deficiencies caused by our diets. (Ironically, a major cause of concern in recent years has been the inadequacy of hospital diets!)

This interest has gathered momentum because of several factors:

- More doctors are realizing that nutritional therapy *works* in treating both mental and physical problems and that nutrients are not only less dangerous than drugs, but much less costly.

- Nutrition is an extremely active science with an information-doubling time of six years—in other words, every six years the amount of new information accrued is equivalent to the previously existing body of information!

- The staggering costs of medical care have finally begun to stimulate interest in alternative health-care systems. Consider the multiplying costs of health—actually disease—care:

1950: $12 billion;
1970: $70 billion;
1980: $247 billion.

The projection for 1990 is $764 billion, and by the year 2000 Americans are expected to spend over $1 trillion on medical care!

A number of factors, then, have reawakened interest in nutritional theory and therapy, and interest is triggering action. Research in the area of nutritional science is beginning to receive more money from federal agencies, the need for nutritional education in our medical schools is getting more attention, and both private industry and the public are becoming increasingly interested and involved in what is called "the wellness movement." As of June 1980, for example, 2,000 hospitals in the U.S. offered some type of wellness program. Major corporations are also adopting wellness and corporate fitness programs for their employees. New York Telephone, which employs 80,000 people, established nine wellness centers eight years ago. In 1980 these programs cost the company $2.84 million; but savings in absenteeism and medical costs alone were estimated at $5.54 million—a net gain of $2.7 million! Blue Cross/Blue Shield in California has a wellness plan and offers a significant decrease in health-insurance premiums for those who participate.

The pendulum has obviously begun its swing back to the other side: Nutritional theory and therapy can no longer be called quackery or dismissed as substitutes for traditional medical treatment. Preventing disease must become as integral a part of our medical care as curing it. For as a nation and as individuals, we can no longer afford to ignore, either from prejudice or ignorance, the overwhelming evidence showing that what we eat and how we live our lives can either kill us—or cure us.

6
Can Nutrition Prevent Alcoholism?

The doctor of the future will give no medicine, but will interest his patients in the care of the human frame, in diet, and in the cause and prevention of disease.

Thomas A. Edison

SEEKING THE LIMITS

WHAT are the limits of nutrition in helping alcoholics recover from their disease? Can good nutrition prevent alcoholism in someone who is beginning to experience problems from drinking? Can a recovering alcoholic who is eating well start drinking again without experiencing the craving to drink more and more often? What about the risk for the children of alcoholics; can they drink safely if they drink moderately and eat wisely?

These are some of the questions that may occur to recovering alcoholics and to those who suspect they might become alcoholics. While there can be no doubt that good nutrition works to relieve many of the physical and "psychological" problems that plague recovering alcoholics, how much can nutrients do to protect a person against alcoholism?

Because we're still not sure exactly what happens inside the cells of an alcoholic to make him susceptible to alcoholism, these questions can't be wholly answered. However, studies show that alcoholism is an inherited disease, meaning that the genes of an alcoholic carry a different message than those of a nonalcoholic, causing different biochemical reactions to alcohol. Thus, the children of alcoholics will run a greater risk of becoming alcoholics themselves if they drink.

We also know that alcoholism is influenced by, and in turn influences, the body's nutritional makeup. For people who have a genetic susceptibility to alcoholism, it appears that providing the cells with the required nutrients may help slow down the disease process. It also appears that "bad" nutrition may facilitate or even speed up the disease. In several different experiments, rats who were fed heavy loads of sugar started drinking excessively; when fed a normal rat diet, these same animals literally turned their noses up when offered a drink. Playing around with a rat's diet, then, will affect the animal's desire to drink alcohol and may have an influence on its susceptibility to alcoholism. Of course, the insides of a rat dance to different biochemical tunes than the insides of a man. But, as shown throughout this book, alcoholics are also affected by what they eat, and cleaning up their diet can do wonders to help them overcome cravings for alcohol and physical and mental symptoms that can undermine sobriety.

Nutrition and genes, then, play a role in the development and expression of alcoholism, but exactly what these roles are and how they interconnect remain a jigsaw puzzle only partly pieced together. Perhaps when we find the precise gene or genes that contribute to alcoholism, we will also be able to find a "cure" for the disease, or at least identify with certainty those people who are at risk. Perhaps, too, when we discover exactly how specific nutrients protect against the specific genetic and biochemical weaknesses underlying alcoholism, we can give susceptible people specific amounts and kinds of nutrients to protect them against alcoholism.

PLUNGING AHEAD

Some scientists believe that we don't need to wait until all the answers are in. Nutrition is such a strong and vital tool, they argue, that it can be used now to protect against and perhaps even prevent alcoholism. Such a thesis is proposed by Roger Williams, a respected American biochemist and a pioneer in alcoholism and nutrition research. In his book *Can Alcoholism Be Prevented?* Williams argues that eating the right foods in the right proportions and taking vitamin and mineral supplements every day can greatly reduce susceptibility to alcoholism. "Without exercising superhuman strength or unusual power," he writes, "any person can avoid becoming entangled in the morass of alcoholism."

Williams believes that certain people can avoid the disease by following specific lifestyle guidelines: guidelines that, in essence, lead to a sound and healthy "internal environment" that protects against alcoholism. These guidelines focus on eating the right kinds of foods, avoiding the wrong kinds of foods, taking vitamin and mineral supplements, getting exercise, and accepting responsibility for one's own health and unique bodily needs.

By carefully examining and commenting on each of Williams's steps,* we hope to further clarify the relationship between diet and the disease of alcoholism, and perhaps get a little closer to the answers of at least two crucially important questions: Can alcoholism be prevented? and What can nutrition do to protect a person against alcoholism?

* For purposes of this discussion, Williams's steps have in some cases been combined and renumbered.

STEP 1: Treat Yourself As the Unique Individual You Really Are

Roger Williams synthesized pantothenic acid, one of the B vitamins, but many physicians and researchers consider his concept of "biochemical individuality" to be his major scientific contribution. In dozens of papers covering hundreds of experiments, Williams has presented compelling evidence that every person in this world is different from everyone else in a variety of ways. We are not carbon copies of each other, he explains, but totally unique individuals. Our organs vary in size and shape, our hormones are produced at different levels, and our reactions to drugs vary dramatically.

Range in Relative Organ Weights of 645 Rabbits

(Grams per kilo of net body weight)

Organ	Minimum	Maximum	Ratio, Max./Min.
Gastrointestinal mass	70.4	452.0	6:1
Heart	1.95	4.42	2.3:1
Liver	23.2	117.0	5:1
Kidneys	3.45	17.28	5:1
Spleen	0.035	2.93	80:1
Thymus	0.248	3.315	13:1
Testicles	0.47	4.93	10:1
Brain	3.33	8.16	2.5:1
Thyroid	0.048	1.23	25:1
Parathyroid	0.001	0.022	22:1
Hypophysis	0.007	0.035	5:1
Suprarenals	0.080	0.572	7:1
Pineal	0.002	0.025	12:1
Popliteal lymph nodes	0.05	0.382	8:1
Axillary lymph nodes	0.019	0.24	13:1
Deep cervical lymph nodes	0.02	0.295	15:1
Mesenteric lymph nodes	0.67	6.91	10:1

Source: Wade H. Brown, Louise Pearoe, and Chester Van Allen, *Journal of Experimental Medicine,* Vol. 43, 1926, pp. 734–738. By permission of the Rockefeller University Press.

This biochemical individuality carries across all species. Williams cites a study conducted in 1926, which compared the weights of body organs in 645 rabbits. The diversity is astonishing, as can be seen in the following chart. Note, for example, that the thyroid gland in one rabbit was twenty-five times the weight of the same gland in another rabbit. Variations in human beings can be just as dramatic. Take a look at the drawings of normal human stomachs below.

Variations in "Normal" Human Stomachs

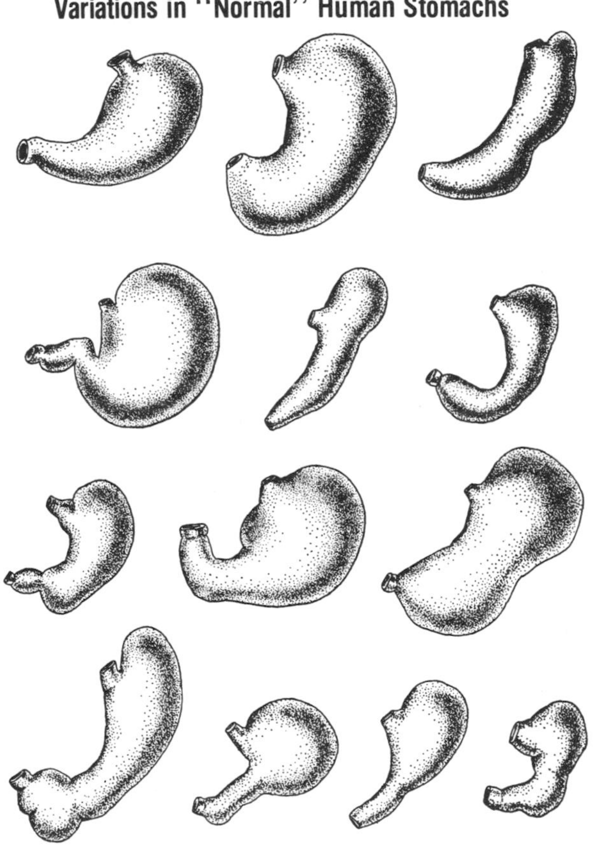

Source: Barry J. Anson, *Atlas of Human Anatomy*, W.B. Saunders Co., Philadelphia, 1951. By permission of the publisher.

Our requirements for nutrients vary as dramatically as the sizes and shapes of our stomachs, with some people needing up to seven times the amount of a specific nutrient required by others. In his book *The Physician's Handbook of Nutritional Science* Williams reports the following variations in adult requirements for nine essential nutrients.

Variation in Adult Needs for Nine Essential Nutrients

Nutrient	Range of needs	Ratio, Max./Min.	Number of subjects
Tryptophan	82 mg–250 mg	3:1	50
Valine	375 mg–800 mg	2.1:1	48
Phenylalanine	420 mg–1,100 mg	2.6:1	38
Leucine	170 mg–1,100 mg	6.4:1	31
Lysine	400 mg–2,800 mg	7:1	55
Isoleucine	250 mg–700 mg	2.8:1	24
Methionine	800 mg–3,000 mg	3.7:1	29
Threonine	103 mg–500 mg	4.8:1	50
Calcium	222 mg–1,018 mg	4.6:1	19

From Roger J. Williams, *The Prevention of Alcoholism Through Nutrition*, Bantam, New York, 1981. By permission of the publisher.

Allergies are another obvious example of biochemical individuality in human beings. Some people sneeze and wheeze over particles of dust, others get an allergic reaction to pollen, penicillin, milk, or shellfish. The same wide range of reactions occurs when different people drink alcohol. One person may take a sip and immediately flush bright red and feel sick to his stomach. In another, a glass of wine may be enough to cause drunken behavior, dizziness, and vomiting. Yet another person can drink three or four times that much and still be sober.

Alcoholism, Williams believes, follows the rules of biochemical individuality: Some people become addicted to alcohol while the majority can drink and never become addicted. And each individual alcoholic reacts differently, with some developing the disease slowly over a period of many years and others reporting blackouts with their very first drink. Because of this extraordinary variability, Williams believes it is crucial that everyone who drinks understand the nature of the disease and how it affects all of us differently. Don't judge your own reaction against someone else's, he cautions, because you will not react in the same way.

In *The Prevention of Alcoholism Through Nutrition,* Williams counsels people to study themselves, their family history, and their own drinking patterns and liking for the taste and effects of alcohol in order to understand their particular individual reactions to alcohol and to guard against alcoholism. He then suggests certain warning signs that may indicate high risk. Be careful, he warns, if:

- You have alcoholic parents;
- You like to drink and look forward to drinking occasions;
- One drink always calls for another;
- You are able to drink a lot without feeling the effects.

Comment. The concept of biochemical individuality is a crucial one, and helps to explain why every alcoholic experiences a slightly different progression of symptoms. Every alcoholic experiences alcoholism differently, and just because someone doesn't have blackouts or never drinks before 5 P.M. doesn't necessarily mean he is safe from alcoholism. Furthermore, alcoholism is a progressive disease, starting out in most cases with a person's subtle preoccupation with alcohol and barely recognizable symptoms. Usually only after years of drinking does the disease progress to the point of obvious and visible symptoms; by then the alcoholic is well on his way to being physically and mentally destroyed by his disease.

Early warning signs can help pinpoint those drinkers who may be high-risk cases, but it's important to remember that early symptoms may actually be signs that the drinker is *already* an alcoholic and not just on his way to becoming one. Someone who enjoys drinking, who experiences a need to keep drinking once started, and who has a high tolerance for alcohol, is probably an alcoholic, for these are not danger signals of a disease to come but actual symptoms of a disease already present.

So to Williams's warning signs add a bright red flag: If you notice these symptoms in yourself or someone you care about, get help immediately. The early stages of alcoholism may not seem like the beginning of a dread and fatal disease, but troubles will multiply as the alcoholic continues to drink. If he waits too long, trying to be sure that he really does have a problem with alcohol, his addiction will increase to the point where he cannot stop drinking by himself. He will become so confused by his painful and uncomfortable withdrawal symptoms, and the ability of alcohol to instantly relieve these symptoms, that he actually will not have the physical capability, let alone the mental desire or motivation, to quit.

Remember, too, that alcohol is not simply the alcoholic's poison, but also his medicine. Both qualities increase in power as the alcoholic drinks and, taken together, they make it increasingly difficult for him to stop drinking. The time to stop is in the early stages before the warning signs of tolerance and craving turn into the more obvious and deadly symptoms of alcoholism.

STEP 2: Eat High-Quality Foods, Avoid Low-Quality Foods, and Use Nutritional Supplements

Williams writes at length about the need to build a sound and healthy "internal environment" to avoid future troubles with alcohol. He suggests several ways to do this:

eat "good" foods, avoid "bad" foods, and take nutritional supplements.

Good foods include eggs, milk, meats, fish, shellfish, cheeses, vegetables, fruits, and whole-grain products—all as fresh as possible. Williams emphasizes that the foods you eat must contain the essential ingredients in the proportions that *you* as an individual need them. Again, the emphasis is on your unique needs, for they will differ dramatically from someone else's.

He suggests avoiding those nutritionally inadequate, low-quality foods such as refined flours, white bread, refined pastas, and refined grains, all of which are nutritionally inferior to the grains from which they are produced. And, he adds, avoid "foreign" chemicals, including caffeine and nicotine, and a wide assortment of what he calls "the outstandingly poor foods"—sodas, candies, cakes, and sugary desserts.

Comment. Williams's enthusiasm for good foods is undoubtedly influenced by some fascinating laboratory experiments with rats. One group of rats was fed a diet consisting solely of whole-grain bread and another group was fed commercially enriched white bread. The rats eating whole-grain bread were sick, but survived; all the rats fed white bread died. In another study, rats given sugar-coated cereal died faster than rats who ate the cereal box!

His excellent dietary advice should be taken to heart by everyone hoping to live a long, healthy life. It makes sense that people who are concerned about their health to the extent that they eat carefully, avoid harmful foods, and take nutritional supplements will also want to avoid alcohol or cut way down on their intake. If such a person found himself drinking more and more often, he would be immediately alerted, because his health is of primary concern to him. In this sense, being concerned with your nutritional health can only be an advantage.

Some additional advice might be included, however, for the special needs of the person with active, unchecked alcoholism. Eating nutritious foods and swallowing fistfuls of vitamin pills can't by themselves stop a raging addiction. Furthermore, because of varying degrees of malnutrition associated with chronic alcoholism, alcoholics should be tested for specific nutritional deficiencies whenever possible; diet and vitamin and mineral supplements can then be individually adjusted. Alcoholics should also, of course, religiously avoid refined sugar and caffeine, both of which aggravate blood-sugar problems and cause a craving for more sugar—or worse, alcohol—to relieve these symptoms (see Chapters 3 and 4).

STEP 3: *Exercise to Promote Nutrition*

Nutrients get to the cells by way of the circulatory system, and sluggish circulation will inevitably hinder the body's supply and distribution of nutrients. Williams counsels regular exercise to get the circulatory system cranked up and flowing strongly, and to ensure a steady supply of nutrients to the cells. He considers exercise an important preventive and protective health measure and notes that "most alcoholics do not consistently take vigorous daily exercise." He argues that people who lead sedentary lives are more vulnerable to alcoholism and cites numerous cases of sedentary alcoholics such as writers, actors, lawyers, and politicians. "Many of these individuals," he writes, "would lose their vulnerability if they routinely engaged in physical exercise, thus strengthening their internal environment."

Comment. Exercise will strengthen the body, helping the cells resist disease, but obviously exercise can't prevent alcoholism all by itself. And while it's true that thousands of sedentary people become alcoholics, it's also true that many of these people led extremely active lives before they started having trouble with alcohol. Alcoholism, in other words, forces people to modify their lifestyles, and the disease will greatly reduce the activities of even the most talented athlete or the most devoted sports enthusiast. It's no fun to jog with a hangover, play squash when your hands are shaking, or concentrate on hitting a golf ball when your whole body is craving a drink.

Drinking alcoholics also tend to be sedentary because sedentary activities allow them to drink. An executive who spends his time sitting behind a desk can have a three-martini lunch without raising eyebrows, but a golf pro or an automobile mechanic would have trouble getting away with such heavy drinking in the middle of the work day. Many alcoholics are able to continue working even into the later stages of their disease by slightly changing the nature of their jobs. Jerry, for example, was a trial lawyer for the first ten years of his practice; then, as he began to drink more and more often, he switched to corporate law. No longer having to appear in court, he could arrange his job around his drinking. Jim was a salesman for a hot-tub company. When his drinking began to get out of control, he arranged to spend most of his time traveling. It was a lot more convenient for him to put down some bourbon on a plane or in a motel room than to sneak it from the flask in his desk.

The point is that alcoholics *become* sedentary because of their disease—*not* because they are more inclined to dislike exercise. They are controlled by an addiction that eventually allows them no choice. But what about all those hard-drinking writers and actors? Why are so many famous creative people alcoholics? The answer is simple—because we hear about them. When famous people do something wrong, their names are splashed in bold print all over the front pages of newspapers and magazines. Actors and actresses make the news when they get drunk in public or are stopped for drunk driving; salesmen and assembly-line workers don't.

Betty Ford, Billy Carter, Dick Van Dyke, Jason Robards, Jr., Wilbur Mills, and William Holden are just a few of the famous names that have been connected in recent years with alcoholic drinking, supporting the myth that certain high-stress professions and lifestyles carry a greater risk of alcoholism. Writers are thought to be susceptible to alcoholism, for example, because their work is demanding, often lonely, sometimes boring, and talent seems to rise and fall with no warning. But loneliness, boredom, and waning talent are only potential *influences* on drinking, not *causes* of alcoholism. The susceptibility to alcoholism is physical, not psychological, and is determined by internal biochemistry, not external psychological problems.

Every drinking alcoholic, of course, has psychological problems, some of which may have preceded the disease but most of which are caused by the addiction itself and alcohol's profound impact on the brain. Alcoholics often use these psychological problems as reasons or excuses to justify continued drinking. "I drink," they say, "because I'm lonely"; or "Nobody cares about me"; or "My father hated me"; or "My mother died when I was ten"; or "I used to be talented, but now I'm just no good." Alcoholics use their problems as excuses to drink not because they are inherently devious or self-destructive, but because they are prisoners to their addiction—as the disease progresses, they must find a way to drink if they are to function at all. But the time will come when their drinking will make the symptoms of loneliness and boredom more unbearable, and their talent and ambition drain out as fast as the bottles they drink, until life becomes a series of miseries. This is the life of an alcoholic, however—not the lifestyle of the average writer; for every legendary alcoholic writer like Ernest Hemingway, F. Scott Fitzgerald, or Eugene O'Neill, there are probably a dozen nonalcoholic writers. Alcoholics can be found in every profession; the famous are simply more visible.

Sedentary or active, if you are physically susceptible to alcoholism and if you drink, igniting your addiction to alcohol, nothing can stop the disease from progressing except abstinence. Exercise, no matter how regular or vigorous, cannot by itself prevent or reduce alcoholism. Nothing yet discovered can stop the disease if the susceptible person keeps drinking.

STEP 4: Cultivate Moderation—and Inner Peace

In offering this last step, Williams says "cultivate moderation *while you can.* After a person becomes an alcoholic, he will not, and literally *cannot,* listen to such words as 'caution' or 'moderation.'"

Comment. Most alcoholics begin their drinking careers as social drinkers. They do not differ significantly from their friends in the way they drink or in the amount they drink. Soon enough, however, they start drinking more and more often, and drinking becomes their favorite social activity. Is this the point where they should try to cultivate moderation? No, because it may already be too late. An early symptom of addiction is the need to drink more and more often; and once a person is addicted, moderation can't stem the tide for long.

Many people believe that if they are able to control their drinking and drink moderately, they will not become alcoholic. But in the early stages of the disease, most alcoholics can and do control their drinking. Even in the middle stage, when the alcoholic begins to lose control over his drinking, most can still drink moderately or even quit drinking for several weeks or months. Eventually, however, the disease will progress into its late stage, when the alcoholic is no longer able to control his drinking; drinking controls him.

Alcoholics often use extraordinary will power in an effort to try to drink moderately. But as the cells become damaged, the alcoholic will lose control over his ability to decide how much to drink or when to stop. This loss of control is in the nature and strength of the disease, *not* the character or weakness of the person. If someone can no longer drink moderately *despite his best efforts,* he and those who care about him should know that he's in deep trouble with alcohol. If he continues to drink, alcohol will cloud his mind and befuddle his logic; the push to get him into treatment must therefore come from others. But the time to get help is in the early and middle stages, before a few episodes of immoderate drinking lead to a complete loss of control.

Conclusions

Will a careful following of Williams's steps lead to prevention of alcoholism? The question is actually misleading because, according to statistics, nine out of ten people are not susceptible to alcohol's addictive effects and will never become alcoholics—even if they blatantly neglect their health. The majority of drinkers have an inherent biochemical resistance to developing the disease. Alcoholics and nonalcoholics are physically different, and it is this physical difference, not psychological characteristics or emotional traumas, that determine whether someone will drink addictively or not.

But can Williams's steps help an alcoholic protect himself against his disease? Yes—if they are used early in the disease, before the addiction takes control. The steps can help people to take a long and careful look at themselves: their biochemical individuality (do they have alcoholic parents, for example, or medical problems such as blood-sugar irregularities, which might increase their susceptibility?) and their lifestyle (eating and drinking patterns, exercise).

After taking a good long look at themselves, some people might decide to stop drinking (or never start) because the risk is simply too great.* Others might actively guard against the disease by watching how much they drink and keeping an eye open for the danger signs—increasing tolerance, preoccupation with drinking, craving, and drinking more and more often. Such a person is, in other words, on guard, prepared to take care of himself, and actively interested in halting the disease in its early stages. In short, he understands the nature of the disease, can spot early warning signs, and can do something about the disease before the addiction takes firm hold.

Can a "prealcoholic"—one with a family history of alcoholism but no clear warning signs of problems—continue to drink if he drinks moderately, and carefully watches his nutrition? It's possible. Not everyone has the same genetic susceptibility to alcoholism. In some, the genetic message is apparently weak and only after years of drinking does the disease take hold; in others the genetic signal is strong and the disease erupts within weeks or months after the person first starts to drink. In those with a strong genetic susceptibility, nutrition is probably powerless to stop the addiction, but in those with a weak signal, good nutrition may be able to protect the cells against alcohol's damaging effects. Obviously, the safest course for a person with early signs is to both eat right *and* stop drinking. Still, it seems possible that some drinkers with a weak genetic susceptibility to alcoholism may actually outlive their disease because they have good biochemical defenses, buttressed in part by good nutrition.

* In alcoholism, something called "the skip factor" is common. This is when the sons or daughters of an alcoholic shun alcohol and thus avoid the risk of becoming alcoholics themselves. Their sons or daughters, however, have not grown up with an alcoholic parent and therefore may not feel the same repulsion towards drinking. They still have the inherited susceptibility to alcoholism, however, and, if they drink, run a fairly high risk of becoming alcoholics. Therefore, when you look at your family tree to determine if there is any alcoholism, be sure to think about the teetotalers; did they avoid alcohol because their parents or other close relatives were alcoholics? If so, the inherited susceptibility continues in your genes—even though your parents may never have touched the stuff.

But for the person who is already an alcoholic—even an early-stage alcoholic who looks and feels healthy and who has as yet suffered no significant, visible damage from drinking—the disease can be prevented only by abstaining from the triggering substance: alcohol. Alcoholics cannot drink safely, for no matter how careful they are, no matter how well they eat or how vigorously they exercise, no matter how many vitamins and minerals they take, they will inevitably suffer the ravages of their addiction *if they continue to drink.* This is the meaning of progression: Once ignited, the addiction catches fire quickly, and only abstinence can put it out.

Abstinence is the only prevention yet discovered that works for alcoholics. Williams himself endorses abstinence for alcoholics in his book when he says, ". . . it is possible, by exercising well-informed care, *for anyone who is not already an alcoholic* to keep on friendly terms with alcohol." He put these words in italics because he wanted the reader to understand their crucial importance—alcoholics cannot drink alcohol without endangering their health and their lives.

Once the alcoholic is abstinent, however, nutritional therapy is a powerful tool to rebuild and restore health. Recovering alcoholics who shore up their nutritional defenses generally feel better, look healthier, and are able to stay happily sober. "To improve an alcoholic's inner environment," Williams writes, "he must not only eliminate alcohol, but he must supply his body, through good food and otherwise, with the approximately 40 hidden chemicals [nutrients] so that rebuilding can take place." The need for that rebuilding has been described in the first six chapters of this book. The specific details on how to accomplish it, and a detailed look at those hidden nutrients, are offered in chapters 7, 8, and 9.

PART THREE

The Diet

7
The Diet for Sobriety

THE diet for sobriety outlined in this chapter has one specific purpose: to help you live sober and feel good while you're at it. Unlike most diets, it's not designed for weight loss (although that can be one of its additional benefits), nor do you have to count calories. This diet concentrates on *gaining,* not losing: gaining valuable nutrients by eating the right kinds of food while avoiding the pitfalls associated with eating the wrong kinds of food.

The diet for sobriety helps the recovering alcoholic's body get back to normal by supplying those nutrients necessary for repairing the damage that drinking has done and by keeping the body—and the mind—strong and healthy. It's not a restrictive diet that you follow for only two weeks or a month until you achieve the desired results; this diet offers many choices and lasts a lifetime. If you want to feel completely well again and be forever rid of the long-term hangover of alcoholism—the anxiety, nervousness, irritability, depression, and sudden cravings for alcohol—you must adopt a new eating lifestyle. Even alcoholics who don't suffer any lingering symptoms can benefit from this diet, for by eating right they can insure their good health and avoid future problems.

About now, many readers are probably groaning and considering closing this book tight. The possibility of changing the eating habits of a lifetime may seem like too much to ask. "I've made a commitment to myself and to my family and friends to give up alcohol," they might be thinking, "but I never thought I'd have to give up favorite foods, too! How much good can a diet do, anyway?" For the reluctant and the doubting, we suggest this plan: Follow the general principles of the food plan listed on pages 162 to 166 for one month. At the end of the month, judge how you feel, and if you find a significant improvement in your energy level, state of mind, and physical well-being, make a longer-term commitment at that point. Let the results convince you that it is worth your efforts.*

For this diet works. It will strengthen your sobriety and help you feel as good as you've ever felt in your life. The proof can be found in those alcoholics who, before they improved their eating habits, were just barely hanging on to their sobriety, felt constantly tired, "bitchy," out of sorts, and never stopped craving alcohol. Within weeks after following the guidelines set forth in this chapter, these alcoholics reported that the craving for alcohol faded, and the headaches, fatigue, depression, and irritability gradually disappeared. Their own statements about how dramatically improved they felt after starting the diet offer the best evidence that it is possible to stay sober and enjoy it.

> Now I understand why I ate handfuls of gumdrops when I stopped drinking—and why I had cycles of depression, crying

*Be aware that many alcoholics who are biochemically "hooked" on sugar and/or caffeine will notice an increase of some familiar physical or mental problems (anxiety, nervousness, irritability, sleep disturbances, cravings, and so on) within the first week. Often this is a period of adjustment for the body as it withdraws from sugar and caffeine. Don't think the diet isn't working—hang tough through this phase and stay firm. Around seven to ten days into the diet you'll notice an improvement, and you'll continue to feel better as the days go on.

jags, and couldn't sleep well. Since my diet has been straightened out, my nerves are strong as steel, my sugar cravings are gone, and I have plenty of energy to do my work. I never thought I'd feel this good.—Bill A.

I'd been faithful with my diet for six months. I ate three good meals every day and carried high-protein nutrition drinks to work in my thermos for snacks. I was feeling good, everyone at work was understanding and helpful, and things were ironing out at home. My wife was feeling a little more secure and was beginning to believe that treatment was going to "take" this time. But then she noticed I was getting cranky with the kids again, flying off the handle, and that I'd suddenly become sullen and withdrawn. She had seen the signs many times before, and she feared the worst. This time, though, she couldn't smell any booze. And I wasn't drinking! But I was snitching some sweets at work and drinking six or seven cups of coffee every day, and I felt and acted like I did when I was drinking. —Stan D.

For two years I was miserable in my sobriety. Scarcely a day went by when I didn't think about drinking. I was constantly tired and many mornings I thought of calling in sick, but I was afraid my boss would think I'd been hitting the bottle again. Life was almost unbearable. I kept myself pumped up with lots of coffee and had a ready supply of candy bars for a quick pick-me-up. It seemed I was happier drinking than sober, but I hung on to the hope that things would get better. And they did when I discovered how sweets, caffeine, and bad nutrition were teamed up against me. The first week after I cut out all the junk food, things seemed much worse, because I still had the headaches, anxiety, and fatigue. It was almost like withdrawal from alcohol. Then things gradually improved, and now they just keep getting better and better.—Betty M.

BUT WHY FOREVER?

Once the alcoholic feels better and has no desire to drink, can he then ease up on the diet and have a candy bar once a day, or perhaps a cup or two of coffee in the morning without paying a penalty? The answer is no, and the reason is this: Alcoholism is a chronic, irreversible disease process that weakens all the major body systems, contributing to biochemical upsets and malnutrition. After the alcoholic stops drinking, his body is able to repair itself, but some of the vital organs are permanently weakened and need continual dietary protection. Alcoholics, in other words, often lose their biochemical "buffer zone" and can't afford to be sloppy in dietary habits. Recovering alcoholics must not be lulled by feelings of good health and well-being into thinking that they are back to normal. They have a chronic disease that they must continually protect themselves against.

To counteract the damage caused by years of heavy drinking, the alcoholic must strengthen his defenses, making himself as strong as possible. An essential part of this building and maintaining body strength is good nutrition. The alcoholic cannot continually cheat on the diet and expect to escape the consequences of unstable body chemistry, low blood sugar, and nutritional deficiencies. For some, it may only require one sugar binge to start the body on a downward spiral; for others, it may take a week or perhaps a month for the symptoms to resurface. But for most alcoholics, poor eating habits will eventually lead to depression, anxiety, nervousness, and a reappearance of the craving for sugar and/or alcohol.

TAKING RESPONSIBILITY

Recovering alcoholics sometimes make the mistake of pinning the responsibility for their sobriety on someone else. "My wife will cook for me," one alcoholic explained to his counselor, "so this diet should be a breeze to follow." But what if his wife gets sick or dies? What if they get a divorce? Is his commitment to the diet also destroyed? Another alcoholic may rely on the example of a friend she meets during treatment. "If Sally can follow the diet, then I certainly can!" But what if Sally gives up and starts drinking again?

Staying sober must become the alcoholic's own responsibility and no one else's. He must commit himself to it, guard himself against the expected pitfalls, and learn to expect the unexpected. Avoiding stress is particularly important, for stressful situations flood the body with adrenalin, creating biochemical imbalances. Stress aggravates hypoglycemia, for example, making the alcoholic cranky, irritable, and nervous, craving sweets or alcohol to calm himself down. Knowing that stress is causing these discomforts and that they will disappear when the stressful situation is resolved will help the alcoholic tough it through. And, by carefully following this diet, the alcoholic can fight off the effects of stress and reduce both the frequency and the intensity of the symptoms associated with stressful situations.

THE FOOD RUSH

The alcoholic, like everyone else, lives in a hurried world where there never seems to be enough time to get everything done. Fast, convenience foods are an easy way to save time on one of life's necessary functions—eating. A candy bar, a few slices of American cheese, a hamburger, or an ice cream cone work just as well as a fruit salad or a piece of chicken to stifle hunger pains, and they're a lot easier to fix. Besides, Americans are brainwashed by constant advertising into believing that "we deserve a break today"—why, then, go to all the trouble to shop, cook, and clean up afterwards when someone else will do it for you, and cheaply, too?

The "food rush" overtakes us in any number of situations:

- It's 1:00 P.M. and you were just about to make yourself a sandwich, but the baby started crying and then the phone rang, and all you could fit in for lunch was a glass of milk and three chocolate chip cookies.

• You forgot to defrost the casserole before you left for work, so you took the family out to Taco Joe's for some nachos and burritos.

• The alarm went off but you went back to sleep, waking up just minutes before you were due at work. No time for breakfast, so you had a doughnut during your midmorning coffee break.

• The softball game started at 5:30 and you figured you'd grab something to eat afterwards. But after some Cokes and popcorn with the team, you weren't really hungry any more.

• It had been a hard day, and you didn't feel like cooking, so you heated up a TV dinner.

• You were ravenously hungry at 5 P.M. and ate half a bag of potato chips. When dinner was ready at 7:00, you weren't really hungry, so you just picked at it, saving room for the strawberry shortcake for dessert.

• You were "starving" and the shopping carts were lined up six deep at each of the supermarket check-out stands. You grabbed a Three Musketeers bar and a bag of M&Ms from the candy display and ate both as you waited in line.

The scenarios go on and on, but they all add up to bad nutrition—skipping meals or waiting until you're ravenous, and then substituting fast foods that supply lots of calories and energy, but not enough nutrients to keep the body in top shape. Fast foods are generally refined, high in fat and sugar, and nutrient-poor; while they work just fine to bring the blood sugar up, they do little to sustain and maintain a healthy body.

PLANNING AHEAD

To avoid these and countless other nutritional traps, be careful to plan ahead. Make up a meal plan for the entire week and then shop ahead for that week. Meal planning is

What You Always Suspected, but Were Afraid to Ask, About Contents of Fast Foods

Item	Calories	Protein (grams)	Carbo-hydrates (grams)	Fats (grams)
McDonald's Big Mac	541	26	39	31
McDonald's Filet-O-Fish	402	15	34	23
McDonald's Egg McMuffin	352	18	26	20
McDonald's Apple Pie	300	2	31	19
McDonald's Chocolate Shake	364	11	60	9
Burger King Whopper	606	29	51	32
Burger King French Fries	214	3	28	10
Dairy Queen Onion Rings	300	6	33	17
Dairy Queen Banana Split	540	10	91	15
Kentucky Fried Chicken Original Recipe Dinner	830	52	56	46
Kentucky Fried Chicken Extra Crispy Dinner (3 pieces chicken)	950	52	63	54
Pizza Hut Thin 'N' Crispy Cheese Pizza (½ of 10-inch pizza)	450	25	54	15
Pizza Hut Thick 'N' Chewy Pepperoni Pizza (½ of 10-inch pizza)	560	31	68	18
Taco Bell Taco	186	15	14	8

Source: Data supplied by food corporations to the Senate Select Committee on Nutrition and Human Needs.

easy and economical once you get into the habit but, more important, it saves wear and tear on your body.

When taking a car trip, you make sure you fill the tank with gas and check the oil and water levels. You wouldn't start out on a long trip with the gas needle on empty and the dipstick showing two quarts low on oil—the car would soon stop dead and refuse to budge until you filled the tank and added oil. When you consider how careful even the careless are with their automobiles, it's incredible how sloppy we can be with our own bodies. Perhaps it's because no red lights flash to warn us when our fuel supply is low, and only the most abused bodies will stop dead in their tracks. But even though we can neglect our health and still function somewhat normally, the lack of attention to diet and nutrition will take its toll, making us feel tired, depressed, and nervous. And, for the recovering alcoholic whose body is damaged and needs special care, the problems caused by neglecting nutrition are greatly increased.

Meal planning helps us treat our bodies with respect; unlike your automobile, the body you have now is the only one you'll ever have.

WHAT DOES THE FAMILY DO WHILE I'M "DIETING"?

Jane has a husband and five kids who looked at her in undisguised dismay when she mentioned the word *diet.* "I suppose this means no more potatoes au gratin?" her husband groused. "Yeah, and what about pancakes and waffles and peanut-butter cookies?" her disgruntled kids chimed in. Just one week after coming home from treatment, Jane was about to call it quits. "How can I stay on this diet when my family is putting so much pressure on me?" she asked herself.

Alcoholism is truly a family disease, and treatment should involve not only the alcoholic but all the affected members of his family. Unless they know what this disease is, and how it affects behavior—both during active drinking and later on, during recovery—the family members may prove more of a burden in recovery than a help. A recovering alcoholic can deal with lots of internal and external pressures, but the family's continual prodding to join in and "just have one piece of cake" can sometimes be disastrous.

Do the family members have to go so far as to watch their eating habits, too? Not necessarily. Some alcoholics are able to stick to their new eating lifestyle without feeling sorry for themselves when they watch other people have dessert after every meal. These alcoholics don't need to continually fight off the urge to cheat or have someone else help them with advice or encouragement. They feel better because they are eating right, and their improved mental and physical health are usually encouragement enough.

But not always. Some alcoholics may need the extra encouragement of their family joining in on the diet and giving up sweets and caffeine. If this is what it takes, the family should make every effort to help, realizing how crucial the diet is to the recovering alcoholic's sobriety and, therefore, to his life. Some recovering alcoholics may also need to get all sugar and sugary foods out of the house, particularly during the early, sometimes rough days of sobriety. The craving for sugar—or alcohol—can arise suddenly and without warning. Alcoholics who suffer from hypoglycemia are particularly vulnerable to these cravings. In addition, many women experience a desire for sweets and/or alcohol before their menstrual cycles. If sweets and alcohol are always readily available in the freezer or kitchen cabinets, the temptation may become too great. In order to prevent a dangerous lapse in control, it's best to keep all alcohol and sweets out of the house.

On the other hand, problems can be created when the alcoholic becomes overly wrapped up in the diet. Some alcoholics feel so much better after starting it that they want to push their new eating habits onto the people they love. Such an alcoholic may watch in dismay as his wife and children skip breakfast, load up on sweets during the day, and eat half a bag of Fritos before dinner. He may feel an overwhelming need to share his new knowledge of nutrition so that his family can also enjoy the mental and physical benefits of eating wisely. Sometimes this works and the entire family can benefit from new eating habits. This diet isn't some new-fangled fad, the family will learn, but a return to the way our grandparents used to eat—processed, refined, and fast foods are out; whole-grain, wholesome foods are in.

But eating habits are deeply ingrained and the alcoholic may find that his family is resentful of any attempts to convert them. If this happens, he should try not to push too hard. He can know that his dramatic physical and mental improvement will affect his family in all kinds of positive ways and eventually they may begin to follow his example and change their own eating habits. Or perhaps he can be satisfied with small victories, like getting his family to cut down on sugar, or substitute decaffeinated coffee or herb teas for caffeinated beverages. Regardless of how the alcoholic's new nutritional lifestyle affects his family, however, he must stick with it—for his first and primary responsibility must always be to himself and to his sobriety.

One Step at a Time

STEP 1: GENERAL PRINCIPLES

The first rule to follow is a simple one: Don't make the diet harder than it is. At first, when you're faced with giving up some of your best food "friends"—sweets, coffee, and junk foods—the whole idea of a diet is distressing. But just as with alcohol, getting some distance from these foods quickly exposes the enemy in disguise. With some basic rules, a touch of resolve, and a few weeks of experience, you'll feel immeasurably better, and sticking to the diet will become second nature.*

* Most alcoholics will notice an improvement in their general stamina and health by following the simple nutritional basics outlined in this chapter. Some alcoholics, however, will need professional direction if they find themselves in a maze of nutritional disorders. If you follow this diet and still feel physically drained and miserable, don't give up—find a doctor to help you. If you need help locating a doctor knowledgeable about nutrition, write the International College of Applied Nutrition, P.O. Box 386, La Habra, California 90631. Be sure to enclose a self-addressed, stamped envelope.

Remember, the diet really is easy. You don't have to count calories or measure foods, and you won't ever have to feel hungry. You can eat as much as you want of most foods; the foods you have to avoid are, for the most part, easy to recognize, and the foods you want to add are available and affordable. Also, by stabilizing your inner biochemistry, this diet can help stabilize your weight; many alcoholics with weight problems have no trouble slimming down on this diet. Another added benefit of the diet is that it bans the most expensive foods—alcohol and refined products—and encourages those foods that are fresh, natural (meaning unprocessed, unrefined, and without additives and preservatives) and, in most cases, relatively inexpensive.

ADD

SUITABLE FOODS. Eat fresh fruits and vegetables, and wholesome, whole-grain foods. Reduce red meats if possible (pages 166 to 168)—try to concentrate on protein from vegetables, grains, nuts, and seeds. Remember, the closer a food is to its natural state—fresh, unfrozen, unhandled, unprocessed, and unrefined—the better it is for you.

SUPPLEMENTS. Taking vitamin and mineral supplements should become as routine as brushing your teeth. For more information on your needs for specific vitamins and minerals and recommendations on supplements, see Chapters 8, 9, and 10.

SNACKS. Three nutritious snacks a day are an integral part of the diet for sobriety, for it is during the periods between meals that the blood sugar drops, bringing on the all too familiar and unpleasant symptoms. Snacking on nutritious foods prevents this drop in blood sugar and keeps the recovering alcoholic's energy level high.

Snacking also reduces the severe hunger pangs that are often responsible for overeating and "bingeing," and can actually contribute to weight loss. The body is better able to digest and absorb small amounts of foods and to put them to good use in the energy and repair needs of the cells. When too much food is taken in at one sitting, the body has to work harder to digest and make use of it. Snacking is not the same as nibbling on junk foods, however, for snacks are actually mini-meals, and should be carefully planned to include protein and nutrient-rich carbohydrates.

Snacks should be taken about two hours after each meal, with a particularly generous bedtime snack, which will help prevent the early-morning blahs. Breakfast is literally a break in a long overnight fast, and a bedtime snack will do wonders to prevent blood-sugar problems in the morning. In the early days of recovery, some alcoholics wake up in the middle of the night, after a restless sleep, feeling sick and shaky, and a snack eaten then often helps them get back to sleep—and a more peaceful sleep.

Snacks are generally nutrient-rich fruits, seeds, and whole-grain bread or crackers in combination with high-protein foods such as peanut butter, cheese, nuts, or small portions of meat. These foods supply a steady, slowly digested source of the all-essential glucose to the cells. Sample snacks are listed starting on page 199 and recipes begin on page 331.

CUT DOWN ON

REFINED FOODS. Reduce your intake of refined foods—those including white flour, white rice, and white pasta products.

PROCESSED FOODS. Processed foods are foods such as sausages, bacon, cold cuts, hot dogs, and salami, which contain preservatives and added salt and sugars.

SALT. Excessive salt intake can cause fluid and mineral imbalances in the body and can increase bouts of high blood pressure.

CANNED FRUITS AND VEGETABLES. Because they usually

contain added sugar and salt, canned fruits and vegetables should be avoided.

CONDIMENTS. Such condiments as mayonnaise, ketchup, pickles, and mustard are on this list because of their added sugar and salt.

AVOID ABSOLUTELY

ALCOHOL. Alcohol and all alcohol products should never be consumed.

SWEETS. Do not eat sweets. This includes table sugar, candy, desserts, and sugar-sweetened drinks.

CAFFEINE. Give up foods that contain caffeine (which is found in coffee, teas, colas, and chocolates).

Now that we've gone through the basic principles, it's time to make a pitch for going on and learning more about how to improve your diet and eating habits. The more you learn about your body and keeping it healthy, the more you will become aware of how much there is to learn. Nutrition is a vast and complex science, and many people find that once they start learning about the effect of nutrients on health, they want to continue learning and practicing what they learn. Good health tends to promote itself; the better you feel, the stronger your commitment becomes to staying fit and healthy.

In this spirit, we offer Steps 2, 3, and 4. These steps are elaborations on the general principles—they will take you into a deeper level of understanding of the mechanics of good health. If you feel overwhelmed at any point, be content with learning and applying the general principles listed in Step 1 and don't worry about the specifics contained in Steps 2, 3, and 4. If you can cut out sugar, caffeine, and refined foods and add an assortment of whole-grain foods, vegetables, nuts, seeds, fruits, and high-quality proteins in three consistent meals each day, and get nutritious snacks between meals, you'll be way ahead of most people who

Summary of Step 1: General Principles

- Three meals and three nutritious snacks every day

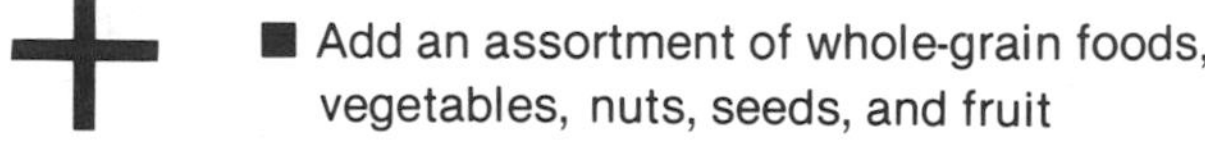

- Add an assortment of whole-grain foods, vegetables, nuts, seeds, and fruit

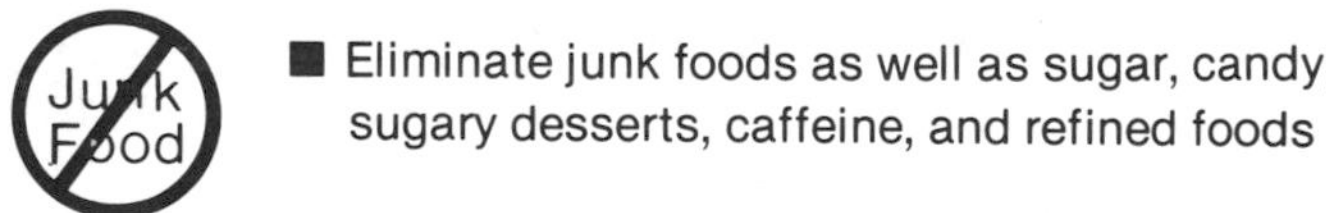

- Eliminate junk foods as well as sugar, candy, sugary desserts, caffeine, and refined foods

have received no nutritional education or training at all. With just a minimum amount of effort, you will enjoy a vast improvement in your physical health and mental and emotional outlook on life.

STEP 2: SOME SPECIFICS

The diet for sobriety originally included lots of protein-rich meat. But research conducted in the last decade on the dangers of eating too much meat, particularly red meat, has resulted in a switch to less meat and more complex carbohydrates and high-quality starches. A look at some of the medical problems associated with meat consumption may help you understand why less meat is better:

• Meat protein is more difficult to digest than the protein available from vegetables, dairy products, nuts, grains, and seeds. Furthermore, many alcoholics have chronic digestive problems caused by long and hard years of drinking and have difficulty digesting heavy loads of meat protein.

• Red meats such as beef and pork are high in saturated fats—those solid fat structures also contained in cream and butter. An imbalance in saturated fats may contribute to improper use and breakdown of fats and cholesterol in the body, promoting hardening of the arteries, heart disease, strokes, and high blood pressure. A healthier balance can be achieved by reducing saturated meat fats, substituting lower-fat meats (fish and fowl), and using a higher percentage of *un*saturated fats, which come from liquid vegetable and seed oils.

• Eating large amounts of protein, particularly meat protein, has been associated with cancer of the colon.

• Meat, particularly red meat, adds more fat to the diet and more calories per gram of food, contributing to such problems as obesity, high blood pressure, and atherosclerosis,* or hardening of the arteries.

If you aren't particularly worried about digestive ailments, cancer, high-cholesterol levels, or obesity, consider one additional drawback to eating red meat: For every pound of beef that we eat, approximately sixteen pounds of grain and legumes—beans and peas—have already been consumed. During the last few weeks of a steer's life, it is pumped up with high-protein feed that turns range-fed beef into marbled-fat beef—beef that tastes and looks great but is astonishingly wasteful of our resources. Not everyone will be moved by this view of meat-eating, but it does merit some thought, considering the fact that many thousands of people in this world, most of them children, die *every day* from malnutrition.

For all these reasons, the diet for sobriety recommended here cuts back on the use of red meats, uses more fish and fowl, limits fats, and encourages the use of dairy products,

* Atherosclerosis is a condition in which fat accumulates on the walls of the arteries, narrowing the passageways, clamping down on the flow of blood to the heart muscle, and eventually leading to tissue death and a heart attack or stroke.

whole grains, vegetables, nuts, and seeds as supporting protein sources. The combination of proteins found in these foods is just as "complete" as that available from red meats. And the right combination of vegetable proteins can supply a major portion of the body's daily protein needs.

The diet for sobriety, then, is high in protein, but it relies heavily on protein from sources other than red meat. It has been called a "complex carbohydrate" diet, but to truly describe it, we would have to use an awkward and cumbersome title like "The Complex-Carbohydrate, High-Quality-Protein, Low-Fat, Nonsugar Diet Specifically Designed For the Recovering Alcoholic." We've settled instead on the short and simple title, "The Diet for Sobriety."

All of the major food groups—proteins, carbohydrates, and fats—are important to this diet, for all supply ingredients unique and essential for life. Nutrients, including vitamins, minerals, amino acids and essential fatty acids, spread themselves throughout the food groups, which is why none of us can live for long on one food or even on the foods contained in one food group. We need foods from all the food groups, but we need some of them less than we do others, and we need them in specific proportions in order to get maximum nutritional value from the foods we eat. Recovering alcoholics have very special nutritional needs based on their disease and its long-term effects on the body organs and biochemical stability; thus the diet for sobriety described in this chapter.

In the following pages the basic food groupings are listed—proteins, carbohydrates, and fats—with food sources for each grouping and guidelines governing the use of these foods. The guidelines are simply that: guides to a better eating lifestyle, not hard and fast rules. Every person will have to make adjustments to this diet based on his or her individual likes and dislikes, allergies to certain foods, family needs, career obligations, and cooking preferences. Find out what works for you and then stay with an eating plan that gives you sufficient calories and energy and makes you feel good—for it you're getting everything you need from this diet, you'll want to stay on it, and staying on it will make all the difference.

A WORD ABOUT PROTEINS

The word *protein* is derived from a Greek word meaning "of prime importance." Every living tissue—plant or animal—contains protein; next to water, protein is the most plentiful substance in the human body.

Protein foods that supply all of the essential amino acids* are known as *complete* proteins and include proteins from animal sources such as meat and dairy products, eggs, fish, and fowl. *Incomplete* proteins are those food sources that cannot supply the body with all the essential amino acids, or building blocks of protein; these are the vegetable proteins found most abundantly in peas, beans, and certain grains. However, a meatless or less-meat diet can still provide all the essential amino acids, because some plant foods have generous amounts of the amino acids which other plant foods lack—eating the two kinds of plant foods together supplies a "complete" source of protein. This is the principle of protein complementarity first publicized by Frances Moore Lappé in *Diet for a Small Planet.* Foods like corn and beans, rice and peas, or bread and beans will, when eaten together, provide high-quality, complete protein: their combined amino-acid pattern has no deficiencies. Because grains are low in the amino acid lysine and high in methionine, for example, a perfect complementary food would be

* Essential amino acids are those protein units that the body cannot produce and that can only be supplied by the food we eat. The essential amino acids are: methionine, threonine, tryptophan, isoleucine, leucine, lysine, valine, and phenylalanine. Two other amino acids, histidine and arginine, are considered essential for growth in children, but the debate continues about whether adults need them.

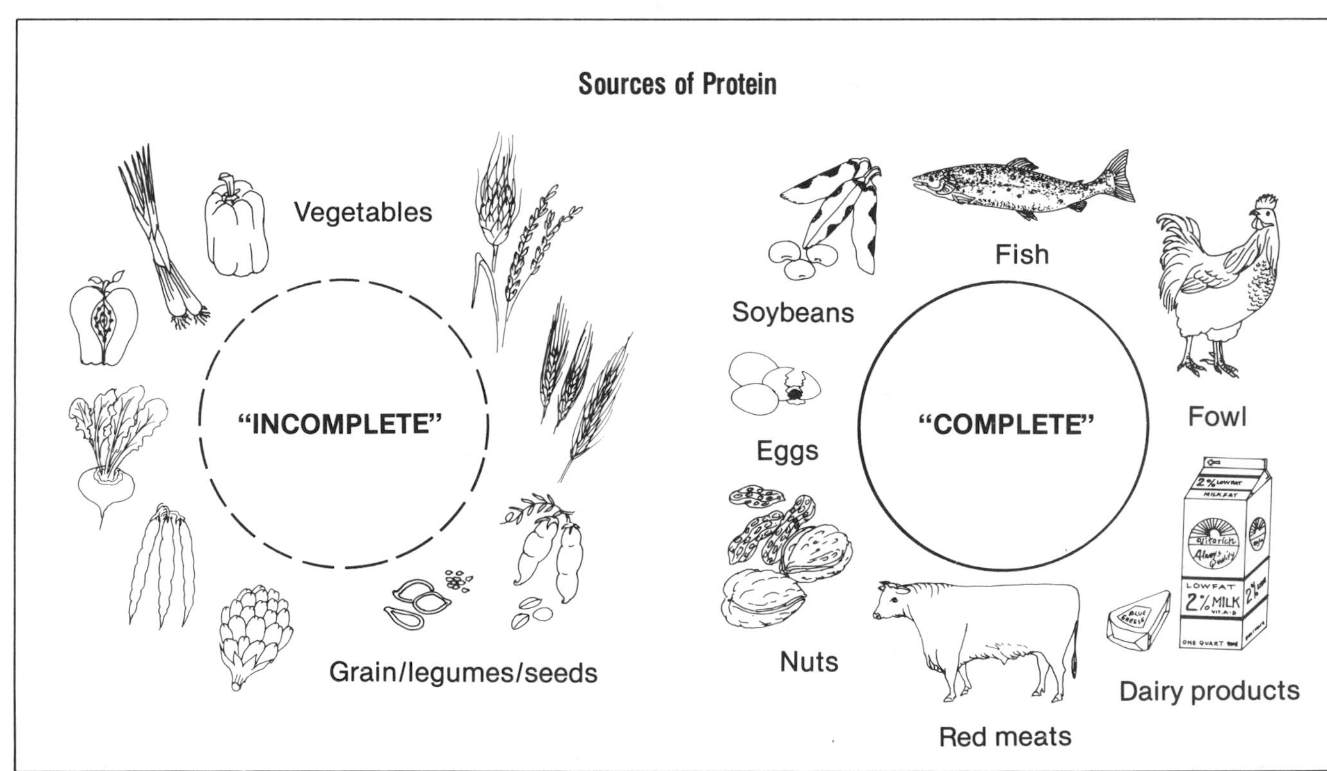
Sources of Protein
Vegetables
"INCOMPLETE"
Grain/legumes/seeds
Soybeans
Fish
Fowl
Eggs
"COMPLETE"
Nuts
Red meats
Dairy products
2% LOWFAT
MILKFAT
LOWFAT
2% MILK
VIT. A·D
ONE QUART
BLUE CHEESE

legumes such as peas or beans, which are low in methionine and high in lysine.

Protein complementarity is demonstrated in the chart on page 172. Alcoholics who are not meat eaters or would like to cut back on meat intake are encouraged to read both Lappé's book and *Laurel's Kitchen,* a comprehensive and delightful cookbook and guide to the meatless lifestyle.

MEAT

Meat supplies vitamin B-12 and fats, in addition to large amounts of protein. Because of the problems associated with eating red meats, outlined above, limit your meat intake to three or four times a week and focus more on fish and fowl when you do eat meat. A good rule of thumb is to eat:

- One meat-based meal a day
- One less-meat meal a day (casseroles, stews, and soups)
- One meatless meal a day (completed grains/vegetables/legumes/seeds, or dairy and egg dishes)

Other meat tips:

- Cut back or eliminate completely processed meats (bacon, ham, cold cuts, hot dogs, salami, and sausages) because they are usually processed with some form of sugar as a preservative and contain numerous chemical additives.
- Stay away from pork whenever possible because of its high fat content.

EGGS

Eggs contain the most perfect protein combination of any food—not surprisingly, since eggs must have all the essentials to make and nurture young chicks. In addition to protein, eggs also supply choline and biotin, both B vitamins, and help the body use fats and cholesterol. The naturally high cholesterol content of eggs has been a cause of con-

Protein Complementarity

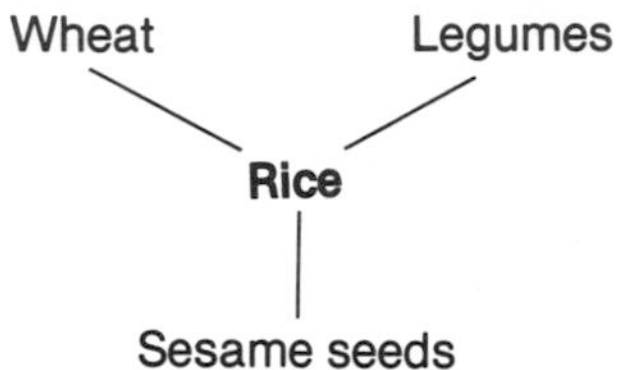

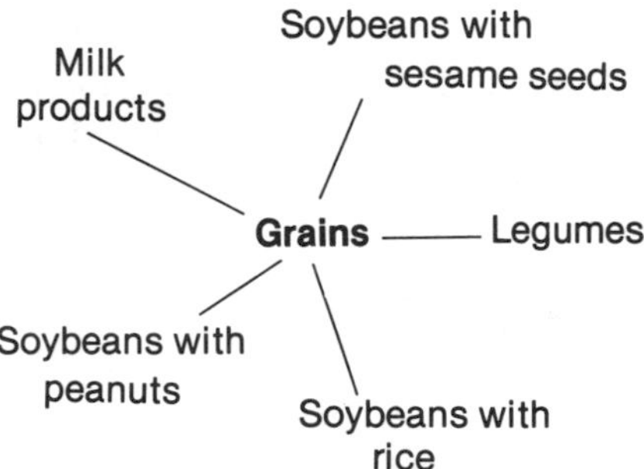

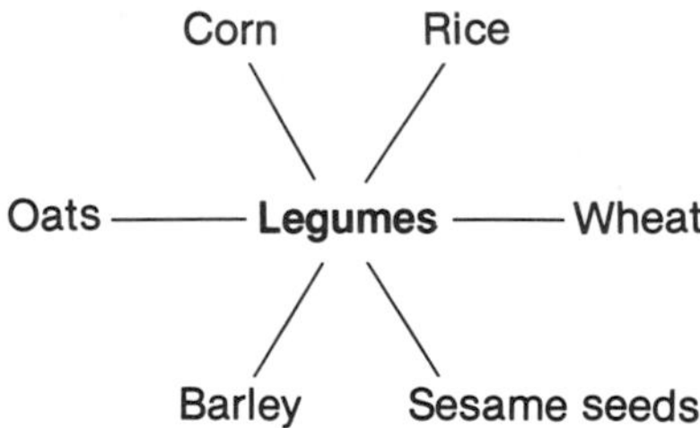

(Legumes include kidney, navy, pinto, and lima beans; chickpeas; soybeans; peanuts; and blackeyed-peas.)

When vegetable proteins are combined this way, there is a gain of 43 percent in protein value.

cern, prompting physicians' warnings to limit eggs. But the large amounts of choline in eggs, when combined with the vitamin inositol, form lecithin; and lecithin works to break up cholesterol and transport it easily through the blood without clogging the arteries. In other words, while eggs contain cholesterol, they also contain substances which help control the buildup of cholesterol in the blood.

An egg a day (or two eggs every other day) should pose no problem for most alcoholics. The alcoholic with cholesterol problems should be under the care of a physician knowledgeable about alcoholism and the dietary imbalances alcoholics typically have. Also, all alcoholics should limit the use of raw eggs (in milk shakes, for example), because of the presence of avidin, a protein substance that interferes with the activities of the B-complex vitamin biotin. (Because avidin is destroyed by heat, cooked eggs pose no problem.)

To cut down on fat, eat your eggs poached or boiled, and avoid frying, scrambling in lots of butter, or adding mayonnaise to deviled eggs.

A WORD ABOUT CHOLESTEROL

Cholesterol, a natural part of the brain, nervous system, liver, and blood, is a fat substance needed to make sex and adrenal hormones, bile, and vitamin D. High blood levels of cholesterol have been associated with arteriosclerosis and, for a time, doctors suggested cutting back on foods that contain cholesterol (eggs, various meats, and other animal products) in order to lower blood cholesterol levels. But even cutting way back on foods containing cholesterol only reduces blood cholesterol levels by 5 to 10 percent. Most cholesterol is actually manufactured by the body, in the liver, and the question researchers are now asking is, "What makes some bodies manufacture too much cholesterol?" The answer appears to be related to the balance in the body of unsaturated fatty acids, vitamin E, vitamin C, lecithin,* and a variety of minerals. It's becoming increasingly clear that control of cholesterol is related to balancing the "mechanics" of the body rather than simply cutting back on cholesterol in the diet.

DAIRY PRODUCTS

MILK. In addition to protein, milk supplies natural carbohydrates (in the form of lactose), fats, calcium, and vitamins B-1, B-6, and B-12.

• Drink two to three cups a day.

• For vegetarians, milk is an extremely important food. It balances the protein from plant sources, making a whole food, or a food that provides all the essential elements for life. It is one of the few naturally rich sources of calcium, and it supplies vitamin B-12, which is totally lacking in an all-plant diet.

• Milk is a source of both fat and natural sugars, and drinking too much can aggravate blood-sugar problems. To cut down on the risk of a hypoglycemic reaction, don't drink more than a quart a day; and to cut down on fat, drink 1 percent, 2 percent, or skim milk (the only difference between 1 percent, 2 percent, nonfat, and whole milk is the fat content).

• Beware of allergies to milk and milk products. Common symptoms are stomach ache, gas, bloated feelings, and diarrhea. If you are allergic to milk, you may be able to tolerate other dairy products such as cheese or yogurt. If not, your calcium needs can be met by enriching your diet with nuts, seeds, and leafy vegetables, or supplementing with calcium tablets.

CHEESE. One ounce of cheese supplies 6.5 grams of protein, but this rich protein comes with a steep price tag:

*Lecithin is contained in many fatty foods but is lost during the process of hydrogenation, when hydrogen is added to liquid oils to make them solid, as in shortening, margarine, and peanut butter.

Cheese is high in saturated fat. Excessive consumption may interfere with cholesterol control and contribute to cardiovascular diseases such as heart attacks and strokes. Some cheeses are significantly better than others—low-fat cottage cheese, for example, is a wonder food, high in protein and low in fat. Soft cheeses (cottage, ricotta) are generally better digested, absorbed, and used by the body than hard cheeses like Swiss, Cheddar, and Parmesan. Avoid processed cheeses like Velveeta or presliced American cheese because of preservatives and added sugar and salt.

BUTTER AND MARGARINE. Butter and margarine both have their problems. Butter, a natural dairy product made from cream, is high in saturated fats; margarine, made from liquid vegetable oils, is hydrogenated, a process which adds hydrogen to the natural oils to make them solid. Margarine, in other words, is actually a man-made saturated fat, although it is not quite as saturated (or solid) as butter. Margarine oils are also heat-processed, which means that, along with containing preservatives and additives, they are less "natural" for the body.

To get a butterlike spread that is lower in saturated fats and not as hydrogenated, make your own "better-butter" (see page 300). Or buy the softtub margarine, which is usually the least hydrogenated, and use liquid vegetable cooking oil for cooking instead of butter or margarine.

YOGURT. Yogurt is a good source of protein and contains "friendly" bacteria that aid in digestion and intestinal function. Yogurt also acts in some as yet unknown way to help lower cholesterol in the body. Since store-bought yogurt usually has lower bacteria activity, and store-bought fruited yogurt contains sugar or honey, homemade yogurt is best of all.

GRAINS, LEGUMES, NUTS, AND SEEDS

Although usually considered carbohydrates, grains,

legumes, nuts, and seeds are also important sources of protein, as well as fat, thiamin, niacin, vitamin B-6, folacin, vitamin E, iron, zinc, magnesium, and fiber. Good stuff!

Legumes (dried beans, peas, lentils) are a rich source of protein and can be the basis of delicious soups and nonmeat casseroles (which have protein values equal to or greater than meat dishes).

Nuts and seeds are healthy snack foods, especially if eaten raw or roasted without salt. They can be used alone or are delicious (and nutritious!) mixed with bits of dried fruit —this is a popular trail snack for hikers, who refer to it as *gorp.*

Sunflower seeds are 25 percent protein and a particularly good source of vitamin B-6. (However, they are also high in oils, and people on a fat-restricted diet will need to limit their intake.) Eat them hulled and raw, as cooking causes loss of nutrients, but be sure to refrigerate them after hulling and watch for signs of their getting rancid or going stale. The seeds should be medium grey; brown, yellow, white, or black seeds may be rancid.*

Unhulled sesame seeds are high in calcium; pumpkin and squash seeds are delicious when roasted, and a good source of protein; almonds, peanuts, and hazelnuts are all excellent protein foods, and almonds are particularly resistant to rancidity.

CARBOHYDRATES

A WORD ABOUT CARBOHYDRATES

Calories have mucked up our thinking about carbohydrates. We think of the two synonymously: carbohydrates = lots of calories. Carbohydrates, in other words, are sup-

*Rancidity occurs when the fatty acids oxidize, creating substances potentially harmful to the body.

posedly fattening and, in that sense, bad for you. But carbohydrates also give us our chief source of energy and help regulate fat and protein metabolism.

The Good and Bad Carbohydrates

	Natural ("good")	**Refined/Processed ("bad")**
Sugars	Fruit Honey	Table sugar (white and brown) Molasses
Starches	Whole grains (wheat, oats, barley, rye) Fresh vegetables	White flour White-flour products (bread and pastas) Processed grains (white rice, pearl barley) Canned and frozen vegetables
Cellulose	Fiber (roughage found in skins of fruits and vegetables)	

Are carbohydrates good, then, or bad? The answer is both, because the category of carbohydrates includes a variety of foods that, like brothers and sisters, are similar but not the same. Potatoes, rice, wheat flour, alcohol, and table sugar are all high in carbohydrates, but they do very different things in and for the body. A banana and a piece of fudge, for example, deliver approximately the same calories —but the banana has twice as much protein, less than one tenth the fat, three times as much iron, ten times as much potassium and niacin, over two hundred times as much vitamin A, seven times as much thiamine, three times as much riboflavin, and fourteen times as much vitamin C. And the fudge contains fifty-four times as much sodium, or salt!

THE "BAD" CARBOHYDRATES

Refined carbohydrates, which include white sugar, white flour, white rice, and white pasta products, provide lots of calories, which in turn provide lots of energy. But besides energy (and those calories), these foods have been stripped of important nutrients. In fact, refined carbohydrates can put big stresses on the body, contributing only minimal amounts of vitamins and minerals and stealing from other foods the nutrients needed to process and use the refined carbohydrates. The "bad" carbohydrates also crowd out other nutritious foods by curbing the appetite; when someone adds 1,000 calories to a day's food by slurping a chocolate milkshake and munching a fistful of French fries, that person isn't going to be particularly hungry for other, more nutritious foods.

Vitamins and minerals aren't the only thing missing in refined foods. When foods such as wheat or rice are refined, the fiber casing is stripped off in processing. With this casing go a number of important nutrients as well as a source of an indigestible but important carbohydrate: cellulose, or fiber. Fiber is the structural part of plants that, because it cannot be

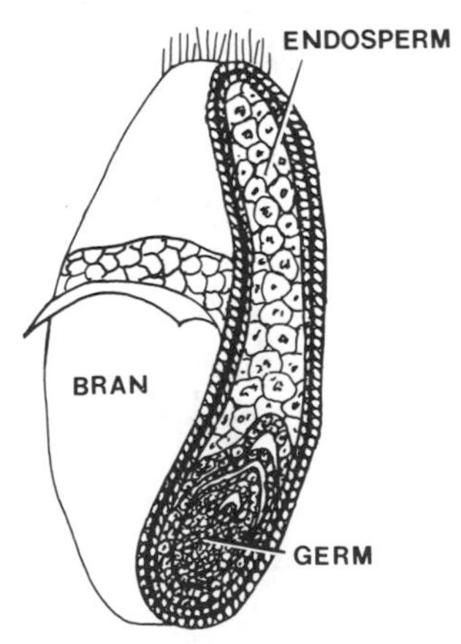

A grain of wheat consists of the *germ*, *bran*, and the *endosperm*. The germ contains polyunsaturated fats, vitamin E, most of the grain's thiamine and much of its ribolflavin, niacin, B-6, and pantothenic acid, and 8 percent of its protein. All this is lost in milling. Also lost is the bran, or fiber part of the grain. What's left is the endosperm, which is primarily starch. Eighty percent of the essential nutrients provided by whole wheat are missing in white bread.

digested, provides bulk or roughage to help the intestines push the partially digested food along. Low-fiber diets are associated with intestinal disturbances, including cancer of the colon.

Cereal fiber, found in whole-grain cereals that include the hulls (the bran), have the added ability to absorb water, keeping stools moist and soft as well as bulky. Most cereals on the market today are so processed that they contain no fiber at all.

Worst of all for the alcoholic, refined carbohydrates also contain simple chains of sugar that are readily broken down and flood the body with a sudden "shot" of glucose. While the cells need glucose for energy, they cannot cope well with large amounts all at once; as a result, the blood sugar goes rapidly up only to come crashing back down. During this blood-sugar roller coaster, the alcoholic may experience slight hyperactivity, rapid heart beat, flushing, nervousness, and anxiety. For some idea of how sugar-laden our foods really are, see the table.

THE "GOOD" CARBOHYDRATES

All digestible* carbohydrates break down to glucose, but the "good" carbohydrates—those in vegetables, whole grains, and fruits—are made up of complex chemical chains that are slowly released and absorbed and thus more easily controlled by the body's blood-sugar mechanisms. In addition to contributing to the slower and more efficient digestive process, natural carbohydrates contain important vitamins and minerals that aid in the absorption and use of glucose. These good, natural carbohydrates must not be confused with the refined, poor-quality, and even hazardous carbohydrates such as table sugar, white flour, and white pasta products. Most people think a carbohydrate is a carbohydrate is a carbohydrate. But as far as nutrients go, the different foods called carbohydrates might as well be classified in completely different groups. Take a look at the table comparing the mi-

*Cellulose is difficult to digest and passes through the intestines basically intact.

neral content of white and whole-grain breads, and then consider the fact that Roger Williams, in a classic experiment, fed sixty-four laboratory rats nothing but commercially enriched white bread; forty died of malnutrition and the survivors were severely stunted in growth. One has to wonder about the "wonder" in Wonder Bread.

Mineral Content of Wheat Bread and White Bread

Trace element	Wheat bread (parts/million)	White bread (parts/million)	Percent lost in milling
Chromium	0.05	0.03	40%
Manganese	46.00	5.9	87%
Iron	243.00	27.3*	89%
Cobalt	.026	0.022	15%
Copper	5.30	2.3	57%
Zinc	35.00	9.7	72%
Selenium	0.63	——	100%
Molybdenum	0.48	0.32	33%

*Enriched bread

Source: adapted from H. A. Schroeder, "Trace Elements after Processing," *American Journal of Clinical Nutrition*, 24, 562, 1971.

SERVINGS AND SOURCES OF "GOOD" CARBOHYDRATES

VEGETABLES

In addition to natural carbohydrates, vegetables also supply amino acids (the building blocks of proteins), fiber, vitamin A, folic acid and other B-complex vitamins, vitamin C, calcium, iron, and many other minerals. Eat five or six servings a day. Other tips:

• Eat fresh, organically-grown vegetables whenever possible—the fresher the vegetable, the higher its vitamin and mineral content and the less you have to worry about chemicals being added to enhance appearance or taste.

• Frozen vegetables are next most desirable; canned are least desirable because of processing and added sugar and salt.

• Beware of "fresh" out-of-season vegetables: They have probably been ripened off the vine and chemically treated to make them look fresh, and they are not as nutrient-rich as fresh fruits and vegetables in season.

• In general, the deeper the color of a vegetable—the greener the leaf, the yellower the flesh—the richer the vitamin content.

• Undercook rather than overcook to spare heat-sensitive vitamins.

• Eat a variety of raw vegetables every day.

FRUITS

Fruits supply natural sugars, vitamin C, potassium, and fiber. Eat four to five servings a day, including fruit juices. Some tips on eating fruits:

• Eat fresh fruits whenever possible—like vegetables, the fresher the fruit, the higher its vitamin content.

• Always wash the fruit, unless you've grown it yourself and know exactly how it's been treated.

• Fresh fruits are preferable, but if using canned fruits, read labels carefully and avoid those that are sugar-packed. Instead, use water-packed fruits or fruit packed in natural juices. If you're stuck for some reason with sugar-packed fruit, drain off the syrup and rinse the fruit with water before eating.

• Drink unsweetened fruit juices, but limit these to one or two small glasses a day, since even unsweetened fruit juice is concentrated and therefore naturally sugar-laden. Squeezing your own is a good alternative—fresh-squeezed juice is fresh, unprocessed, and delicious.

• Limit your intake of dried fruits such as raisins, prunes, dried apples or pears, because the natural sugar is heavily concentrated during the drying process.

GRAINS, NUTS, AND SEEDS

Besides supplying bran and fiber, grains, nuts, and seeds

are rich sources of B vitamins, vitamin E, amino acids, minerals, and essential unsaturated fatty acids.

To get sufficient grain, eat two or three slices of bread a day, and cereal three or four times a week (alternating it with an egg- or meat-based breakfast). As for nuts and seeds, use them as colorful, crunchy additions to cereals, casseroles, or by themselves as snacks. Other tips:

• When cooking, use whole-grain products (brown rice, rye, barley, and whole-grain noodles, macaroni and spaghetti) because they contain the germ of the grain and are rich in nutrients.

• Chew whole grains, nuts, and seeds carefully in order to break down the outer shell or kernel and release the nutrients within.

• When buying cereals, choose hot, whole-grain types (oatmeal, rice, or wheat); they are less processed than cold or commercial cereals. Besides, most cold cereals also have added sugar, although some, like Shredded Wheat and Grapenuts, are more nutritious and contain minimal amounts or no added sugar (see chart on page 185 listing the sugar content of popular commercial cereals).

• Peanut butter is an excellent source of B vitamins and protein, but be sure to use "natural" peanut butter with no salt or sugar added (or make your own), and watch out for the calories—⅓ cup (about five tablespoons) delivers a whopping 430 calories.

• Eat *un*salted nuts and seeds. They're usually as easy to find as the less healthful salted ones.

• Sunflower seeds, unhulled sesame seeds, and almonds are all excellent foods. Remember, though, that nuts and seeds are high in fats (although primarily the less hazardous unsaturated types).

SWEETENING AGENTS

The body has no need for refined sweetening agents; it

Sugar in Foods and Beverages

	Size of portion	Teaspoons of sugar
Beverages		
Chocolate milk	8 ounces	6
Cola drinks	6-ounce glass	3½
Ginger ale	6-ounce glass	5
Beer	8-ounce glass	2
Highball cocktail	6-ounce glass	2½
Kool-Aid	8-ounce glass	6
Cakes/cookies		
Angel food cake	1 piece (4 ounces)	7
Chocolate cake (iced)	1 piece (4 ounces)	10
Chocolate cookies	1	1½
Oatmeal cookies	1	2
Doughnut	1	6
Candies		
Chewing gum	1 stick	½
Fudge	1-ounce square	4½
Lifesavers	3	1
Gumdrop	1	2
Chocolate bar	1 ounce	7
Ice cream/sherbet		
Ice cream	½ cup	3–6
Ice cream sundae	1	7
Ice cream cone	1	3½
Sherbet	½ cup	6–8
Jams/jellies		
Jelly/jam	1 tablespoon	4
Apple butter	1 tablespoon	1
Honey	1 tablespoon	3
Pastry		
Apple pie	1 slice	7
Cherry pie	1 slice	10
Pumpkin pie	1 slice	5

Sources: American Dental Association, American Dietetic Association, U.S. Department of Agriculture, and others.

can meet all its carbohydrate needs with grains, vegetables, and fruits. Yet the average consumption of refined sugar in the U.S. is over 125 pounds per person per year—or about 650 calories every day. The average American adolescent eats over 3 pounds of sugar every week, or more than 150 pounds every year—between a quarter and a half of his daily calories.

Sugar and sweetening agents are not only unnecessary, they can be hazardous to your health, tampering with the body's finely tuned sugar-regulating system. Since the appetite is satisfied by calories alone, large amounts of "empty" calorie foods will crowd out other foods necessary for nourishment and steal from other foods the nutrients needed to put the sugar to use. In these ways, refined sugar products can actually contribute to vitamin and mineral deficiencies.

Everyone in this country should watch his refined sugar intake, but recovering alcoholics have an added incentive: Sugar causes most alcoholics to have blood-sugar problems that can cause depression, mental confusion, and irritability and create a strong and sometimes irresistible desire for a drink. In the initial two to three months of recovery, the alcoholic should avoid sweets completely in order to allow his body to pull itself back together again. If at all possible, it's best to stay away from sweets forever. Realistically, however, it's almost impossible to completely avoid sweets in a culture like ours; many of our traditional holidays—Halloween and Easter, for example—have evolved into ritual celebrations of candy and other sweets. For those who cannot completely avoid sugar, consider the following suggestions:

- Have a *planned* dessert once—or at most, twice—a week.
- Eat sweets at the end of a nutritious meal. If you're full of good food, you'll be better able to control your sweet tooth and you'll have nutritious food "on board" to help offset the effect of concentrated sweets.
- Plan desserts that are less disturbing to the body's biochemical balance. In general, the rich and gooey sweets like ice-cream sundaes, chocolate cakes, tortes, pastries, and

Sugar in Cereal

Cereal	Total sugar (percentage of dry weight)
Sugar Smacks	56.0
Apple Jacks	54.6
Fruit Loops	48.0
Cocoa Krispies	43.0
Sugar Frosted Flakes	41.0
Cap'n Crunch	40.0
Honey Comb	37.2
Trix	35.9
Golden Grahams	30.0
Raisin Bran	29.0
C.W. Post	28.7
Frosted Mini-Wheats	26.0
100% Bran	21.0
All-Bran	19.0
Life	16.0
Grape-Nuts Flakes	13.3
Buc Wheat	12.2
Product 19	9.9
Wheaties	8.2
Grape-Nuts	7.0
Special K	5.4
Corn Flakes	5.3
Kix	4.8
Cheerios	3.0
Shredded Wheat	0.6
Puffed Wheat	0.5
Puffed Rice	0.1

Source: U.S. Department of Agriculture

doughnuts are particularly upsetting to the body. Desserts like custard, puddings, and apple crisp will treat you much better. See the recipe section for dessert suggesions.

TIPS ON SWEETENING AGENTS

• While honey is not much better for your body than refined sugar (it influences the blood-sugar levels in exactly the same way), good-quality honey (Tupelo honey, for example) contains some vitamins and minerals. Honey is also about two times sweeter than sugar, so use about half as much. But don't be fooled into thinking that because honey is a natural substance, you can eat as much as you want. Sugar is sugar, and honey is full of it.

• Brown sugar is white sugar with coloring—same product, same effect. Some people claim it tastes better and some insist it's better for you than white sugar. The taste is up to you, but don't be fooled by the few extra nutrients brown sugar contains—you'd have to eat several cups to get enough nutrients to amount to anything.

• Artificial sweeteners such as saccharin are an alternative to sugar and honey, but because of the unsettled controversy over the possible bad effects of these sweeteners, use them sparingly. A new sweetening agent, sold under the brand names Equal or NutraSweet, is being promoted as safer and better-tasting than either saccharin or cyclamates. This sweetener is actually a natural protein product, aspartame, plus lactose (milk sugar). Although it is more expensive than the other nonsugar sweeteners, we recommend it as a better sugar substitute, since no health risk is known at this writing.

• If at all possible, learn to enjoy your food without added sugar and whenever you feel an urge for sugar, try eating fruits, which have a high natural sugar content.

FATS

Sources of Fat

Diary products	Meat fats
Eggs	Vegetable, nut, and seed oils

A WORD ABOUT FATS

What a word is *fat*! And what images it suggests—puffed-out cheeks, belly rolls, stretch marks, and flabby thighs. But fat has special roles in the body that go far beyond the extra padding on our bellies and buttocks. Fat, and fat alone, can fulfill several crucial roles:

- Fats provide the most concentrated source of energy of any food group—about twice the number of calories per gram as carbohydrates and protein;
- Fatty tissues in the body can store and transport substances like fat-soluble vitamins which, because they are insoluble in water, can't be carried by the blood;
- Because fat doesn't mix with water, it can't be washed away by body fluids, and is therefore perfect for storing energy that can be continually burned and replaced;
- Because fats are packed with calories and slow down digestion, the stomach stays full longer, the appetite is satisfied, and the eater stops eating—so in this sense, fat can actually help dieters by getting rid of hunger pains;
- Fat absorbs flavor, making foods taste better;
- Fat provides three essential nutrients that no other food group can provide: linoleic, linolenic, and arachidonic fatty acids—all polyunsaturated fatty acids. As long as these are present, the body can make all the other fatty acids it needs. These crucial nutrients also help regulate clotting mechanisms in the blood and distribution of cholesterol in the body.
- Fats protect and surround the internal organs (kidneys, heart, liver).

As valuable as fat is, though, a little bit truly goes a long way. And, like carbohydrates and proteins, the kind of fat we eat is crucial. Fats are essentially made up of two types: saturated and unsaturated. The "bad" fats are the saturated fats, which are primarily from animal sources and include lard, bacon fat, and butter. The typical American diet is rich in these saturated fats (see graph), which may contribute to blood cholesterol problems and lead to cardiovascular diseases such as heart attacks and strokes. Unsaturated fats—

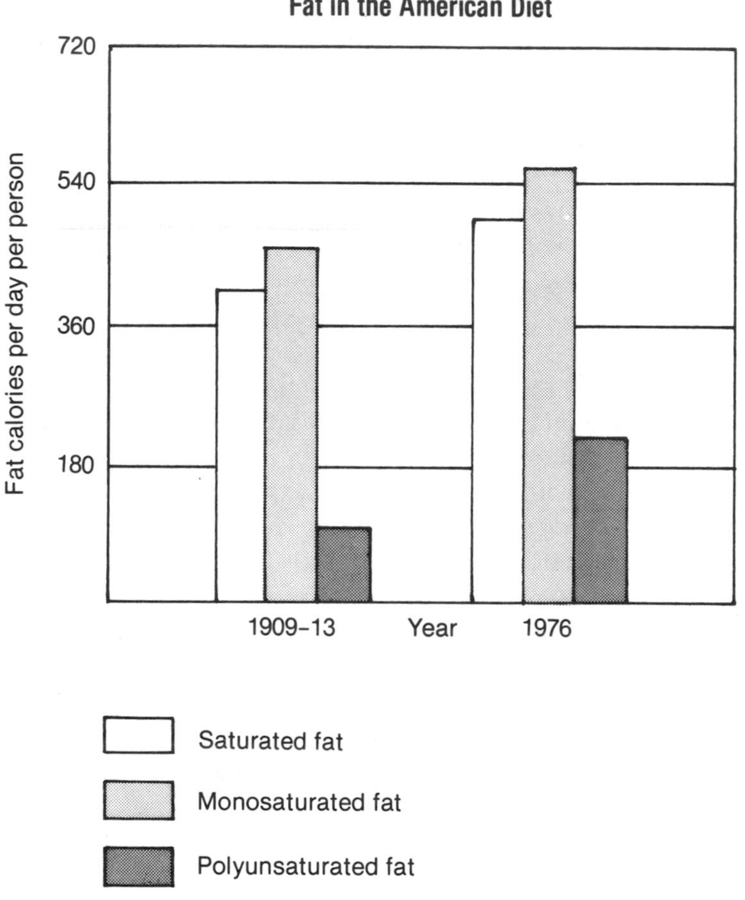

From Jane Brody, *Jane Brody's Nutrition Book*, New York, Bantam Books, 1981. By permission of the publisher.

oils like corn, peanut, sesame, safflower, and sunflower oil, all of which come from vegetables, nuts, and seeds—are less disturbing to blood cholesterol levels, and some unsaturated fats, particularly the essential fatty acid, linoleic acid, can actually help lower blood chlesterol. For a more detailed discussion of cholesterol, see page 173 to 176.

It's also important to watch out for hydrogenated fats, those oils that have been artificially saturated for commercial reasons such as keeping the oil from separating in peanut butter or turning liquid vegetable oils into solid margarines or shortening. Hydrogenation is a chemical process that increases the ratio of hydrogen to carbon; the more hydrogen, the more saturation and the more solid the product. Hydrogenated oils (shortening and margarine, for example) are actually manmade saturated fats.

SOME "FAT" TIPS:

• Limit fat foods to 25 to 30 percent of your total calories—or less if you want to work at it. (Most Americans consume between 40 to 50 percent of their calories in fat and

Which Foods Contain the Most Fat?

75 percent fat or more (mostly saturated fats)

Bacon
Beef: choice grade of chuck, rib, sirloin, and loin untrimmed; hamburger (regular, not lean)
Cold cuts: bologna, salami
Cream: heavy, light, half-and-half, sour
Cream cheese
Head cheese
Hot dogs
Olives
Pork: sausage, spareribs, butt, loin, and untrimmed ham
Salt pork

75 percent fat or more (mostly unsaturated fats)

Avocados
Coconut
Cole slaw dressing
Nuts
Peanut butter
Seeds: pumpkin, sesame, sunflower

50 to 75 percent fat

Beef: rump, corned
Cake, pound
Canadian bacon
Cheese: blue, Cheddar, American, Swiss, etc.
Chicken roasted with skin
Chocolate candy
Cream soups
Eggs
Ice cream (rich)
Lamb chops, rib
Oysters, fried
Fresh-water fish, fried
Pork: ham, loin, and shoulder (trimmed lean cuts)
Tuna with oil
Tuna salad
Veal

40 to 50 percent fat

Beef: T-bone steak (lean only)	Pumpkin pie
Hamburger (lean)	Salmon, canned
Cake, devil's food with chocolate icing	Turkey pot pie
Chicken, fried	Yogurt (whole-milk)
Ice cream	
Mackerel	
Milk, whole	

30 to 40 percent fat

Beef: flank steak, lean chuck pot roast	Milk, 2 percent
Cake, yellow, white (without icing)	Pizza
Chicken roasted without skin	Seafood: scallops and shrimp (breaded and fried)
Cottage cheese, creamed	Soup, bean with pork
Fish: flounder, haddock (fried), halibut (broiled)	Tuna in oil, drained
Granola	Turkey dark meat, roasted
Ice milk	Yogurt (low fat)

20 to 30 percent fat

Beef, sirloin (lean)	Pancakes
Corn muffin	Soups: chicken-noodle, tomato, vegetable
Fish, cod (broiled)	Wheat germ
Liver	
Milk shake, thick	
Oysters, raw	

Less than 20 percent fat

Beans, peas, and lentils	Fruit
Bread	Grains
Buttermilk	Milk, skim
Cabbage, boiled	Seafood: scallops and shrimp (steamed or boiled)
Cakes: angel food, sponge	Soups: split pea, bouillon, consomme
Cereals	Tuna in water
Cottage cheese, uncreamed	Turkey white meat, roasted
Fish: ocean perch (broiled)	Vegetables

Ibid. By permission of the publisher.

maintain a 2:1 ratio of saturated to unsaturated fats.)

In order to cut down on fats, and particularly saturated fats:

- Trim off meat fat;
- Select lean cuts of meat;
- Minimize fried foods (to no more than once or twice a week);
- Remove the skin of poultry before eating;
- Eat less red meat (beef and pork) and eat more fish and fowl;
- Use 1 or 2 percent milk or nonfat milk;
- Limit eggs as a main course to three or four times a week;
- Use oils instead of butter or margarine in cooking.

AND THE EXTRAS . . .

BEVERAGES

CARBONATED. Carbonated beverages (Coca Cola, Dr. Pepper, Pepsi, and other colas) are usually high in sugar and caffeine. These beverages also contain phosphates that can create calcium/phosphorus and hormone imbalances in the body, and artificially-sweetened colas contain chemicals that have not yet been proven safe. For all these reasons, limit carbonated beverages to two or three a week or less. As an alternative, try unsweetened carbonated water mixed with an unsweetened concentrated fruit juice like apple or orange juice. Simply dilute the concentrate with carbonated water and you'll have a delicious homemade "sparkling cider."

COFFEE. Use decaffeinated coffee to eliminate the stimulant effects of caffeine. Large amounts of caffeine speed up metabolism, deplete the body of valuable nutrients, and can affect blood-sugar levels. Because of the oils and acids found in both caffeinated and decaffeinated coffee, however, it's best to limit coffee drinking to one or two cups a day.

Caffeine in Beverages

Beverage	Caffeine in 6-ounce cup
Coffee, brewed	100–150 mg
Coffee, instant	60–80 mg
Sanka, instant, freeze-dried, or ground-roast	3-5 mg
Tea	40–100 mg
Cola beverages	17–55 mg

TEA. Teas are similar to coffee in that most contain caffeine. Herbal teas usually don't contain caffeine (be sure to read the label, however) and may provide some therapeutic benefits: anything from steadying the nerves to settling the stomach to stimulating blood circulation.

CHOCOLATE AND COCOA. Most chocolate products are prepared with large amounts of sugar. Chocolate also contains two stimulants, caffeine and theobromine, which can cause stress to the central nervous system and can aggravate hypoglycemia. Try carob, which tastes and looks like chocolate, as a substitute. Carob is a natural sweetener containing no caffeine and is high in B vitamins and minerals. Many commercially prepared carob products also contain sugar, however, so be sure to read labels.

FRUIT JUICES. Limit yourself to one to two glasses a day because of concentrated and natural sugars.

VEGETABLE JUICES. An excellent source of vitamins and minerals, these juices have a quarter to a third less carbohydrates than fruit juices. Drink one to three glasses a day.

MILK. Drink two or three cups a day of 1 or 2 percent or nonfat milk.

CONDIMENTS AND SALT

Pickles have added sugars and salt; salad dressings and mayonnaise are high in fats and have added sugars; sauces (chili sauce and hot sauce, for example) are usually high in salt and have extra sugar—so use these foods sparingly. Better yet, make your own sauces and condiments (see recipes starting on page 306).

Salt (sodium chloride), our most common seasoning, is simply too common. Excess salt intake can contribute to abnormal fluid retention, resulting in dizziness and swelling of the legs; high blood pressure, increasing the chance of heart disease; loss of blood potassium; and improper use of protein foods in the body.

For all these reasons, lightly salt when you cook and keep the salt shaker off the table at mealtime. Sea salt, which contains important trace minerals, is a good alternative, and commercial products such as No Salt and other salt substitutes can give you the taste of salt without the penalties of excessive sodium.

How Much Sodium Do You Eat?

The average American consumes between 10 to 20 grams of salt every day. That's between 2 to 4 teaspoons a day and about 15 pounds a year! Yet we actually need only 220 milligrams—about a tenth of a teaspoon—of salt daily.

Take a look at the table and add up the amount of salt you take in every day, bearing in mind that a teaspoon of table salt contains 2,132 milligrams of sodium.

Product	Amount	Sodium (in mg)
Breads and pastries		
White, enriched	1 slice	142
Whole-wheat	1 slice	121
Rye	1 slice	139
Biscuit	1 slice	272
Corn bread	2-inch square	283
Danish pastry	1	275
Canned soups		
Beef broth or bouillon prepared with equal amount of water	1 cup	782

	Amount	Sodium (in mg)
Chicken noodle		
prepared with equal amount of water	1 cup	979
Cream of celery, chicken, mushroom		
prepared with equal amount of milk	1 cup	955–970
Minestrone		
prepared with equal amount of water	1 cup	995
Tomato		
prepared with equal amount of milk	1 cup	1,055
Vegetable cup-a-soup	1 cup	1,058

Dairy products

Butter	1 tablespoon	140
Margarine	1 tablespoon	140
Cheese, Cheddar	1 ounce	198
cottage cheese, creamed, not packed	1 cup	850
Swiss	1 ounce	74
Swiss, pasteurized and processed	1 ounce	388
American, pasteurized and processed	1 ounce	406
Eggs, large	2	122
Milk, whole	1 cup	120
skim	1 cup	126
low-fat (2%)	1 cup	122
Yogurt, whole-milk	1 cup	115

Vegetables

Asparagus, raw	1 cup	2
canned	1 cup	570
Beans, snap, raw	1 cup	8
canned	1 cup	319
Broccoli	1 stalk	18
Carrots, raw	1	34
canned	1 cup	366
Cauliflower, raw	1 cup	13
Corn, fresh	1 ear	trace
canned, whole-kernel	1 cup	496
Peas, raw	1 cup	3
canned	1 cup	401
frozen	1 cup	184
Potato, raw	1 cup	5
scalloped	1 cup	870
mashed with milk	1 cup	632

	Amount	Sodium (in mg)
Spinach, raw	1 cup	39
canned	1 cup	484
Tomatoes, raw	1	4
canned puree	1 cup	1,000
Tomato juice	1 cup	486
Fruits		
Apple	1	2
Avocado	1	9
Blackberries	1 cup	1
Blueberries	1 cup	1
Strawberries	1 cup	1
Meats and seafood		
Bacon, sliced	1 pound	3,084
Beef frankfurters	1	425
Bologna	1 slice	369
Chicken, dark or light meat	1 pound	377
Crab, canned, drained, packed	1 cup	1,600
Ground beef, lean, cooked	12 ounces	228
Lobster, cooked	1 pound	1,359
Pork sausage	1 pound	3,357
Round steak, lean, cooked	1 pound	318
Salmon, fresh	1 pound	217
canned	1 cup	850–1,150
T-bone steak, lean	1 pound	217
Tuna, in oil	6½-ounce can	1,472
in water	6½-ounce can	75
Canned and frozen dinners		
Beans and franks	8 ounces	1,224
Frozen chicken or turkey dinner	1 dinner	1,500–2,500
Frozen cheese pizza	6½ ounces	925
Spaghetti, canned	1 cup	955
Fast foods		
Arthur Treacher's Fish Sandwich	1	836
Burger Chef Hamburger	1	393
Burger King Vanilla Shake	1	159
Burger King Whopper	1	909
Kentucky Fried Chicken Dinner, original recipe (3 pieces chicken)	1 dinner	2,285
McDonald's Big Mac	1	1,510
McDonald's Egg McMuffin	1	914
McDonald's Apple Pie	1	414
McDonald's Chocolate Shake	1	329

	Amount	Sodium (in mg)
	Snacks	
Peanuts	1 ounce	132
Potato chips	1 ounce	230
Pretzel sticks	1 ounce	735
Saltines	1 ounce	430
	. . . And the extras	
Baking powder	1 tablespoon	1,205
Barbecue sauce	1 tablespoon	127
Ketchup	1 tablespoon	156
Mustard	1 tablespoon	195
Oil (corn, peanut, safflower, etc.)	1 bottle	0
Olives, green, large	10	926
Peanut butter	2 tablespoons	150–200
Pickles, dill, medium	1	928
Salad dressing, Blue/Roquefort	1 tablespoon	164
French	1 tablespoon	219
Italian	1 tablespoon	314
Mayonnaise	1 tablespoon	84
Russian	1 tablespoon	130
Soy sauce	1 tablespoon	1,319

Sources: Data compiled from *The Nutrition Almanac,* revised edition (McGraw-Hill, 1979), *The Intelligent Person's Guide to Calories and Nutrition* (Jeffrey Weiss Group, 133 Fifth Ave., New York, NY 10003), and analyses by the Center for Public Interest, the Consumers Union, and manufacturers.

EXTRACTS AND COOKING WINES

Natural extracts (vanilla, almond, maple, and so on) contain alcohol. For absolute protection, use imitation extracts instead. Learn to read labels, however, for some imitation extracts also contain alcohol.

Cooking wines, like most wines, contain 11 to 12 percent alcohol. While this alcohol is generally cooked out when food is baked, boiled, or steamed, a bottle on the shelf is a temptation that most alcoholics can do without. Why make it harder on yourself, particularly during those first, sometimes shaky, months of sobriety? Keep cooking wine, sherry, port, liqueurs and anything else containing alcohol out of the house—and concentrate on the thousands of delicious recipes that don't call for alcohol.

Summary of Step 2: Specific Principles

Protein foods:	
Rules of thumb:	• 1 meat-based meal • 1 meatless meal • 1 less-meat meal
Meat	Concentrate on more fish and fowl; eat less beef and pork
Eggs	2 every other day
Milk	2–3 glasses every day
Cheese	Unprocessed, low-fat, soft cheeses are best
Fats:	
Rules of thumb:	• Choose leaner cuts of meat • Trim off meat fat • Drink 2% milk • Skin chicken • Use margarine or Better Butter (page 300) • Use cooking oils when possible instead of butter, margarine, or shortening
Carbohydrates:	
Fruits	4–5 servings a day, including juices Unsweetened fruit juices Fresh fruit preferable
Vegetables	5–6 servings a day Use an assortment of deep-green leafy and dark-yellow/orange vegetables and raw vegetables every day Eat vegetables raw whenever possible Undercook rather than overcook
Grains & cereals	Use whole-grain products Limit cold cereals and use sugar-free brands
Sugar	Eliminate sweets and sugary desserts and pastries Use sugar substitutes in moderation

STEP 3: THE EXCHANGE SYSTEM

Once you understand the basic guidelines, the diet for sobriety can be taken one step further by following a formula called *the exchange system*. In this system, foods are divided into six major categories: milk, meat (protein), vegetable, fruit, bread (starches), and fat.

The exchange system is sort of a mix and match in which you can pick from a number of foods in each category—as long as you include the right proportions of foods from all the food groups. Any food within a group can be exchanged for another food within the same group. For example, every day you should eat nine servings, or exchanges, from the bread group. To fulfill the nine exchanges, you can choose from dozens of foods, all containing approximately the same nutrients and calories. As you can see, the bread group includes foods primarily known as starches—breads, cereals, and starchy vegetables. A sampling of just some of the bread exchanges shows the wide variety available: 1 slice of whole-wheat bread, ½ cup of brown rice, ½ cup of rolled oats, ¼ cup of wheat germ, 1 small white potato, 1 small ear of corn on the cob, 4 whole-grain crackers, or dozens of other bread exchanges.

The exchange system appeals to many alcoholics who feel they can better understand the requirements of the diet for sobriety if they follow a rigid guideline. Some use the system for several weeks or a month to help them sort out which foods are allowed in which amounts. Then, when they've learned the principles through practice, they no longer need a rigid system and can easily make the right food choices on their own. Of course, the "right" foods will vary depending on individual likes and dislikes and specific medical problems and nutritional requirements. Some alcoholics have special health problems requiring a specialized diet that must be watched over by a physician or other health-care professional. Others will need to adapt the exchange system for

The Diet for Sobriety

Approximate Composition

Protein: 25 percent
Carbohydrates: 45 percent
Fat: 30 percent
Calories: 2,000

Meal plan	Total exchange	Breakfast	Snack	Lunch	Snack	Dinner	Snack
Milk (2%)	3	½	½	–	–	1	1
Meat (protein)	11	2	1	4	1	2	1
Vegetable	6	–	–	3	–	2	1
Fruit	6	2	1	1	1	1	–
Bread (starches)	9	2	–	3	1	2	1
Fat	6	2	–	2	–	2	–

Sample Menu

Breakfast (meatless)

½ cup 2% milk
2 eggs, boiled or poached
½ cup orange juice
½ grapefruit
1 slice whole-grain toast
½ cup oatmeal
2 teaspoons margarine or Better Butter*

Mid-morning snack

6 ounces high-protein shake*

Lunch (meat-based)

1 cup vegetable juice
4 ounces sirloin steak
½ cup mixed vegetables
1 baked potato
1 whole-wheat roll
2 teaspoons margarine
½ cup pineapple–orange gelatin salad*

Mid-afternoon snack

1 ounce unprocessed cheese
1 small apple
4 squares rye crackers

Dinner (less-meat)

Chicken casserole*
½ cup cole slaw with dressing*
½ cup cooked broccoli
1 slice whole-grain bread
½ cup fruit cocktail in natural juices

Before-bed snack

Celery sticks with 2 tablespoons natural peanut butter
4 squares stone-ground wheat crackers
1 cup 2% milk

*See recipe section

low-fat diets, diabetic diets, low-cholesterol diets, or low-salt diets. So, once again, this system of eating is offered as a guide and can easily be adapted to fit special needs. The diet we describe in this section is a middle-of-the-road plan intended to meet most alcoholics' needs most of the time.

The preceding table lists the total exchanges allowed in each food group and then breaks these down into breakfast, lunch, dinner, and three snacks. This is a menu plan. The sample menu then shows how a day's menu can be drawn up using this plan.

The following pages list foods according to groups (milk, meat, vegetable, fruit, bread, and fat), and the amount of food making up an exchange is indicated at the beginning of each section. From these food lists you can select your choice and amount of food to make your own menus, following the meal plan described in the preceding table. Look for recipes beginning on page 288.

MILK GROUP

Exchanges per day: 3. One exchange is approximately 8 grams of protein, 12 grams of carbohydrates. Fat and calories will vary depending on type of milk.

A. NONFAT MILK

8 grams protein 0 grams fat 12 grams carbohydrate

Skim milk	1 cup
Nonfat powdered (before adding liquid)	⅓ cup
Canned evaporated	½ cup
Buttermilk (made from skim milk)	1 cup
Yogurt (made from skim milk)	1 cup

B. LOW-FAT MILK

8 grams protein 4 grams fat 12 grams carbohydrate

1% fortified milk	1 cup
2% fortified milk	1 cup
Yogurt (2% milk)	1 cup

C. WHOLE MILK

8 grams protein	8 grams fat	12 grams carbohydrate
Whole milk		1 cup
Whole evaporated		½ cup
Buttermilk (made from whole milk)		1 cup
Yogurt (made from whole milk)		1 cup

MEAT AND PROTEIN GROUP

Exchanges per day: 11. One exchange (1 ounce) contains approximately 7 grams protein, 3 grams fat, and 55 calories.

A. MEAT (lean only)

beef
elk
lamb
liver
moose
pork
rabbit
veal

B. POULTRY (take skin off to eliminate extra fat)

chicken
Cornish game hen
duck
eggs (1 egg = 1 exchange)
goose
turkey

C. CHEESE

cottage cheese (¼ cup serving)
hard cheese — Cheddar, mozzarella, Swiss, etc. (1 ounce or a 1-inch cube = 1 exchange)

D. LEAN FISH

bass
bluefish
catfish
cod
flounder
haddock
halibut
ocean perch
pike
rockfish
smelt
snapper
sole
trout
tuna
yellow fish

E. FATTY FISH

albacore	salmon
bluefin tuna	sardines
eel	shad
herring	swordfish
mackerel	whitefish

F. SHELLFISH (high in cholesterol)

clams	lobster
crab	oysters
	shrimp

G. OTHER SOURCES OF PROTEIN

dried beans and peas ½ cup serving = 1 exchange

natural peanut butter (no preservatives or additives) 2 tablespoons per serving

tofu, 3 ounces

VEGETABLE GROUP

Exchanges per day: 6. One exchange is ½ cup, contains approximately 1 to 5 grams carbohydrate, 2 grams protein, and 5 to 25 calories.

Vegetables that are low in carbohydrates, high in water, and can be used as desired:

chicory	garlic
Chinese cabbage	lettuce
cucumber	parsley
endive	radishes
escarole	watercress

Vegetables that are slightly higher in carbohydrates:

asparagus	cabbage
bean sprouts	carrots
beets	cauliflower
broccoli	celery
Brussels sprouts	eggplant

green pepper	onions
greens	peapods
beet greens	rhubarb
chard	rutabaga
collards	sprouts (all kinds)
dandelions	string beans (yellow or green)
kale	summer squash
mustard greens	tomatoes
spinach	tomato juice
turnip greens	turnips
mushrooms	vegetable juice cocktail
okra	zucchini

FRUIT GROUP

Exchanges per day: 6. One exchange contains approximately 10 grams carbohydrate and 40 calories.

apple	1 small
apples, dried	1 package
applesauce (unsweetened)	½ cup
apricots, fresh	2 medium
apricots, dried	4 halves
apple juice	⅓ cup
banana	½ small
berries	
blackberries	½ cup
blueberries	½ cup
raspberries	½ cup
strawberries	¾ cup
cherries	10 large
dates	2
figs, fresh	1
grapefruit	½
grapefruit juice	½ cup
grapes	12

grape juice (unsweetened)	¼ cup
mango	½ small
melons	
cantaloupe	¼ small
honeydew	⅛ medium
watermelon	1 cup
nectarine	1 small
orange	1 small
orange juice (unsweetened)	½ cup
papaya	¾ cup
peach	1 medium
pear	1 small
persimmon	1 medium
pineapple	½ cup
pineapple juice (unsweetened)	⅓ cup
plums	2 medium
prune juice	¼ cup
prunes	2 medium
raisins	2 tablespoons
tangerine	1 medium

BREAD GROUP

Exchanges per day: 9. One exchange contains 15 grams carbohydrate, 2 grams protein, and 70 calories.

A. CEREALS (whole-grain, containing no preservatives, no refined sugar)

Grape Nuts	½ cup
rolled oats	½ cup cooked
seven-grain	½ cup cooked
Shredded Wheat	½ cup cooked
wheat germ	¼ cup

B. BREAD—1 slice

barley	rye
gluten	soy
millet	100% wheat
oat	any other whole-grain bread

C. MISCELLANEOUS

barley	½ cup cooked
brown rice	½ cup cooked
rye wafers	3 (2″ x 3½″)
whole-grain bagel	½
whole-grain bun	½ slice
whole-grain crackers	4
whole-grain muffin	½
whole-grain noodles	½ cup
whole-grain pancake	1 (5″ x ½″)
whole-grain roll	1
whole-grain waffle	1 (5″ x ½″)

D. STARCHY VEGETABLES

corn	⅓ cup
corn on the cob	1 small ear
dried beans or lentils	½ cup cooked
lima beans	½ cup cooked
parsnips	⅔ cup
peas, green	½ cup
potato	1 small
potato (mashed)	½ cup
pumpkin	¾ cup
squash	
acorn	½ cup
butternut	½ cup
winter	½ cup
yam or sweet potato	¼ cup

FAT GROUP

Exchanges per day: 6. One exchange contains approximately 5 grams fat and 45 calories.

avocado (4″ diameter)	⅛
butter	1 teaspoon
cream, light	2 tablespoons

cream, heavy	1 tablespoon
cream, sour	2 tablespoons
cream cheese	1 tablespoon
margarine, soft, tub, or stick	1 teaspoon
nuts, natural	2 to 10 (varies according to kind)
nuts, mixed	6
olives	5 small
salad dressing	
French, homemade	1 tablespoon
mayonnaise, homemade	1 tablespoon
oil-vinegar	1 tablespoon
seeds—sunflower, sesame, pumpkin, etc.	2 ounces
vegetable oil	1 teaspoon

STEP 4: KEEPING NUTRIENTS SAFE

Vitamins and minerals are surrounded by enemies that can rob them of their strength and power. Light, heat, cold, and moisture are the primary problems. While it's impossible to preserve all nutrients, it is possible to minimize loss by reducing their exposure to enemy elements. The following guide to food selection, preparation, cooking, and storage will give you some valuable hints on how to increase the nutrient value of foods and keep nutrients safe. Some of this information has already been discussed in previous pages, but we include it again here in summary form.

FOOD SELECTION

- Fresh fruits and vegetables in season are best.
- Watch out for "fresh" fruits and vegetables out of season—they may be marked fresh, but chances are good they've been subjected to storage and lots of handling.
- Frozen foods are next best to fresh, although freezing will cause a loss of nutrients, particularly vitamin C and thiamine. Wrap your frozen foods tightly. Boil-in-the-bag frozen

vegetables are preferable if you can afford them, because some of the nutrients are preserved in the sauces.

• Stay away from commercially canned foods—fruits, vegetables, and soups. The high temperatures used in canning destory water-soluble vitamins (the B vitamins and vitamin C), and storage destroys additional vitamins. You can expect canned foods to contain half or less of the original vitamin content of the food. Most canned foods also have added sugar and salt.

• Read labels carefully, avoiding those canned goods with added sugar and salt. Sugar has been added to a product if the words *syrup, dextrose, fructose, glucose, hexitol, lactose, maltose, manitol, sorbitol* or *sucrose* are listed. As a general rule, words ending in *-ose* and *-ol* indicate sugar. Corn syrup is another sugar-laden additive. Salt may be disguised as sodium, monosodium glutamate, or the chemical symbol Na. Baking powder and baking soda contain significant amounts of sodium, i.e. salt.

• Condiments such as ketchup, soy sauce, barbecue sauce, chili sauce, mayonnaise, mustard, and salad dressing contain sugar and salt.

• Avoid precooked foods like TV dinners, chicken pot pies, frozen pizzas, and so on, because valuable nutrients are lost in the processing of flour, as well as in precooking, storing, and freezing.

• When purchasing margarine and skim or nonfat dry milk, look for ones that have been fortified with vitamins A and D, since these are lost when fat is removed.

PREPARATION, COOKING, AND STORAGE

• If a recipe calls for wine, sherry, or cooking alcohol, adapt the recipe and substitute broth or water.

• Eat your fruits and vegetables raw whenever possible.

• Don't soak raw vegetables or fruit before eating because water (and other liquids you drain out) also drain the nutrients out.

• Don't wash rice before cooking—you'll lose some of your water-soluble vitamins and minerals (iron, for example).

• In general, the shorter the cooking time, the more nutrients retained. Pressure-cooking is a good cooking method, as is steaming—but you'll lose significant amounts of vitamin C, thiamine, niacin, and folacin when you steam. Stir-frying your vegetables and meats is a good technique (but go easy on adding oils!).

• Avoid frying foods in oil, as a lot of fat is soaked into the food, and fats are broken down to potentially harmful substances at high temperatures—particularly with deep-fat frying methods. Frying also destroys some vitamin C.

• Broiled, roasted, and fried meats retain more of the B vitamins than stewed or braised meat. If you drink the broth of braised or stewed meats, however, you'll recapture the lost vitamins.

• If you eat your meat rare, you'll get more thiamine than in well-done meat—but the rare meat will have more fat.

• Cook your potatoes in the skin, a handy jacket that holds in most of the vitamins and minerals.

• If you cook in water, find a way to use the vitamin-rich water in soups, casseroles, or gravies.

• Prolonged high-temperature baking of bread can destroy lysine, an essential amino acid. If bread is steamed or baked in a microwave oven, significant amounts of lysine will not be destroyed.

• If you toast bread, toast lightly. Dark toast has about a third the nutritional value of lightly toasted bread.

• Avoid spicing food heavily—you'll overstimulate your palate and lose your sensitivity to subtler flavors and textures. Spicing also tends to upset a sensitive stomach. Some ulcer patients, for example, can't tolerate highly spiced foods.

• Copper pots, unless heavily lined, can destroy vitamins C and E and folacin.

• Keep milk in the refrigerator and make sure it's in an opaque or light-tight container—light destroys riboflavin, an essential B vitamin.

Vitamin and Mineral "Thieves" in the Kitchen

- **Vitamin B-1** (thiamine) is destroyed by processing (chopping, peeling, cutting, and other types of handling prior to cooking), air, and water.
- **Vitamin B-2** is destroyed by light and water.
- **Vitamin B-6** is destroyed by water, processing, long storage, and, in meat, by canning, roasting, and stewing.
- **Vitamin B-12** and **Vitamin B-15** are destroyed by water and sunlight.
- **Biotin** is destroyed by water and processing.
- **Vitamin C** is destroyed by water, cooking, heat, and light.
- **Pantothenic acid** is destroyed by heat, processing, and canning.
- **Choline** is destroyed by water and processing.
- **Vitamin E** is destroyed by heat, freezing, oxygen, and processing.
- **Folic acid** is destroyed by sunlight, processing, boiling, and heat (particularly boiling).
- **Inositol** is destroyed by processing and water.
- **Vitamin K** is destroyed by freezing.
- **Niacin** is destroyed by water and processing.
- **PABA** is destroyed by water and processing.
- **Selenium, iodine,** and **cobalt** are lost in processing.

8

The Vitamins

VITAMINS are to food as matches are to a pile of kindling: they ignite it, allowing the food to be put to use, its energy released. These chemical "igniters" help food move along the pathways of biochemical reactions, providing energy for tissue repair and regeneration and all the other processes necessary for life. Without vitamins, food would be useless, for no matter how much we ate our bodies could not release the energy, or nutrients, in the food—a sort of starvation in the midst of plenty.

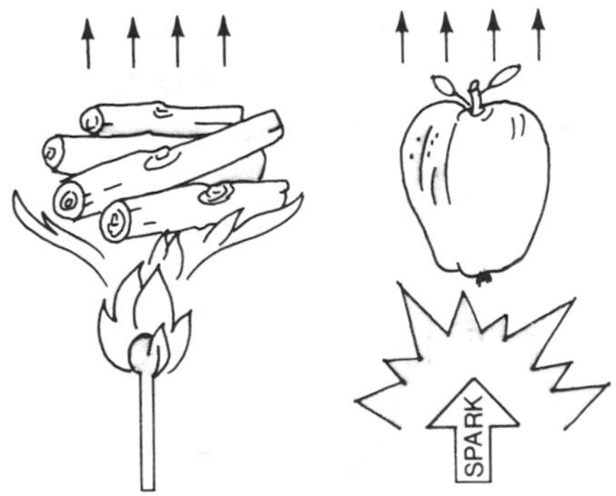

Vitamins are linked to protein chains, called enzymes, and together they help to initiate and regulate chemical reactions in cells. The average cell contains approximately 3,000 different enzymes, each of which includes co-factors that allow the enzyme to do its job. Vitamins and minerals, in their role as co-factors, literally give enzymes their get-up-and-go. Without them, enzymes are grounded and useless, miniature power plants with no juice to get things going.

WATER-SOLUBLE AND FAT-SOLUBLE VITAMINS

Vitamins C and the B-complex vitamins* are soluble in water, allowing them to mix with the water component of blood and be transported to the cells. While their ability to mix with water allows these vitamins to be highly mobile, it also presents a drawback because they cannot be stored to any significant extent, and vitamin excesses are washed out in the urine.

The fat-soluble vitamins (A, D, E, and K), which require dietary fat for absorption into the body, are not as mobile, but they can be stored in the body's fatty tissues and in cell membranes. The body can then draw on these stores when it needs them. But storage presents its own problems, for unlike the water-soluble vitamins, which are conveniently eliminated even when taken in large doses, the fat-soluble vitamins—particularly A and D—can build up to potentially hazardous levels when taken in very large amounts. More on these potential hazards when we describe the vitamins in detail later in this chapter.

VITAMIN DEFICIENCIES

Vitamins are needed in very small amounts, but their power is life-sustaining, and their absence can be life-threatening. When one or more vitamins are absent or deficient in

*The B-complex vitamins include thiamine (B-1), riboflavin (B-2), niacin (B-3), pyridoxine (B-6), B-12, folic acid, pantothenic acid, biotin, choline, inositol, PABA (para-amino-benzoic acid), B-15 (pangamic acid) and B-17.

the diet, the biochemical pathways dependent upon that particular vitamin cannot be completed and cell function falters. Cells may be unable to put together or break down sugars, or repair themselves with new proteins; they may starve because the vitamin necessary to release the energy in food is missing. Imagine the body as a train, with all its moving parts in perfect shape, derailed because one rail on the track—a single vitamin—is missing. Vitamins are the rails that move food along to nourish the body, and when they are missing or are available only in inadequate amounts, the body machinery simply begins to fall apart.

A vitamin deficiency will eventually result in tissue damage, showing up first in the parts of the body where the vitamin is most active. Thus, vitamin deficiencies make themselves known in a wide range of malfunctions, and the symptoms of deficiency are diverse, including loss of appetite, fatigue, mental confusion, dizziness, paranoia, abnormal heartbeat, ruptured blood vessels, loose teeth, rashes, and sores. These symptoms can easily be overlooked or, in the case of severe vitamin deficiencies, can be confused with other mental and physical illnesses. Because deficiencies of certain vitamins (most notably the B vitamins, which are essential to the health of nerve cells) cause damage to the cells of the brain and nervous system, the sufferer can be misdiagnosed as mentally ill or psychologically troubled.

A dramatic example of this confusion and misdiagnosis can be found in the history of the treatment of pellagra, a disease caused by a severe deficiency of niacin, or vitamin B-3. The pellagra story is particularly interesting to alcoholics, for pellagra victims, like alcoholics who also suffer from nutritional deficiencies, were typically diagnosed as mentally ill and presumed deficient in personality or character. Misdiagnosis has caused pellagra victims and alcoholics much suffering, as victims of both diseases came to believe that the cause of their affliction was somehow within their control;

misdiagnosis has also prevented effective treatment, causing many people to suffer and die unnecessarily.

PELLAGRA: A CASE OF MISTAKEN IDENTITY

Pellagra became a problem of epidemic proportions at the turn of this century, particularly in the South where pellagra victims were crowded into insane asylums. "Like a mushroom, pellagra is coming up overnight, spreading everywhere," wrote Dr. Claude H. Lavinder of the U.S. Public Health Service in 1908. Victims typically suffered from vomiting, loss of appetite, and diarrhea. Their tongues became red and sore, and their mouths became inflamed, with cracks and sores appearing in the surrounding skin. Skin on the back of the hands, as well as on the neck and chest, was often red, thick, and scaly. The mental and psychological problems of the victims were obvious and sometimes dramatic. Pellagra victims were often depressed and suffered from insomnia, headaches, irritability, and general anxiety. Some victims would go into a stupor; others were violent and irrational.

Commissions established to study pellagra concluded that the disease was caused by infection, probably in the intestinal tract, and communicable from person to person by some unknown means. The infectious agent eluded investigators, however, and in 1914 Dr. Joseph Goldberger, a bacteriologist, was assigned by the surgeon general to head a pellagra task force.

Goldberger visited orphanages, insane asylums, and prisons in the South, where the disease was most prevalent, and concluded that pellagra was not an infectious disease at all but a nutritional disorder caused by a diet deficient in meat, milk, and eggs. To prove his point, Goldberger put twelve volunteer convicts on the high-carbohydrate, high-fat, and extremely low-protein diet of the Southern poor, feeding them cornmeal, grits, pork fat, rice, cane syrup, sweet potatoes, and turnip greens. Six of the twelve convicts developed pronounced pellagra and two more showed signs of it.

Goldberger was so convinced of his theory and met so much resistance to it that he concocted an extraordinary experiment to prove his point: He, his colleagues, and his wife injected themselves with the blood of pellagrins and swallowed skin scrapings, feces, and urine of pellagra patients. When none of them developed any signs or symptoms of the disease, he had conclusive proof that pellagra was not a communicable, infectious disease.

Despite these dramatic experiments and Goldberger's pronouncement that "pellagra may be prevented completely by a suitable diet without intervention of any other factor, hygenic or sanitary," his findings were ignored and pellagra deaths multiplied. The racially prejudiced statements of another respected scientist, Charles Benedict Davenport, were primarily responsible for suppressing the truth about pellagra. Davenport, a zoologist and founder and leader of a quasi-religious cult called the American Eugenics Movement, claimed that all insanity is hereditary and that certain strains of the Nordic race were genetically superior to other, "inferior" strains (such as poor Southern whites). Completely ignoring Goldberger's experiments, Davenport insisted that pellagra appeared primarily in white people whose genetically inferior blood lacked the gene for resistance to the pellagra "germ." He was able to get control of the final report of the Pellagra Commission and used the report to spread his theory that pellagra was not caused by bad diets but by bad genes, dismissing Goldberger's work as meaningless.

In 1929, when Goldberger died, pellagra deaths had increased eightfold since 1914, when his findings were first presented. So strong was the opposition to the vitamin-deficiency theory that even when Goldberger discovered in 1922 that the amino acid tryptophan* could cure pellagra

*Tryptophan is converted to niacin in the body.

when added to the diet, the information was ignored, as was his eventual discovery that niacin could prevent pellagra. Not until 1939 did the Council on Foods and Nutrition of the American Medical Association call for the fortification of white flour, white bread, and other staples with niacin, thiamine, riboflavin, iron, and calcium. This fortification, along with rising incomes after World War II and improvements in the diets of the poor, helped eradicate pellagra in the United States.

LESSONS TO BE LEARNED

The history of pellagra victims and their treatment in this country is a fascinating example of the power of prcjudice to distort reality. It also dramatizes the resistance many people have to accepting vitamin therapy as a cure for such afflictions. This resistance continues on today, fueled by a lack of emphasis and focus in medical schools on the practice and application of nutrition, and by the continuing belief that "mental" symptoms are primarily caused by psychological, not physiological, problems.

For alcoholics, who suffer from numerous vitamin deficiencies caused both by their diet and their excessive drinking, the exclusive psychological focus of mental illness can be particularly dangerous. Instead of being treated for vitamin deficiencies, the recovering alcoholic is presumed nutritionally sound once he stops drinking and is usually released from treatment with no information about adequate and continuing nutritional therapy. If he continues to have psychological problems, they are assumed to be just that—psychological, in his head. "Alcoholics are lonely, depressed and anxious individuals" is the refrain heard all too often, "and that's why they started drinking too much in the first place." Any continuing problems are presumably something the alcoholic will have to learn to live with. All too often, however, the alcoholic's lingering symptoms are a result of unfinished repair and healing of the body.

When the depression, anxiety, irritability, headaches, and insomnia are recognized for what they are—symptoms of tissue damage caused by vitamin deficiencies—and when the alcoholic is restored to health through diet and vitamin therapy, these so-called psychological problems frequently disappear. No better support for using nutritional therapy in alcoholism treatment can be found than the fact that it works.

In the remainder of this chapter, the major vitamins are discussed from two viewpoints: what they do for us, and what a deficiency does to us. The effect of chronic alcoholism on specific deficiencies is explained, daily requirements are given, and food sources for each vitamin are listed. In discussing daily requirements, we've provided the recommended amounts both for adults and for recovering alcoholics and have used the term *RDA*s—shorthand you'll find on numerous food containers that means *recommended daily allowances* (recommended *dietary* allowances in the 1980 Food and Nutrition Board listings).*

Be aware that recommendations regarding specific doses is a tricky business, since every one of us is different, and a dosage that works beautifully for 98 percent of recovering alcoholics may not be right for the remaining 2 percent. Because of this individuality, alcoholics (and, in fact, anyone who regularly takes vitamin and mineral supplements) should consult a physician before increasing the recommended amounts and should be aware of the potential hazards of taking very large or disproportionate amounts. Most vitamins are safe even in large doses but, again, there are individual differences in reactions.

*The RDAs we've used are from the 1980 listings of the Food and Nutrition Board and cover men and women from age 23 to 50. Because the 1980 revisions sometimes use different units of measurement than those currently listed on supplement labels, we've translated the measurements when necessary into those most commonly used. See Appendix 3 for the most complete table of 1980 U.S. RDAs.

For quick reference regarding RDAs, see the summary of nutrients at the end of the chapter.

The Fat-Soluble Vitamins

VITAMIN A

Roles. Active in the fatty membranes of the cells that cover the outer and inner surfaces of the body—like the skin and lining tissues of the mouth, respiratory passages, digestive and urinary tracts—vitamin A is essential for the proper growth and health of these soft tissues. Vitamin A is also necessary for building strong bones and teeth and for the light-sensitive pigments in the eye that make night vision possible.

Deficiencies. One of the most common symptoms of vitamin A deficiency is night blindness, an inability of the eyes to adjust to darkness. Vitamin A deficiency may also affect the skin, which becomes dry and warty like a toad's. In countries where starvation is rampant, vitamin A deficiency can cause serious problems. The lining cells of the respiratory tract, which protect the lungs and airways, can become dried up, scaly, and easily infected. An increased susceptibility to pneumonia and tuberculosis may result from prolonged vitamin A deficiency; also, the eyes often become infected, and growth is sometimes stunted because of the part the vitamin plays in bone formation.

Vitamin A deficiencies are not uncommon in alcoholics, especially in patients with liver disease, because the decreased synthesis of protein in the liver reduces the binding capacity and use of vitamin A in the body. Also, the enzyne used to process alcohol is the same used to metabolize vitamin A. Because of this competition, the enzyme may be overused or even burnt out in alcoholics, and thus unable to efficiently use vitamin A. Further, heavy use of alcohol appears to accelerate the breakdown of vitamin A and interferes with its storage in the liver, resulting in a vitamin A deficiency in the body.

Recommended Amounts. For adults the recommended daily allowance of vitamin A is approximately 3,000 IU—international units.* For some vitamins, IU is used as a measurement rather than milligrams or micrograms. The IU measures the *activity* of the vitamin rather than the quantity. Most alcoholics can safely double this RDA, and many may require as much as 25,000 units or more daily. But high doses should be taken only under medical supervision, and special caution must be taken when cirrhosis or advanced liver disease exists.

Symptoms of vitamin A excess are headaches, diarrhea, irregular menstruation, loss of appetite, blurred vision, and hair loss.

Sources. Vitamin A can be manufactured by animals (including man) from carotene, the substance that give plants like carrots, squash, and sweet potatoes their yellow-orange color. Carotene is also found in dark, green leafy vegetables like kale, broccoli, and spinach, although its color is masked by the green chlorophyll. Other food sources of vitamin A include liver, eggs, whole milk, cream, and cheese.

VITAMIN D

Roles. The action of sunlight on the skin transforms certain substances in the body to Vitamin D. Vitamin D is necessary for the absorption and use of calcium and phosphorus, both of which are essential for the growth and maintenance of bones. Vitamin D also contributes to other calcium-dependent activities of the body, including proper functioning of the nerves, heart, and blood-clotting mechanisms.

*Actually, the 1980 RDA is listed in REs or *retinol equivalents.* The adult RE is 1,000 for men and 800 for women. This translates into approximately 2,700 to 3,300 IU.

Deficiencies. When vitamin D stores are inadequate, the body can't effectively absorb the calcium needed for the bones or supply the body with adequate calcium—even if calcium is plentiful in the diet. Rickets, a childhood disease, is caused by a severe vitamin D deficiency. The bones grow soft, and the result is various degrees of deformity including nodules on the ribs and bending of the bones; the softened bones simply can't support the weight of the body. Rickets is common in parts of the world where the winter is especially long, where smoke and fog constantly block out the sun, and in impoverished countries where food is scarce and dietary deficiencies are common. Working indoors for long hours and getting little or no exposure to the sun can also cause vitamin D deficiencies. However, most people are able to store enough vitamin D in sunny weather to last through normal dark and cloudy winters.

Fortification of milk with vitamin D has done away with this deficiency problem for most Americans. Too much vitamin D can also be a problem, however, producing high levels of calcium in the body, which are then deposited in places like the blood vessels and kidneys and can contribute to hardening of the arteries and kidney stones.

Recommended Amounts. The recommended daily allowance of vitamin D is set at 200 IU per day, an amount that meets the needs of nearly all healthy people.

The standard dosage in almost all multiple vitamins and mineral supplements is 400 IU (the 1974 RDA) and this should be sufficient for alcoholics.

Sources. The best source of vitamin D is not food at all, but sunlight. Milk fortified with vitamin D is also an excellent source, with one cup of whole milk providing 100 IU.

VITAMIN E

Roles. Vitamin E has been called the "miracle" vitamin and a listing of some of its reported roles in the body shows why. Vitamin E:

- supplies oxygen to the muscles (including the heart), promoting strength and endurance;
- acts as an "anti-oxidant," meaning that it opposes oxidation and keeps fatty substances from going "rancid" in the body. This anti-oxidant property of vitamin E is credited with slowing down the aging process of cells and thus helping people to look younger;
- acts as a natural anticoagulant, dissolving blood clots and restoring the blood to its proper consistency;
- slows down the aging process of red blood cells;
- can, by working with vitamin A, protect the lungs against air pollution;
- can lower the blood pressure;
- improves circulation and resistance to cold;
- heals scar tissues and prevents thick scar formation (both externally and internally);
- lowers levels of cholestereol in the blood.

Add to vitamin E's wonders its reported ability to prevent diseases of reproductive glands, miscarriages, sterility, still-births, spontaneous abortions, symptoms of menopause (hot flashes, sweating), cystic breast disease, coronary heart disease, angina pectoris, varicose veins, ulcers, thrombosis, phlebitis, some eye diseases, and kidney disease, and the word *miracle* seems somewhat tame.

Deficiencies. Less than a decade ago most doctors and scientists believed vitamin E was not essential to health and considered it "a vitamin looking for a disease." But, while a clear-cut disease resulting from vitamin E deficiency has not been defined, growing evidence points to the body's dependency upon vitamin E: use of it as a supplement has been found to relieve the symptoms of, and perhaps even prevent, over eighty ailments.*

Recommended Amounts. The adult RDA of vitamin E is 12 to 16 IUs. Alcoholics who have evidence of cardiovascular disease (poor circulation, elevated blood fats, or high blood pressure, for example) may benefit from doses of 300 to 600 IUs a day under a physician's supervision. Hypertensive (high-blood-pressure) patients and people with rheumatic heart disease, however, need to increase their dosage slowly to avoid aggravating their disease with sudden high doses. For alcoholics who suffer from skin rashes or rough, dry skin, vitamin E oil may be applied as a skin salve to promote healing.

Sources. Polyunsaturated fats such as safflower, sunflower, and wheat-germ oil provide an excellent source of vitamin E,** as do almonds, walnuts, and sunflower seeds. Asparagus, beet greens, broccoli (especially the leaves), leeks, spinach, sweet potatoes, and turnip greens are vegetables high in vitamin E; fruits high in the vitamin include apples, wild blackberries, and pears.

VITAMIN K

Roles. Vitamin K is essential to helping the liver produce substances necessary for normal blood clotting. Specifically, vitamin K promotes the manufacture of prothrombin, also called "the clotting factor."

* *The Nutrition Almanac* (compiled by John D. Kirschman, McGraw-Hill Book Co., New York, 1973), lists eighty-three ailments for which vitamin E may be beneficial.

**Cold-pressed oils are superior, since the heat-treated oils lose a lot of vitamin E during processing. Most oils available in supermarkets are heat-treated, but cold-pressed oils are available in most health food stores.

Deficiencies. Vitamin K deficiencies are common in alcoholics with severely damaged livers, because the liver is unable to produce sufficient amounts of bile acids, which are necessary to absorb fats. Poor absorption of fats leads to decreased absorption of fat-soluble vitamins, particularly vitamin K. Vitamin K is manufactured in the intestine by intestinal bacteria; alcoholics with intestinal damage and absorption problems may have deficiencies of vitamin K. Symptoms of a deficiency of vitamin K include bleeding and hemorrhaging.

Recommended Amounts. The normal adult requires only a small amount of vitamin K because the vitamin can be manufactured in the intestinal tract. No RDA has been established, but dosages in the range of 70 to 140 micrograms (.07 to .14 milligrams) are considered safe by the Food and Nutrition Board. When the alcoholic's liver or intestinal lining is severely damaged, however, 1 to 10 milligrams injected directly into a muscle or the blood stream may be necessary during the first days of treatment.

Sources. Green leafy vegetables (especially spinach and cabbage), egg yolks, milk, and safflower oil are all excellent sources of vitamin K. But the most dependable source is produced by "friendly" bacteria in the intestines. Yogurt, kefir, and acidophilus milk can contribute to this bacterial manufacturing of vitamin K.

The Water-Soluble Vitamins

Because any excess of the water-soluble vitamins (C, and the B-complex vitamins) is excreted in the urine, it's difficult to take too much, even if the dosage is increased tenfold or more. Megavitamin therapy* is, however, a controversial subject, with the majority of doctors and scientists arguing that until we know all the risks and benefits associated with taking massive doses of a particular vitamin, we should not megadose.

But biochemist and Nobel Prize winner Linus Pauling vehemently disagrees with this majority view and outspokenly defends taking megadoses of the water-soluble vitamin, vitamin C. Pauling believes that vitamin C is essential to the health of every cell in the body, protecting against diseases such as cancer, hardening of the arteries, and arthritis. Every animal except man can manufacture his own vitamin C and most animals produce between five and twenty grams a day; Pauling believes man needs approximately the same amount per kilogram of body weight that animals produce. His opponents, for the most part representing conventional medicine, argue that Pauling's theory needs extensive testing to make sure that vitamin C supplements do, indeed, positively affect health and that megadoses are not toxic to some people.

The vitamin C controversy underscores how much we still have to discover about vitamins and their roles in cell function. The controversy also reveals the hostility that often erupts between traditional medical practitioners and pioneers like Pauling who challenge established ideas by introducing startling and unusual ways of looking at diseases and their treatments. This friction is not without its benefits, however, for it has always been the conflict between the old and the new that encourages controversy and stimulates research, thereby pushing science along to new discoveries.

* *Megavitamin therapy* is a rather loose term used to describe vitamins taken in large doses—doses as large as thousands of milligrams, many times the RDA.

VITAMIN C

Roles. Scientists like Pauling and Szent-Gyorgi, who was the first to prepare pure L-ascorbic acid (vitamin C) in 1928 and later won a Nobel Prize for his work, believe that vitamin C participates, or is required, in all cellular metabolism and therefore can affect virtually every activity in the body. Pauling suggests that vitamin C stimulates the body's natural protective mechanisms and improves the functioning of the body in general, helping to protect against such diseases as heart disease and cancer. Szent-Gyorgi theorizes that vitamin C is much more than a vitamin, being one of the most fundamental substances in the body, taking part in the most basic processes essential for life and good health.

Vitamin C appears to be the superman of the vitamins, capable of some stunning heroics. Vitamin C:

- is essential for the efficient working of the immune system, the patrol force of the body that blocks and destroys harmful substances and keeps foreign cells in check, preventing the development of malignant growth.
- acts in several other ways as an anticancer substance, in addition to its role in the immune system. It helps surround and wall off tumors, keeping them from spreading; controls infection; detoxifies harmful substances; and increases production of interferon, a protein capable of stopping viruses from multiplying.
- helps the body fight against infectious diseases, both viral and bacterial (vitamin C's role in fighting the common cold has received the widest acclaim). It appears that the body can successfully defend itself against foreign attackers only when enough vitamin C is present to enable the natural protective mechanisms to operate properly.
- works to detoxify or render harmless foreign substances such as cancers, drugs, germs, and viruses. It helps convert toxic substances into nontoxic substances and then eliminate them in the urine.

• is required for the manufacture of collagen, the "cement" found in connective tissue that literally holds our body cells together. Without vitamin C, broken bones cannot knit themselves together, surgical incisions cannot heal, and cuts and scratches cannot be repaired. Lack of collagen can also cause the tissues to appear loose and watery, allowing germs and viruses to travel more easily throughout the body. People with infections have a reduced amount of vitamin C in their tissues, leading many researchers to believe that vitamin C, in adequate amounts, helps combat infections.

• acts, like vitamin E, as an anti-oxidant, preventing fatty acids from breaking down into substances irritating and potentially dangerous to the heart and blood vessels; vitamin C also helps control cholesterol in the body. In these ways, the vitamin helps protect against cardiovascular disease.

Deficiencies. Like all vitamin deficiencies, even a slight deficiency of vitamin C can cause problems that, because of their varied and hidden nature, may not be recognized for what they are. Mild vitamin C deficiencies may include easy bruising, listlessness, fleeting joint pains, and poor endurance. A prolonged deficiency can cause the body's tiniest blood vessels to rupture, producing little red spots under the skin.

Severe deficiency leads to scurvy, which causes bleeding and swollen gums, loose teeth, and hemorrhaging, and may result in anemia, extreme weakness, soreness of the arms and legs, an abnormally rapid heartbeat, and labored or difficult breathing and even death.

Recommended Amounts. The RDA is set at 60 milligrams for both men and women, a dose approximately midpoint between the level needed to prevent symptoms of mild deficiency and replace what the body uses in one day (10 milligrams), and the point at which saturation appears to occur (100 to 200 milligrams). *Saturation* means that any vitamin C above 200 milligrams will simply be excreted and the amount of vitamin C in the blood will not go any higher. But saturation is not a constant factor, and saturation levels will vary from person to person. Bodily demands for vitamin C increase with illness, infection, stress, injury, cigarette smoking, air pollution, and physical exercise. Furthermore, to make use of the vitamin's ability to protect against disease, larger doses may be necessary. This is Szent-Gyorgi's theory and the reason why Pauling himself takes 10 grams (10,000 milligrams) every day. Besides, vitamin C is one of the least toxic substances known to man, even in extraordinarily large doses. A common side effect from taking these megadoses (or thousands of milligrams) is diarrhea, which can be treated by reducing intake until the diarrhea disappears. Some scientists' reports linking megadoses of vitamin C to kidney stones and diabetes have been discounted by other medical researchers, although in very rare cases someone may have an intolerance to large doses—or may be allergic to the fillers in the vitamin pill.

Alcoholics can take 500 to 1,000 milligrams of vitamin C a day and, under a doctor's care, may increase that amount to between 2 and 10 grams a day. Alcoholics who smoke should be absolutely sure to get enough vitamin C, as one cigarette alone destroys about 25 milligrams—a pack, then, will use up about 500.

Anyone who regularly takes high doses of vitamin C should know about the so-called "rebound effect." Taking lots of vitamin C cranks up the activities of certain enzymes, which are then used to help put the vitamin to work in the body. If the intake of vitamin C is dramatically reduced or stopped altogether, the overactive enzymes keep right on working and use up all the vitamin C in the body. This enzyme hyperactivity lasts only a few days, but during that time a person may be more susceptible to infection. So, if you decide to stop taking vitamin C and, especially, if you are taking megadoses, gradually lower the amount over a few days' time.

Sources. The best sources of vitamin C are fresh fruit, particularly citrus fruits, and fresh vegetables such as Brussels sprouts, broccoli, cauliflower, raw cabbage, and green and red peppers. Fruits have the reputation of being full of vitamin C, but certain vegetables are even better: an orange has about 65 milligrams of vitamin C, for example, while one stalk of broccoli contains 160! Remember, though, that heat destroys vitamin C, so eat your vegetables raw whenever possible.

THE B VITAMINS

The B vitamins, although differing chemically and performing different functions in the body, are grouped together because they have similar biochemical structures and are always found together in nature.

A deficiency in only one of these vitamins is rare because if a person is deficient in one, it's almost certain that he will be deficient in the others. A person deficient in thiamine, for example, is almost certainly deficient in folic acid, pantothenic acid, niacin, and all the other B vitamins.

The B-complex vitamins are necessary for the cell to convert carbohydrates into glucose, the fuel which the body burns for energy; they are essential for the breakdown and use of fats and proteins; and they maintain the health of the nervous system and other vital organs such as the liver and the heart. These vitamins can be thought of as the oil that keeps the cogs in the inner parts of the cell running smoothly.

An interesting story about the B vitamins involves biochemist Casimir Funk, the man who coined the word *vitamin.* Funk was studying pigeons and, being poor and struggling, fed them the hulls of rice scraped up off the laboratory floors.

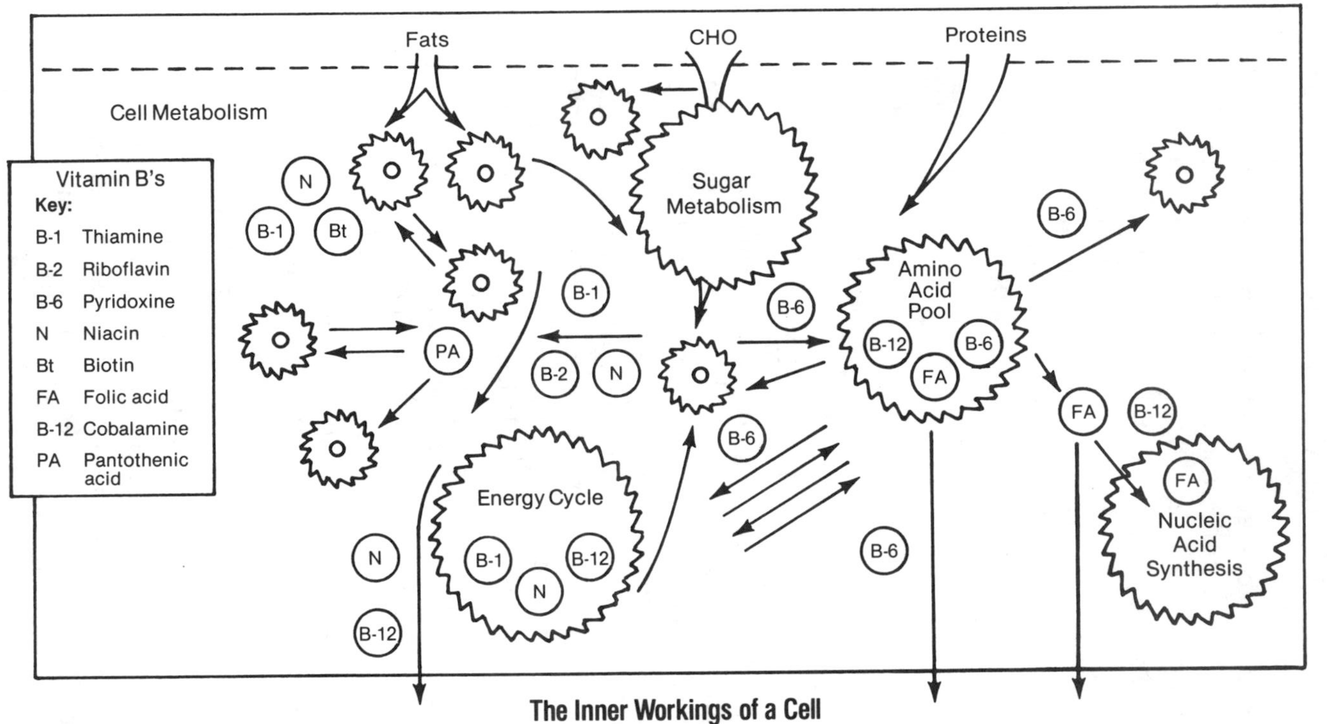

The Inner Workings of a Cell

The B vitamins are needed in every essential reaction in the body—they provide the "lubrication" which keeps the wheels and cogs of cell machinery going and working smoothly. If any one of the B vitamins is absent or in low supply, the body machinery will begin to grind and slow down, working with more effort and less efficiency and accuracy; if the deficiency goes on for too long, the body machinery will eventually burn itself out.

The pigeons didn't mind the indignity, and in fact they were fat, healthy, and reasonably content. Later, Funk had a little extra money, and decided to treat his birds to the more esthetic and expensive polished rice. But after a while the pigeons began to go lame. Funk was convinced that their affliction was somehow related to their diet, and he began investigating the differences between polished and unpolished rice. In the hulls of the rice he discovered a chemical compound known as an *amine,* which he called the *vital amine;* this term then came to be known as *vitamin* and was later identified as the B-complex vitamins, including B-1, B-2, B-3, B-6, and so on.

Funk's pigeons, as he eventually discovered, got sick on a diet of refined rice because, during processing, the rice has most of its B vitamins removed. Other processed grains (those in white bread and white spaghetti, for example) also have most of their B vitamins removed. Even though processed grains are now fortified with selected B vitamins (B-3, for example, to prevent pellagra), not all the vitamins lost in processing are added back. As a result, a consistent diet of highly processed foods may present some health risks and hazards. Furthermore, sugar and alcohol use up the B vitamins much faster than the typical American diet replaces them. And since the B vitamins are water soluble, they can't be stored and must be replaced continually. All these facts make marginal deficiencies in the B vitamins a potential problem for many Americans—and, obviously, not just American pigeons.

Alcoholics are faced with serious B vitamin deficiency problems because:

- they drink large amounts of alcohol, an infamous destroyer of B vitamins, usually over a long period of time;
- their diet is typically high in processed and refined foods and low in whole grains, cereals, liver, nuts, and seeds—foods that are naturally rich in B vitamins;

• their drinking causes gastrointestinal problems that interfere with absorption of the B vitamins;

• when alcohol is in the body, it receives immediate attention while the B vitamins and other essential substances are left waiting in the wings and are often washed out before the body gets a chance to use them.

The following table shows what a study of 210 alcoholics revealed about just how common (and severe) these B vitamin deficiencies are.

B-Vitamin Deficiences in Chronic Alcoholics

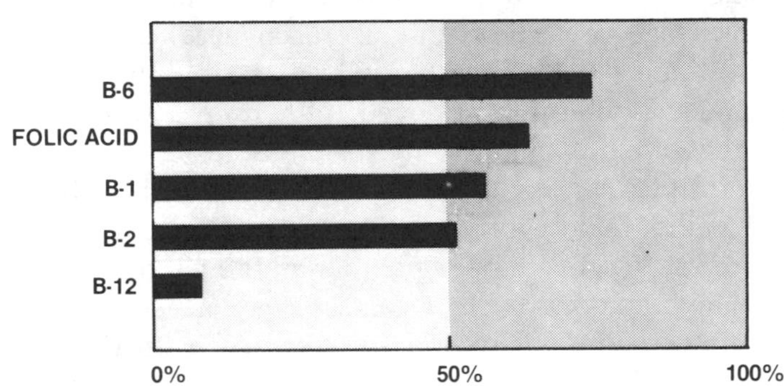

Source: Allan D. Thomson, "Alcohol and Nutrition," *Clinics in Endocrinology and Metabolism*, Vol. 7, 1978, pp. 405–428.

THIAMINE (B-1)

Roles. Thiamine is needed to break down and release energy from carbohydrates, and to help make use of protein as a back-up "fuel" supply. Thiamine is called the morale vitamin because it contributes to the health of nerve tissue and has a beneficial effect on mental attitude and outlook.

Deficiencies. Alcohol, a pure, refined carbohydrate, contributes to thiamine deficiency in four major ways: (1) alcohol supplies none of the vitamin itself*; (2) the calories in alcohol

* Refined foods, unless fortified, contain no thiamine, because the vitamin is a part of the germ and bran of wheat and husks of rice—the parts that are discarded in the refining of grains to make alcohol as well as white flour, white rice, sugar, and so on.

satisfy the appetite and crowd out other, healthier, foods; (3) thiamine is needed to help the body process and eliminate alcohol—so that, in this sense, alcohol actually "eats up" thiamine; and (4) alcohol interferes with the absorption and use of thiamine in the body.

When not enough thiamine is taken in, carbohydrates can't be properly processed, and the glucose (energy) flow is interrupted. The brain and central nervous system are particularly sensitive to a lack of thiamine; the symptoms of a deficiency will show up as depression, anxiety, irritability, and inability to concentrate. These are the same symptoms often associated with unstable blood-sugar levels, and in fact, a thiamine deficiency, combined with a diet high in sugar, can compound the brain's problems.

Symptoms of deficiency can be produced after only ten days of reduced thiamine in the diet. The symptoms, in order of appearance, include loss of appetite, lack of interest and concentration, irritability, muscle cramps, fatigue, and depression. Prolonged thiamine deficiency advances to a disease known as beriberi, in which the victim's feet and legs grow stiff and painful, with numbness and tingling. Other effects of beriberi can be swelling of the heart and heart failure. A related nutritional disorder caused by deficiencies of B-1 and other B-complex vitamins is polyneuropathy, in which the peripheral, or branching, nerves to the arms and legs are damaged. This disorder is common in late-stage alcoholics; in a survey of thirty-five alcoholic patients hospitalized with polyneuropathy, 55 percent showed B-1 deficiencies* (see page 67 for a more detailed discussion of polyneuropathy).

Recommended Amounts. Because thiamine is directly involved in the release of energy from foods, particularly carbohydrates, individual requirements for thiamine vary accord-

*"Detection and Incidence of B and C Vitamin Deficiencies in Alcohol-Related Illness," *Annals of Clinical Biochemistry,* Vol. 15, pp. 307–312.

ing to how much carbohydrate a person eats. If you eat a lot of carbohydrates, you will need more thiamine. Refined carbohydrates provide little, if any, thiamine and a diet high in refined carbohydrates will actually increase the body's need for thiamine while contributing nothing to relieve that need.

The adult RDA is 1.0 milligram for women and 1.4 milligrams for men, levels that even those on low-carbohydrate diets should not fall below. Recovering alcoholics should supplement their diets with additional B-1—at least 2 to 5 milligrams a day—because of their typically prolonged deficiency and because thiamine is so crucial in glucose metabolism. Sicker alcoholics may require up to 100 milligrams a day in the first days of recovery and then 10 to 50 a day for the next several weeks of treatment.

Sources. The richest source of B-1 is brewer's yeast. Other excellent food sources are wheat germ, barley germ, whole-wheat grain, oatmeal, whole brown rice (or just the hulls), nuts, nut butters, soybeans, meat (especially pork, kidneys, and heart), and most vegetables.

RIBOFLAVIN (B-2)

Roles. Riboflavin plays a role in the metabolism of all living cells: It is essential to releasing energy, synthesizing protein, and causing other reactions that promote the body's growth and repair.

Deficiencies. Riboflavin deficiency is one of the most common deficiency diseases in the U.S. because B-2 is contained only in small amounts in only certain foods, and these are foods Americans seldom eat—liver, tongue, other organ meats, and brewer's yeast. Symptoms include cracking and open sores at the corners of the mouth, a purple-red inflamed tongue, swollen membranes in the mouth and throat, irritable, watery and bloodshot eyes, and a scaly rash on the face. Brain and nervous-system problems include personality disturbances, depression, and hysteria. Alcoholics frequently show the tongue, mouth, and membrane-lining disturbances of B-2 deficiencies* and may well also have nervous-system disorders resulting from vitamin deficiencies. These disorders are not easily distinguished from the direct effects of alcohol on the brain (see the discussion of neuropsychiatric disorders in Chapter 4, page 68).

Recommended Amounts. The adult RDA of riboflavin is 1.2 milligrams for women and 1.6 milligrams for men. Recovering alcoholics should take at least 2 to 5 milligrams daily and may safely increase their dosage to 10 to 50 milligrams a day in the initial phases of recovery. The best source of riboflavin is milk, but since riboflavin is easily destroyed by light, milk and milk products should be stored in dark places like the inside of a refrigerator and in opaque or cardboard containers that repel light. Clear glass should not be used to store milk.

Sources. For most Americans, milk is the primary source of riboflavin; cottage cheese, vegetables (beans, broccoli, mushrooms, asparagus, spinach, avocados), yogurt, and brewer's yeast are other good sources.

NIACIN (B-3) (NICOTINIC ACID, NIACINIAMIDE)

Roles. Niacin is crucial to the breakdown of food for energy and vital for the functioning of the brain and nervous system. In large enough doses it improves circulation and lowers cholesterol.

Deficiencies. Cells are completely unable to release energy if niacin is absent in the diet, resulting in tissue damage

*The studies previously mentioned regarding alcoholics hospitalized with polyneuropathy reported 23 to 50 percent of alcoholics showing deficiencies in B-2.

throughout the body, particularly in the skin, digestive tract, and nervous tissue. Mild deficiency symptoms include nervous irritability, headaches, insomnia, digestive disorders, and a swollen, sore, red tongue. In cases of severe and prolonged niacin deficiency, the result is pellagra, once a major deficiency disease in the U.S. and the cause of thousands of deaths in the first third of this century, as detailed earlier in this chapter.

Recommended Amounts. The adult requirement for niacin is set at 13 milligrams a day for women and 18 milligrams for men. Alcoholics can safely increase this to 100 to 200 milligrams, a dosage frequently found in many multivitamin supplements. Large doses of niacin—3,000 to 4,000 or more milligrams daily—have helped diminish alcohol cravings, mood swings, and insomnia as reported in studies by Russell F. Smith, M.D.* However, because of the possible side effects associated with megadoses of niacin, alcoholics should take these large doses only under medical supervision. (The three synthetic forms of niacin are niacinamide, nicotinic acid, and nicotinamide).

Sources. Lean meats, poultry, fish, and peanuts are rich in both niacin and tryptophan, a substance from which niacin can be manufactured in the body. Among other good sources are eggs, dried peas, beans, and whole-grain and enriched cereals, pastas, and breads.

PYRIDOXINE (B-6)

Roles. Vitamin B-6, like the other B vitamins, wears a number of different hats, although its primary role is in metabolism. It helps break down and use fats, carbohydrates,

* R. F. Smith, "A Five-Year Field Trial of Massive Nicotinic Acid Therapy of Alcoholics in Michigan," *Journal of Orthomolecular Psychiatry,* Vols. 3 and 4, 1974.

and proteins, and helps release glycogen for energy from the liver and muscles. Pyridoxine is also involved in converting tryptophan to niacin, the absorption of vitamin B-12, burning protein for energy, converting glycogen to glucose to provide energy for muscle tissues, producing red blood cells, and proper functioning of nervous tissue.

Deficiencies. Symptoms of pyridoxine deficiency are similar to those of niacin and riboflavin deficiencies and include a rash around the eyes, cracking and soreness around the corner of the mouth, and a red, sore tongue. Anemia, dizziness, weakness, depression, nausea, vomiting, weight loss, irritability, mental confusion, and convulsion may also result. Brain chemicals called *amines* or *neurotransmitters* are dependent upon vitamin B-6 for the proper transmission of nerve impulses; a deficiency may contribute to the alcoholic's brain disturbance, including depression and sluggish thinking or, in some cases, hyperactivity or manic behavior.

Recommended Amounts. Like thiamine, the required amount of pyridoxine varies according to what you eat. Because pyridoxine is essential for protein metabolism, a person on a high-protein diet would require additional B-6. The RDA is 2.0 milligrams for women and 2.2 for men, but because so many alcoholics are deficient in B-6 (see graph on page ____), doses may be increased up to 30 or 50 milligrams a day in initial recovery, with sicker patients needing more. Doses in the range of 100 to 200 milligrams daily have been cited as therapeutic for alcoholics with Dupytren's contractions, a condition which causes tightening and shortening of the ligaments running to the fingers, with contraction, or curling up, of one or more fingers. Recommended maintenance dosages for alcoholics are 2 to 5 milligrams.

Sources. Whole grains such as whole-wheat flour, brown rice, rice bran, and wheat germ are a rich source of pyridoxine, as are legumes (navy beans, lentils, garbanzos, lima beans, pinto beans, and black-eyed peas) and certain vegetables, particularly spinach, asparagus, broccoli, cauliflower, and beet greens.

VITAMIN B-12 (COBALAMIN)

Roles. The activity of vitamin B-12, which contains the metal cobalt, is closely associated with that of another B vitamin, folacin (or folic acid). Like folacin, B-12 is essential in the functioning of most cells, but is particularly important in the manufacture of the nucleic acids DNA and RNA, which enable cells to divide and multiply. In addition, B-12 aids in the formation of red blood cells and helps the nervous system to function properly.

Deficiencies. With too little vitamin B-12, cells cannot divide properly, a problem that first affects those tissues that multiply rapidly. The bone marrow will eventually produce large, immature red blood cells (megaloblasts), which are inefficient carriers of oxygen and may cause megaloblastic anemia.

Another area where tissues multiply rapidly is the digestive passages, and deficiency symptoms here include indigestion, abdominal pain, constipation, and diarrhea. These are only warning symptoms, however, of the eventual deterioration of nervous tissue that occurs with lack of B-12, leading to numbness and tingling in the feet, a sore back, unsteadiness, poor memory, confusion, moodiness, delusions, and eventually death. Alcoholics deficient in vitamin B-12 have shown abnormal EEG (electroencephalagram) tracings in over 60 percent of the cases studied.*

Recommended Amounts. The adult RDA is 3.0 micrograms for both men and women, a generous amount since 0.1

*Allan D. Thomson, "Alcohol and Nutrition," *Clinics in Endocrinology and Metabolism,* Keats Publishing, Inc., New Canaan, CT, 1978, Vol. 7, pp. 405–428.

microgram will prevent deficiency symptoms in a normal healthy person. Since B-12 is abundant in foods commonly consumed and a little bit goes a long way, deficiency states are not too common, except in problems of absorption. Some people, lacking the digestive substances in the stomach necessary to aid B-12 absorption, will develop pernicious anemia. Also, alcohol can hinder the body's ability to absorb B-12, and some severely malnourished alcoholics may suffer deficiencies of this vitamin; in such cases, B-12 injections are required to counteract these defects.

Sources. Most milk products, except butter, are excellent sources of B-12; two glasses of milk will provide two micrograms, or two-thirds of the recommended daily allowance. Liver, kidneys, fish, oysters, eggs, and nutritional yeast will also provide substantial amounts of B-12.

FOLACIN (FOLIC ACID)

Roles. One of the B-complex series, folacin, like cobalamin, is essential in the formation of DNA and RNA, which allow cells to divide and make new cells, and in the manufacture and breakdown of amino acids, also necessary for cell reproduction. Folacin is also necessary for proper formation of red blood cells.

Deficiencies. Folic acid deficiency is common in alcoholics. When malnourished alcoholics are hospitalized, they are frequently found to have folic acid anemia. A high percentage of drinking alcoholics (80 percent or more) will show enlarged, immature red blood cells, which cannot effectively transport oxygen; anemia may be present. Causes of these abnormalities and deficiencies are due to any one of several causes: (1) a folic acid deficient diet; (2) alcohol competing with folic acid for absorption in the intestine; (3) alcohol interfering with the bone marrow taking in folic acid; or (4) direct effects of alcohol on bone marrow and red-blood-cell formation. Symptoms are the same as those seen in B-12 deficiency, since the two vitamins work together and in similar ways.

Recommended Amounts. The adult RDA for both men and women is 400 micrograms a day (.4 milligram); alcoholics may need to supplement this with 1 to 4 milligrams a day in the first few months of recovery, but the alcoholic should be monitored by a physician for the amount and duration of folic acid supplementation, since excessive intake of folic acid can cover up a B-12 deficiency.

Sources. The richest source of folacin is dark green leaves, with romaine lettuce and spinach leaves being the richest of all. Since normal cooking temperatures destroy up to 65 percent of the folacin in vegetables, and three days' storage at room temperature can destroy 70 percent, it's best to eat your dark green leafy vegetables uncooked and as fresh as possible. Other good sources include liver, kidneys, wheat germ, and dried peas and beans.

PANTOTHENIC ACID

Roles. Panto means *everywhere,* and pantothenic acid is needed in literally every cell of the body to help with the metabolism of fat, protein, and carbohydrate. A close correlation exists between pantothenic acid and adrenal-gland functioning. Pantothenic acid can support the body during stress, and is often referred to as one of the anti-stress vitamins.

Deficiencies. Alcoholism eats away at the body's supply of pantothenic acid. Deficiency symptoms are as varied as the vitamin's activities and include fatigue, headaches, nausea, sleep disturbances, abdominal cramps, vomiting, muscle cramps, and impaired coordination.

Recommended Amounts. No RDA of pantothenic acid has been established, but the Food and Nutrition Board considers 4 to 7 milligrams a day a safe and adequate dosage. Recovering alcoholics with "adrenal exhaustion" and hypoglycemia may respond well to therapeutic doses of 100 to 300 milligrams daily. Recommended maintenance doses for alcoholics are 50 to 100 milligrams a day.

Sources. Pantothenic acid is found in most foods, and even inadequate diets will usually provide enough of this vitamin to meet the RDA. However, the best sources of pantothenic acid are yeast, liver, kidneys, milk, egg yolks, and vegetables. Freezing and milling destroy a large part of the pantothenic acid content of food, so fresh, unrefined foods are best.

And the Lesser-Known (But Still Important) B-Complex Vitamins

BIOTIN

Roles. Biotin assists in the breakdown and use of fats in the body as well as the use of protein, folic acid, and pantothenic acid. It's active throughout the body and is needed for normal growth and for the health and maintenance of skin, hair, nerves, bone marrow, and sex glands.

Deficiencies. Deficiency symptoms are rare, since biotin is widely available in common foods and only small quantities are needed. Deficiency conditions have been reported in restrictive diets that contain large amounts of raw eggs—the substance avidin, which is present in raw eggs, destroys biotin. (Avidin is destroyed by heat and, in fact, cooked egg yolks are one of the richest sources of biotin.) Deficiency symptoms include: nausea, poor appetite, depression, muscle pains, skin problems (dry skin, excema, and dermatitis, for example), sleep disturbances, and general lack of energy.

Recommended Amounts. No RDAs have been established, but safe and adequate dietary intakes are listed at 100 to 200 micrograms (0.1 to 0.2 milligrams) for both men and women. This amount is sufficient for most alcoholics.

Sources. Biotin is found in all animal and plant tissues, but the richest sources are cooked egg yolks, beef liver, dark green vegetables, whole-grain rice, and brewer's yeast.

CHOLINE

Roles. Choline is present in all living cells and is essential to making fats and cholesterol usable, preventing fats from building up in the liver, and allowing fats to be transported into the cells. Choline also keeps the nerve fibers healthy, helps in the transmission of nerve impulses, and regulates and improves liver and gallbladder function.

Deficiencies. Because choline is widely found in food and can be synthesized in the body with the help of vitamin B-12, folic acid, and the amino acid methionine, deficiencies are rare. Insufficient supplies of choline can contribute to liver, heart, and kidney disorders, and may cause high blood pressure, cirrhosis, and atherosclerosis (hardening of the arteries).

Recommended Amounts. No RDA has been established, although the average diet contains between 500 to 1,000 milligrams of choline, which should be sufficient for most recovering alcoholics. But some recovering alcoholics may benefit from supplements in the range of 500 to 1,500 milligrams a day to aid in fat decomposition in the liver. Large doses of choline taken alone may cause a deficiency of B-6, so all the B-complex vitamins should be taken together and in relative strengths.

Sources. Good sources of choline include lecithin, liver, brewer's yeast, wheat germ, and egg yolks.

INOSITOL

Roles. As a partner with choline, inositol helps "dissolve" fats. It also can contribute to weight reduction and stop hair from thinning and falling out (nutritionist Adelle Davis recommends that balding men take inositol in substantial amounts); and it's necessary for cell growth and health in the intestines, eye membranes, and bone marrow.

Deficiencies. An inositol deficiency may cause constipation, eczema, and eye abnormalities, and may contribute to hair loss and high cholesterol levels in the blood. Because of inositol's role in controlling fats, a deficiency can contribute to artery and heart disease.

Recommended Amounts. No RDA has been established. Some alcoholics might benefit from supplements in the range of 500 to 1,500 milligrams daily.

Sources. Inositol is present in most plant and animal food sources, especially fruits and cereals; processing, however, destroys it. Liver and brewer's yeast, citrus fruits, and unprocessed whole grains are rich sources of this vitamin.

PANGAMIC ACID

Roles. Although pangamic acid is widely used (and praised for its effects) in Russia and Europe, it's not familiar to most Americans. In fact, it has been on and off the market in this country, and the Food and Drug Administration has, in the past, considered it ineffective. Nevertheless, pangamic acid has some important functions in the body. It helps regulate fat and sugar metabolism, and stimulates glucose oxidation, and it promotes protein metabolism (especially in the muscles of the heart), supplies oxygen to the heart, helps stimulate the glandular and nervous systems, and aids in treating high cholesterol levels in the blood, poor circulation, and premature aging.

Deficiencies. Little is known about deficiency symptoms, but because of pangamic acid's known role in oxidation and metabolism in the heart and glandular and nervous systems, a deficiency may cause or contribute to various disorders in these systems.

Recommended Amounts. No RDA has been established although doses up to 10 milligrams have proved completely nontoxic and pangamic acid is probably safe even if taken in very large amounts. Alcoholics can safely include this vitamin in their daily supplement and may well benefit from its support to bodily systems commonly damaged by alcoholism.

Sources. Natural sources of pangamic acid include whole grains, whole brown rice, brewer's yeast, and pumpkin and sesame seeds.

PABA (PARA-AMINO-BENZOIC ACID)

PABA is unique in that it is not really a vitamin by itself, but is a basic constituent of folic acid. It's a "vitamin within a vitamin." Furthermore, by stimulating intestinal bacteria, PABA helps produce folic acid, and folic acid aids in the manufacture of pantothenic acid—another example of the interdependence of the B vitamins.

Along with folic acid, PABA aids in the breakdown and use of proteins in the body and in the formation of blood cells. When added to a salve and applied to the skin, PABA protects against sunburn; it may even prevent skin cancer. PABA has also been used successfully for skin disturbances like eczema and loss of pigmentation in the skin. More controversial is PABA's role in restoring natural hair color and lustre to prematurely gray hair.

PABA is manufactured by "friendly" bacteria in the intestines. Best food sources are liver, brewer's yeast, yogurt, milk, eggs, whole-grain rice and cereals, whole wheat, wheat germ, and molasses.

No RDA has been established.

VITAMIN B-17 (NITRILOSIDES, OR LAETRILE)

The health-contributing roles of this vitamin, which is also called laetrile, are hotly debated. Many researchers believe laetrile is harmless in large amounts, although others caution of potential cyanide poisoning due to its natural cyanide content. The federal government takes a middle road and claims there's no proof vitamin B-17 is beneficial to health. Research on vitamin B-17 is pitifully scanty, and we know very little either about its roles in the body, or its deficiency symptoms. No RDA has been established.

Laetrile is found in high concentrations in the seeds or kernels of almost every fruit, including apricots, apples, plums, peaches, cherries, and nectarines; citrus fruits contain only trace amounts.

Vitamin Summary

Major roles of the vitamin	Deficiency symptoms	Food sources	RDA	Safe maintenance doses for alcoholics
		The fat-soluble vitamins		
		VITAMIN A		
Essential for proper growth and health of skin, mouth, respiratory passages, digestive and urinary tracts. Needed for building strong bones and teeth and for the light-sensitive pigments in the eye, which allow night vision.	Night blindness; dry, pimply skin; infection of lining cells in the respiratory tract; increased susceptibility to pneumonia and tuberculosis; eye infections; stunted growth.	Vitamin A is "preformed" in animal foods: liver, eggs, whole milk, cream. In plants, the substances called carotenes are converted to active vitamin A in the body. Carotene is found in dark, green, leafy vegetables: broccoli, spinach, kale; and in carrots.	3,000 IU	5,000–10,000 IU (under medical supervision if patient has chronic liver disease)
		VITAMIN D		
Necessary for fat absorption and use of calcium and phosphorus; essential for formation and growth of bones and teeth. Contributes to proper functioning of nerves, heart, and blood-clotting mechanisms.	Bones grow soft. Rickets is a Vitamin D deficiency disease seen in children: bowed legs, nodules on ribs, malformed teeth. In adults, softening of bones can lead to shortened bones and fractures.	Fortified milk, egg yolks, liver, tuna, salmon, cod liver oil.	200 IU	400 IU

VITAMIN E

Acts as an anti-oxidant, protecting fatty acids from going "rancid" in the body; a natural anticoagulant; supplies oxygen to the muscles, promoting strength and endurance. Heals scar tissue.	No clear-cut vitamin deficiency disease has been defined.	Polyunsaturated fats (safflower, sunflower, wheat-germ oils). Almonds, walnuts, sunflower seeds; asparagus, beet greens, broccoli, leeks, spinach, sweet potatoes; apples, blackberries, pears.	12–16 IU	100 IU

VITAMIN K

Essential for normal blood clotting.	Symptoms are seen in alcoholics with severely damaged livers. Symptoms include bleeding and hemorrhage.	Green leafy vegetables (especially spinach and cabbage), egg yolks, milk, safflower oil. Yogurt, kefir, and acidophilus milk promote manufacture of vitamin K in the intestine.	No RDA, but 300–500 mcg considered safe and adequate.	Supplements not usually required

The water-soluble vitamins

VITAMIN C

Essential for efficient working of the immune system. Fights infections, detoxifies harmful substances, is necessary for the manufacture of collagen, prevents fatty acid oxidation.	Early symptoms include bruising, listlessness, joint pains, poor endurance. Severe deficiency leads to scurvy: bleeding and swollen gums, loose teeth, hemorrhage, extreme weakness, sore arms and legs, abnormal heart beat, labored breathing.	Fresh fruit, particularly citrus fruits, and fresh vegetables (broccoli, cauliflower, cabbage, peppers).	60 mg	500 mg–1 gm

Major roles of the vitamin	Deficiency symptoms	Food sources	RDA	Safe maintenance doses for alcoholics
VITAMIN B-1 (thiamine)				
Needed to break down and release energy from carbohydrates; contributes to healthy nervous tissue.	Loss of appetite, muscle cramps, fatigue, anxiety, inability to concentrate, depression. Beriberi, the vitamin-deficiency disease of B-1, causes mental confusion, stiff and painful legs, "flabby" heart, and heart failure.	Milk and milk products, organ meats, brewer's yeast, dark green vegetables, mushrooms, yogurt.	1–1.4 mg	2–5 mg
VITAMIN B-2 (riboflavin)				
Essential for releasing energy from foods; aids in protein synthesis.	Skin disorders, particularly around mouth. Irritated, watery and bloodshot eyes. Brain and nervous-system problems, including personality disturbances, depression, and hysteria.	Lean meats, poultry, fish, peanuts, eggs, whole grains, dried peas and beans.	1.2–1.6 mg	2–5 mg
VITAMIN B-3 (niacin)				
Crucial to breakdown of food for energy; vital for brain and nervous-system functioning. Improves circulation and lowers blood cholesterol.	Mild: nervous irritability, headaches, insomnia, digestive disorders, swollen, sore tongue. Pellagra is the severe deficiency disease: skin disorders, diarrhea, irritability, insomnia, mental confusion.	Lean meats, poultry, fish, peanuts, eggs, whole grains, dried peas and beans.	13–18 mg	100–200 mg

		VITAMIN B-6 (pyridoxine)		
Helps the body break down and use fats, carbohydrates, and proteins; helps release glycogen for energy. Needed for formation of red blood cells and proper functioning of nervous tissue.	Skin disorders, cracks around the mouth, sore red tongue. Anemia, dizziness, weakness, depression, nausea, vomiting, weight loss, irritability, mental confusion, and convulsions may also result.	Whole grains, legumes, spinach, asparagus, broccoli, cauliflower, beet greens.	2–2.2 mg	2–5 mg
		VITAMIN B-12 (cobalamin)		
Works closely with folacin to to manufacture DNA and RNA; necessary for proper formation of red blood cells. Helps the nervous system to function properly.	Anemia; digestive problems including indigestion, abdominal pain, constipation, diarrhea. More severe deficiencies lead to nervous-system deterioration: unsteadiness, numbness and tingling in feet, sore back, mental confusion.	Milk products, liver, kidney, fish, oysters, eggs, and nutritional yeast.	3 mcg	Supplements not usually required
		FOLACIN (folic acid)		
Essential in formation of DNA and RNA and for proper formation of red blood cells.	Common in alcoholics. Symptoms same as for B-12 (above).	Dark green leafy vegetables; liver, kidneys, wheat germ, dried peas and beans.	400 mcg	400 mcg

Major roles of the vitamin	Deficiency symptoms	Food sources	RDA	Safe maintenance doses for alcoholics
		PANTOTHENIC ACID		
Helps in metabolism of carbohydrates, proteins, and fats; important for proper functioning of adrenal glands.	Common in alcoholics. Fatigue, headaches, nausea, vomiting, sleep disturbances, abdominal cramps, muscle cramps, impaired coordination.	Yeast, liver, kidneys, milk, egg yolks, vegetables.	4–7 mg*	20–50 mg
		BIOTIN		
Assists in the use of fats, carbohydrates, proteins, folic acid and pantothenic acid. Necessary for the health and maintenance of skin, hair, nerves, bone marrow, and sex glands.	Deficiency symptoms are rare, but can be caused by eating large amounts of raw eggs, which destroy biotin. Symptoms include: nausea, poor appetite, depression, muscle pains, skin problems, sleep disturbance, lack of energy.	Egg yolks (cooked), liver, whole-grain rice, brewer's yeast, dark green vegetables. Found in all animal and plant plant tissues.	100–200 mcg*	100–200 mcg
		CHOLINE		
A basic constituent of lecithin. Essential for the use of fats and cholesterol in the body. Helps keep nerve fibers healthy, assists in transmission of nerve impulses, and regulates liver and gallbladder function.	Deficiencies are rare. Insufficient supplies may contribute to liver, heart, and kidney disorders.	Lecithin, liver, brewer's yeast, wheat germ, egg yolks.	None established	100–200 mg

*No RDA has been established, but this is considered a safe and adequate dosage.

INOSITOL				
With choline, helps dissolve fats. Necessary for cell growth and health in the intestines, eye membranes, and bone marrow.	May cause constipation, eczema, eye abnormalities, hair loss, high blood cholesterol levels.	Whole grains, lecithin, citrus fruits, brewer's yeast, liver.	None established	100–200 mg
PANGAMIC ACID				
Helps regulate fat and sugar metabolism, stimulates glucose oxidation, promotes protein metabolism, supplies oxygen to heart, stimulates glandular and nervous systems.	A deficiency may contribute to various disorders in the heart, glandular and nervous systems.	Whole grains, brewer's yeast, pumpkin and sesame seeds.	None established	Unknown
PABA (para-amino-benzoic acid)				
Aids in breakdown and use of proteins in body and in formation of blood cells. Can protect against sunburn and skin disturbances; may prevent skin cancer.	Not known	Liver, brewer's yeast, yogurt, milk, eggs, whole-grain rice and cereals, whole wheat, wheat germ, molasses.	None established	Amounts less than 30 mg are considered safe. High doses over a period of time may be toxic to liver, heart, and kidneys.
VITAMIN B-17				
Unknown at this time.	Not known	Seeds of most fruits (but citrus fruits contain only small amounts.)	None established	Unknown

9
The Mighty Minerals

THE minerals, which make up only 4 percent of the body's weight, have hefty responsibilities. Their three major roles in the body include:

• Giving strength and substance to cells. While all tissues and internal fluids contain minerals, the bones, teeth, muscles, blood, and nerve cells are particularly dependent upon minerals for vitality and health.

• Working with vitamins and enzymes to start chemical reactions. Many chemical reactions in the body are activated when minerals work in partnership with vitamins and enzymes; zinc, for example, triggers more than seventy different enzyme reactions, including the chemical reactions involving the breakdown of alcohol. Minerals are also important in the manufacturing of hormones and antibodies.

• Circulating in internal fluids to help maintain the body's proper water balance and prevent it from becoming too acid or alkaline.

The twenty or more minerals that form the mineral composition of the body are divided into two categories: the *macrominerals*—sodium, potassium, chloride, calcium, phosphorus, magnesium, and sulfur—which are required by the body in relatively large quantities (100 milligrams or more every day); and a dozen or so *trace minerals*, which are required in amounts ranging down from 100 milligrams to a few micrograms. (A microgram is a thousandth of a milligram, about the weight of a grain of sand.)

*The Macrominerals**

SODIUM, POTASSIUM, AND CHLORIDE

Roles. These minerals function as traffic cops lining the cell membranes. Sodium and chloride are stationed outside the cell while potassium stands guard inside. Blood, with its crucial passengers—nitrogen, oxygen, water, and nutrients—is allowed to pass into the cell, where it delivers its goods, picks up the cell's waste products, and then exits. Other substances, including toxins and waste products, are barred from entering the cell.

Sodium, along with potassium, also helps regulate the body's water balance. The flow of sodium, potassium, and water is monitored by the kidneys. Water is retained when sodium levels are high and excreted when the sodium level is too low, an action that keeps the right concentration of salt (or sodium) in the body's internal fluids. Continually high sodium levels can lead to serious problems: As the kidneys add water to the blood stream to dilute sodium to its proper concentration, the volume of fluid in the blood vessels increases and the excess fluid gets into body tissues, producing swelling in the feet, legs, hands, and other areas. This build-up of fluid and pressure in the blood vessels may contribute, eventually, to high blood pressure.

Sodium is found in virtually all foods, but it is especially concentrated in salt, or sodium chloride. Innocent-looking

*Sulfur is not discussed in this section because it's so plentiful in foods that deficiencies are not a problem.

salt, which is found on every table and in every cupboard, can be a very dangerous enemy indeed, aggravating high blood pressure and leading to heart attacks and strokes. But a salt shaker is only the most visible source of sodium. Snack foods—pretzels, potato chips, salted peanuts, corn chips—are heavily laced with salt, as are processed breads, butter, cheeses, and margarine, canned foods, and convenience foods like the French fries, fried onion rings, and hamburgers sold at thousands of fast-food stands.

Deficiencies. Of these three minerals, potassium deficiencies are most common in alcoholics and cause the most concern. A deficiency in potassium can be caused by excessive sodium intake, which leads to increased urinary output of potassium. Prolonged vomiting and/or diarrhea will also deplete the body's supply of potassium. And alcoholics, who tend to retain fluid and suffer from high blood pressure, are often treated with diuretics, pills that wash away potassium as well as sodium.

A severe potassium deficiency can be life-threatening by causing an irregular heart rate. Lesser problems are general weakness and fatigue. Most multivitamin and mineral supplements contain potassium; doses higher than in those supplements should be taken only under a physician's advice and supervision, since too much potassium in the body can also be dangerous, causing the heart to beat unevenly or even to stop.

CALCIUM AND PHOSPHORUS

Roles. Calcium and phosphorus help make the bones and teeth hard and strong. Ninety-nine percent of the body's calcium is found in the bones and teeth, but calcium also "moonlights" in other part of the body, assisting in the flow of nerve impulses, the coagulation of blood, the relaxation and contraction of the heart muscle, and the transfer of fluids through cell walls. Phosphorus is found in every cell of the body; it's a particularly important ingredient in all energy-yielding reactions, and it combines with calcium to form and strengthen bones.

Deficiencies. Alcoholics are prone to become calcium-deficient because:

• Their diets are often low in calcium-rich foods like milk and milk products;

• Their digestive systems are damaged by excessive drinking and their organs are unable to absorb calcium efficiently.

• Alcohol greatly increases the excretion of calcium. Just twenty minutes after he drinks one ounce of alcohol, the alcoholic's urinary output of calcium is increased by 100 percent. (Magnesium loss is increased by 167 percent!)

X-ray studies of alcoholics' bones show softer, less dense bone structures, indicating premature loss of minerals in the bones. Alcoholics in their mid-40s have bone densities comparable to those of nonalcoholics in their 60s. Alcoholics tend to break bones easily because of this lessening of density in their bones and also because heavy drinking, leading as it does to poor muscle control, slow reflexes, and a puzzled brain, increases the susceptibility to bone-breaking accidents.

Calcium deposits also plague alcoholics. To be properly absorbed and used, calcium depends on the right balance of other minerals and vitamins, particularly phosphorus and vitamins A, C, and D. With these nutrients in short supply due to chronic drinking, the body machinery falters and calcium may even be deposited in places where it doesn't belong—the joints, arteries, and kidneys.

Other symptoms of calcium deficiency include numbness or tingling in the arms and legs, insomnia, headaches, unhealthy teeth and gums, brittle nails, heart palpitations, and "neuro-muscular" irritability, as in muscle and menstrual cramps.

Recommended Amounts. Because of alcohol's disruptive effect on the body's calcium balance, alcoholics may take ½ to 1 gram of calcium every day for the first month of recovery. Daily dosages of 1 gram or more taken for longer than one month, however, should be continued for longer periods of time only under medical supervision; and alcoholics with a tendency to develop kidney stones should be under a doctor's care. Finally, calcium supplements should be taken with a magnesium supplement of *half* the calcium dosage to keep these two minerals in proper balance. Magnesium is closely related to calcium in the way it's used in the bones; by weight, it's half as abundant in the body as calcium, and the recommended daily allowance is half that of calcium.

MAGNESIUM

Roles. Magnesium helps enzymes do their work, particularly those enzymes involved in the transfer of energy. It is also required for protein manufacture, muscle contraction, and conducting nerve impulses smoothly. And it is needed for the absorption and use of the B vitamins as well as vitamins C and E.

Deficiencies. Alcoholics are often deficient in magnesium since alcohol promotes excessive excretion and loss from the body, and because the alcohol-battered digestive system is often unable to efficiently absorb minerals. Deficiency symptoms include twitching muscles, tremors, hormone imbalances, hyperexcitability, and mental confusion. A magnesium deficiency is believed to contribute to more severe and life-threatening withdrawals, causing seizures and delirium tremens (the D.T.'s). Studies have shown a correlation, for example, between the occurrence of delirium tremens and low magnesium levels in the fluid surrounding the brain and spinal cord.

Recommended Amounts. During the first month of recovery, magnesium should be given in doses of 250 to 500 milligrams (approximately half the calcium dosage). Larger doses over longer periods of time should be under a doctor's supervision. Multiple-vitamin and mineral supplements usually contain lower dosages that are appropriate for maintenance therapy.

The Trace Minerals

Trace minerals, also known as trace elements, are so named because they are needed in tiny amounts, often measured in parts per million.* But they are needed; at least some of them are. To understand this ambiguous statement, you have to be aware that trace minerals are both good and bad, and can generally be divided into four categories:

1. Those trace minerals required in well-defined amounts for normal human growth and development. These include iron, zinc, and iodine.

2. Other trace elements known to be essential for human development, but whose required amounts have not been clearly established. These include chromium, manganese, copper, selenium, cobalt and molybdenum.

3. Certain trace minerals that have been identified in plant and animal tissues, are *suspected* to have an influence on growth and development, but whose value to human nutrition is uncertain at this time. These include fluorine, silicon, vanadium, nickel, tin, and possibly arsenic and cadmium.**

*As biochemist Jeffrey Bland notes, a part per million would be something like a jigger of vermouth per tank car of vodka—a very dry martini, indeed!

**Arsenic and cadmium, while considered toxic for humans, have been found, when used in very small amounts, to stimulate growth and development in *animals.*

4. All the above elements—which could be harmful and toxic if consumed in large amounts. However, another category of trace minerals includes the *toxic metals*, which have no currently established value to human nutrition. Our present-day environment contains several of these minerals, the most common of which are lead, mercury, arsenic, and cadmium.

Imbalances of Trace Minerals Commonly Found in Chronic Alcoholics

Mineral	Significance to Alcoholic
Manganese and chromium	Deficiency can disturb blood-sugar control.
Zinc	Zinc is a necessary partner for 25 to 30 different enzymes involved in digestion and metabolism. Also partners with the enzyme alcohol dehydrogenase, which breaks down alcohol. Low blood levels of zinc are found in alcoholics with cirrhosis. Decreasing levels of zinc are associated with loss of taste and appetite.
Copper	Alcoholics, particularly those with addictions to other central-nervous system drugs in addition to alcohol, have high levels of copper, which are associated with brain and nervous-system irritability.
Iron	Deficiency results in anemia, usually associated with blood loss.
Calcium and magnesium	Deficiency results in neuro-muscular irritability (as in cramps); can be a contributor to withdrawal seizures, D.T.'s, weak bones, and susceptibility to broken bones.

These mineral imbalances are determined by hair-mineral analysis; blood tests will also often show deficiencies in iron, calcium, magnesium, potassium, sodium, and chloride.

Of the fourteen trace minerals known or suspected to be essential to life, four receive the most attention:

- Iron, particularly valuable for iron-deficiency anemias;
- Iodine, which contributes to thyroid function;
- Cobalt, for its role in Vitamin B-12 activity;
- Zinc, for its role in insulin metabolism.

The other ten essential trace minerals have basically been ignored; but in the last decade evidence has rapidly accumulated about their value and nature. The role of chromium in fat and sugar metabolism, and the value of selenium as an anti-cancer substance, are just two examples of exciting discoveries regarding these often neglected substances.

It's been easy to overlook the trace minerals because they're present in such tiny, infinitesimal amounts. Looking for them in the body is somewhat like searching for a needle in a haystack. Only specialized laboratory techniques can detect such small amounts, and even then only in tissues where the elements are most concentrated. Trace elements in the blood are often too sparse for reliable readings.

Even if they could be measured in blood samples, these levels of trace minerals circulating in the blood are not very helpful in determining what concentrations are in the tissues and cells where the minerals are most active. For example, the blood level of calcium, the most plentiful mineral in the body, does not tell much about calcium saturation in bones, where 99 percent of the body's calcium resides. Tissue analysis has the potential of providing much more information because tissues are where minerals are more concentrated and where they are at work. Hair, which is an easily available body tissue, can be painlessly sampled for mineral analysis at specialized laboratories. This innovative analytic technique, though still in its developing stages, offers potential benefits in helping evaluate the mineral status of the body. Examination of hundreds of alcoholics, through the use of hair–mineral analysis, tends to confirm suspected imbalances in calcium, magnesium, and zinc. Hair tests of alcoholics often show excesses of copper, particularly in alcoholics with long and heavy drinking careers, and also show low levels of chromium, manganese, and iron.

Recommended Amounts. Many multiple-vitamin and mineral supplements now contain an array of minerals, including some of the trace elements. Self-treatment with higher doses of minerals than the supplements provide is *not* recommended, because the mineral status of the body can be thrown out of balance by prolonged excessive amounts of any given mineral. The interplay between the various minerals in the body is in very delicate balance. Too much chromium, for example, will decrease the body's store of manganese; calcium and magnesium have their proper interdependent balance, as do copper and zinc, and manganese, chromium, and iron. Once again, the alcoholic should consult a knowledgeable physician who can help in the fine tuning of the body with these specific nutrients.

The Toxic Metals

The three most common toxic metals in our present-day environment are lead, mercury, and cadmium.* Even minute, microscopic amounts of these metals can be harmful or fatal. Lead poisoning used to be a real problem, with lead-based paints, toys, pencils, and toothpaste tubes providing children with an easily accessible, edible—and deadly—source of lead. Products containing lead have now been banned, and unleaded gasoline is now required for new cars, since lead fumes contribute mightily to the contamination of our air.

*Chances are good that within the next year or so several more toxic metals will be added to the list; and the following year will add even more. Such is the nature of our increasingly technical and synthetic environment.

Mercury poisoning is another example of the lethal nature of the toxic metals. Certainly the most tragic story involving mercury is that of the inhabitants of the small Japanese fishing village of Minamata. The first sign of trouble came when the villagers watched in horror as their cats died horrible deaths, writhing in excruciating pain. It wasn't long before the villagers learned why their animals were dying, but for many of them the knowledge came too late. The cats had eaten fish that had washed up on the beaches of Minamata Bay; the fish were poisoned with mercury wastes that were being dumped into the bay from a chemical factory. Those unlucky villagers who had unknowingly eaten the fish caught by themselves, their families, or their neighbors suffered the same horrible fate as their cats. Many died; many were paralyzed; many more were brain-damaged.

Death, paralysis, and mental retardation cannot be ignored, and strict environmental laws have been enacted in many countries to protect us from large amounts of the toxic metals. But concern has been growing about small amounts of toxic metals, amounts that affect us in less obvious ways. For example, many of us may suffer from low-level toxic-metal poisoning. The symptoms are often subtle and difficult to recognize, and can be confused with any number of other illnesses since these metals are stored in every organ in the body. It would require the skills of a particularly alert and imaginative physician to diagnose less-than-lethal lead or mercury poisoning as the cause of a kidney malfunction, an irregular heartbeat, a nervous malfunction, or a child's learning disability—and yet these disorders are now being associated with "subtoxic" levels of lead.

Lead and mercury levels in our environment have increased in only the past few years, and these toxic metals appear in our water and soil as well as in the plants we eat. Mercury is contained in industrial pesticides, fungicides, and vapors from smokestacks.

People who live near chemical factories or industrial areas are obviously at risk, but even a rural environment does not promise safety. Take the case of Times Beach, Missouri, a town of 2,400 people. In the 70s, Times Beach had a problem with dust; dioxin, a chemical by-product of herbicide production, was mixed with waste oil and sprayed on the streets to keep the dust down. In 1983, the federal government found itself buying out the town of Times Beach for $33.1 million and moving its residents to protect them from lingering chemical contamination, which causes kidney, spleen, and liver ailments in laboratory animals.

Of course, not everyone reacts to these deadly chemicals in the same way, a fact that often complicates diagnosis. One person who works around mercury might become diseased, while another remains healthy. Some people are so sensitive to mercury that they can't tolerate the mercury compound used for ordinary dental work. Another toxic metal, cadmium, may be even more deadly than lead or mercury, because it's found almost everywhere: in our water and soil, and thus in our foods, and in the air, due to petroleum, coal dust, smoke, and certain gasolines. Cadmium also resides in tin and aluminum cans and in corroded galvanized pipes. Cadmium is one of the ingredients in cigarettes. Sugar, instant coffee, and instant tea contain cadmium, as do many other foods. Whole-grain foods, however, can protect again cadmium poisoning because they contain zinc, a cadmium "antagonist" that displaces the toxic metal so that it can be excreted. Other antagonists include pectin (as in apples) and vitamins C and E.

Recommended Action. To avoid these toxic metals, we can all begin by cleaning up our own environment. Whenever possible, walk or ride a bicycle to avoid adding to the pollution caused by automobiles. Don't start smoking cigarettes, and if you already smoke, get help to quit or cut down drastically. Limit your coffee drinking, but remember it isn't just the caffeine you have to worry about—decaffeinated coffee contains the oils and acids found in caffeinated coffee, and is often treated with chemicals to remove the caffeine. If you have to take medications, make absolutely sure that you are not taking pills that interact dangerously with each other; your physician will be able to tell you about these drug contraindications.

Eat natural, unprocessed and unrefined foods whenever possible. Be sure to wash and scrub carefully anything that isn't taken directly out of your garden—even the scruffy raccoon scrubs his food until it shines. The same goes even for the food that *is* from your garden, unless you are absolutely sure that the soil is clean and uncontaminated. And watch out for those chemicals that are so familiar they seem totally innocent: air fresheners, shoe polish, deodorants, soap, hair spray, shampoo, furniture polish, cleaning compounds, bug sprays, and so on.

Be sensitive to your body's reactions. If you tire easily, don't automatically assume that you need more sleep or that job or marriage pressures are wearing you down. Keep track of your moods and learn to look for possible environmental causes that might contribute to irritability, stress, moodiness, depression, fatigue, and headaches.

And don't assume that something is safe just because it's allowed to stay in business. Don't drink out of streams, ponds, or lakes just because the water looks or smells clean or because government standards label it clean and safe to drink. If you live near a chemical factory, look into its dumping practices. If you believe the factory may be contaminating your environment, consider moving. The people who were contaminated at Love Canal should serve as a reminder to all of us: it *can* happen to you.

The government may not be doing enough to protect our environment, but pay attention to what it does do. If the Environmental Protection Agency declares the air unsafe, take heed. You can't see the deadly toxins, but they are there. Sick and elderly people should be especially careful.

This conscientious watchdogging is important for any group of people concerned with their own health and the health of their loved ones; but it is crucial for alcoholics who must guard their outer environment in order to protect their inner environment and stay strong and purposeful in their sobriety.

Mineral Summary

Major roles	Deficiency symptoms	Food sources	RDA	Safe maintenance doses for alcoholics
CALCIUM				
Builds strong bones and teeth; maintains cell membranes; important for muscle contraction, normal heart action, nervous-system functioning, blood clotting. Involved in enzyme activity. Helps metabolize iron.	Distorted bone growth in children; softening and loss of bones in adults, with increased risk of broken bones. Retarded tooth development. Stunted growth. Cramps, spasms, heart palpitation, insomnia, nervous-system irritability.	Dried beans and peas, cheeses, milk, dark leafy vegetables, bone meal, yogurt, buttermilk, sesame seeds, sardines, nuts.	800 mg	500–1,000 mg for initial 1–3 months. Further dosages under medical supervision.
PHOSPHORUS				
Involved in virtually all physiological chemical reactions. Builds bones and teeth, is essential for release of energy from food. Essential to formation of cell membranes, enzymes, and genetic material. Needed for transmission of nerve impulses and muscle contraction. Functions with calcium.	Poor mineralization of bones. Poor growth. Weakness, loss of appetite and weight.	Seeds, nuts, dried beans and peas, dried fruit, meat, poultry, fish, eggs, milk, milk products.	800 mg	Supplements not usually required.

Major roles	Deficiency symptoms	Food sources	RDA	Safe maintenance doses for alcoholics
		MAGNESIUM		
Builds bones. Aids in manufacture of proteins and carbohydrates and in conducting nerve impulses to muscles. Aids in regulation of acid–alkaline balances. Partner in some enzyme reactions and in energy production. Releases energy from muscle glycogen; aids in adjustment to cold.	Common in alcoholics. Muscle cramps, spasms, seizures, irregular heart beat. Sensitivity to noise, confusion, marked depression, failure to grow, pallor, weakness. Kidney damage.	Leafy green vegetables, meat, milk, nuts (especially almonds and cashews), legumes, whole grains, soybeans, seeds.	300–350 mg*	250–500 mg for initial 1–3 months. Further dosages under medical supervision.
		POTASSIUM		
Transmits nerve impulses; aids in muscle contraction; normalizes heart rhythm; maintains fluid and mineral balance in cells; releases energy from food.	Water retention (edema), irregular heart beat, nervous system upsets, muscular weakness, hypoglycemia, sodium imbalances.	Meats, fish, coffee, tea, most vegetables, citrus fruits, dried fruits, dried peas and beans, bananas.	1,875–5,625 mg*	Supplements not usually required.
		SODIUM		
Essential for normal growth; involved in mineral balance, body-fluid volume, and nerve-impulse conduction. Helps nerves and muscles function properly.	Overabundance is greater problem, but deficiency symptoms include nausea, vertigo, mental apathy, heat prostration, muscular weakness, cramps, respiratory failure.	Salted and pickled foods, salt, shellfish, cured ham, bacon, bread, crackers, most canned foods, carrots, beets, artichokes, kelp.	1,100–3,300 mg*	Not required.

SULFUR				
Helps maintain oxygen balance necessary for proper brain functioning; aids liver in bile secretion; essential for healthy hair, skin, and nails.	Eczema, rashes, dermatitis, sluggishness, brittle hair and nails.	Meat, fish, soy beans, cabbage, eggs, wheat germ, dried peas and beans, peanuts, clams.	An adequate protein diet provides sufficient amount.	Not required.
CHLORINE				
Maintains and regulates balance of body fluids, electrolytes. Stimulates production of hydrochloric acid in stomach; activiates enzymes in saliva.	Disturbed digestion, carbon dioxide build-up. Loss of hair and teeth.	Table salt, tomatoes, celery, kelp, olives.	1,700–5,100 mg*	Not required.
IRON				
Essential to formation of hemoglobin (in blood) and myoglobin (in muscles), which supply oxygen to cells. An essential part of certain enzymes, thus helping to promote protein metabolism.	Anemia: fatigue, weakness, shortness of breath.	Liver (pork, calf, beef, chicken), kidneys, red meat, molasses, egg yolks, green leafy vegetables, dried fruits, dried peas and beans.	10 mg (M) 18 mg (F)	RDA is usually adequate.

Major roles	Deficiency symptoms	Food sources	RDA	Safe maintenance doses for alcoholics
IODINE				
Assists in energy production; part of thyroid hormones; essential for normal reproduction; promotes healthy hair, nails, skin and teeth.	Fatigue and apathy, low blood pressure, slow pulse, weight gain, lack of energy. Goiter (enlarged thyroid, with low hormone production). In newborns, cretinism (retarded growth, protruding abdomen, swollen features).	Seafood, seaweed, Swiss chard, turnip greens, iodized salt, sea salt.	.15 mg (150 mcg)	Supplements not usually required.
COPPER				
Functions with iron in the body's hemoglobin formation. Necessary for production of RNA; aids in development of bones, brain, nerves, connective tissue, pigment formation. Essential for utilization of vitamin C.	Anemia, abnormal development of bones and nervous tissue. Loss of hair, skin rash, heart damage.	Shrimp, most seafood, liver, kidney, nuts, raisins, prunes, dried peas and beans, corn oil margarine.	2–3 mg*	1–3 mg
COBALT				
Essential for red blood cells; a necessary component of vitamin B-12.	Anemia, though deficiencies are rare.	Meat, kidney, liver, milk, oysters, clams.	None established	Not required.

MANGANESE				
Activates numerous enzymes; plays a role in the metabolism of carbohydrates, proteins, and fats; essential for proper functioning of nervous system, reproduction, and normal bone structure. Needed with choline to utilize fat; necessary for utilization of some B vitamins and vitamin C.	Deficiencies can affect glucose tolerance and may cause failure of muscle coordination, dizziness, and hearing loss.	Nuts, whole grains, green leafy vegetables, wheat germ, bran.	2.5–5.0*	10–15 mg
ZINC				
Found in liver, bones, skin and hair tissues, blood, pancreas, kidneys, and pituitary glands. A constituent of insulin. Essential for protein synthesis and carbohydrate metabolism. Effects transfer of carbon dioxide and maintains blood cholesterol levels. Aids in wound healing. Constituent of numerous enzymes in the body.	Retarded growth, low resistance to infection, delayed wound healing, loss of appetite, loss of fertility. A deficiency interferes with formation of RNA and DNA.	Meat, liver, poultry, eggs, milk, whole grains, nuts, green leafy vegetables, wheat germ.	15 mg	15–25 mg

Major roles	Deficiency symptoms	Food sources	RDA	Safe maintenance doses for alcoholics
		MOLYBDENUM		
Constituent of certain enzymes; aids in carbohydrate and fat metabolism. Antagonist of copper.	None known in human beings. In animals: weight loss, shortened life span.	Legumes, liver, kidneys, cereal grains, yeast.	.15–.50 mg*	RDA is usually adequate.
		SELENIUM		
Acts as an anti-oxidant, preventing fats from breaking down to harmful substances. Works closely with vitamin E.	Deficiency symptoms unknown in human beings. In animals: protects against liver damage and muscle degeneration. In humans may slow down aging process and protect against cancer.	Seafood, whole grain cereals, meat, chicken, wheat germ, bran, tuna, egg yolk, milk, onions, tomatoes, broccoli.	None established	25–50 mcg
		CHROMIUM		
Metabolism of glucose, integral part of some enzymes and hormones.	Abnormal sugar metabolism; may contribute to onset of diabetes in adulthood.	Meat, shellfish, cheese, whole grain breads and cereals, brewer's yeast, dried beans, peanuts.	.05–.20 mg*	RDA is usually adequate.
		FLUORINE		
Forms strong teeth, hardens tooth enamel, maintains bone strength.	Tooth decay. In large doses, fluorine is highly poisonous.	Fish, tea, fluoridated water, most animal foods, green leafy vegetables.	1.5–4.0 mg*	Not required.

*These are estimated safe and adequate amounts.

OTHER TRACE ELEMENTS FOUND IN THE HUMAN BODY FOR WHICH DEFICIENCIES HAVE NOT BEEN ESTABLISHED:

Aluminum	Mercury
Argon	Neodymium
Arsenic	Neon
Berylium	Nickel
Boron	Rubidium
Bromine	Scandium
Cadmium	Silicon
Cerium	Strontium
Helium	Tin
Lanthanum	Titanium
Lead	Vanadium
Lithium	

10

Supplements: Who Needs Them, What's in Them, How to Choose Them

Who Needs Supplements?

IT COULD be argued that everyone needs to take nutritional supplements of one kind or another. Carlton Frederick, Ph.D., makes the case quite persuasively in the May 1983 issue of *Prevention* magazine:

> A recent advertisement in a medical journal lists some of the candidates for vitamin and other nutritional deficiencies. These include 10 million alcoholics, over 25 million geriatric patients and over 23 million surgical patients, plus 5 million infected hospital patients. Added to these are the incalculable millions on calorie-reduced diets . . . one could [also] add those who are on medically restricted diets for digestive and other disorders, those who have vitamin dependency (creating requirements so high that they can't be satisfied by any conceivable diet) and those taking the long list of medicines which interfere with vitamin (or mineral) utilization. Another group, whose numbers must run into the millions, are those with [problems of] malabsorption.

Alcoholics need to take dietary supplements because

their disease has so thoroughly and pervasively affected the nutritional balance of their bodies. They also need to take supplements if they smoke, are sick, injured, elderly, pregnant, or are nursing mothers. Some people argue, however, that vitamin and mineral supplements are unnecessary because most Americans can afford to eat regularly and because many of the foods we eat are now heavily fortified. But carefully consider these facts:

- Enriched bread has only four artificially added nutrients. In "fortified" bread, the B-complex vitamins are woefully depleted; significant amounts of vitamin E are lost; and, of the minerals, 40 percent of the chromium, 87 percent of the manganese, 89 percent of the calcium, 57 percent of the copper, 72 percent of the zinc, and 33 percent of the molybdenum are missing.
- Seventy percent of the food we eat today has undergone some form of processing, which invariably destroys nutrients.
- Thirty percent of the money we spend on food is for food eaten outside the home—and a large percentage of this is for fast foods, which are heavily processed and rich in fat, sugar, and salt.
- In 30 to 50 percent of American families, one or more members are regularly absent from breakfast—the most important meal of the day.
- Eighty-five percent of the breakfasts we eat provide less than 25 percent of our total daily calories. (Ideally, breakfast should provide us with about a third or more of our daily calories.)
- Twenty-five to 30 percent of the women at home skip lunch.
- Fifty percent of the total snack-food market is cookies and crackers; 20 percent is potato chips.
- The average American consumes over 150 pounds of sugar a year—almost half a pound a day for every man,

woman and child! Sugar gives the body nothing nutritious—in fact, the body has to use up valuable nutrients to process sugar.

• Toxic insecticides, which leave harmful residues on food and compound body chemistry problems, are being used more and more often.

• Synthetic fertilizers "tie up" minerals, making them unavailable to plants; if the plants we eat don't contain minerals, we don't get them either.

• Overworked soils are being sucked dry of minerals.

Who needs vitamin and mineral supplements? Alcoholics, definitely. But given just the sampling of facts listed above, it's a pretty good bet that virtually everyone in this country could benefit from some type of nutritional supplement. We're not eating as well as we should, we're not getting what we should from the plants we eat, most of the food we eat is heavily processed and thereby stripped of nutrients, and our increasingly technological society robs our foods of vital nutrients. Fortifying foods with a few vitamins and minerals can't make up for these significant losses and destruction of nutrients.

What's in a Supplement?

The crowded world of vitamin and mineral supplements can be overwhelming to a newcomer—take vitamin C as an example. Is vitamin C with rose hips best? What are rose hips? What are bioflavinoids and why are they paired with vitamin C? If you take 1 gram of C a day, should you take 500 milligrams twice a day, a 1,000 milligram pill once a day, or five 200 milligram pills throughout the day? If you smoke, should you take more vitamin C? What about time-release pills? Powder or tablet form? Natural or synthetic? Organic or inorganic?

Vitamins and minerals come in all sorts of shapes, sizes, and prices; choosing between them requires some knowledge about the needs of your individual body as well as the specific ingredients in each supplement. The way you live, the environment you live in, the food you eat, the exercise you get, and the illnesses that afflict you all influence the kind and amount of supplements you should take. If you get an upset stomach from oil, or suffer from acne or other skin conditions aggravated by oil, for example, you might want to take your oil-soluble vitamins (A, D, E, and K) in "dry" or water-soluble forms. Also, because fat-soluble vitamins require fat for proper assimilation, people on a low-fat diet may benefit from the dry form.

Another factor to consider: taking too much of certain vitamins will increase the need for others. The B vitamins are notoriously interdependent, and taking large amounts of just one B vitamin while ignoring the others can cause trouble. Adelle Davis tells the story of a woman who took excessive doses of thiamine for fatigue. At first she felt better, but the good effects soon wore off. So she took higher and higher doses until her skin began to crack, her hair fell out, her eyes became bloodshot, she developed a serious case of eczema, and she was almost too tired to move. In this case, very high doses of thiamine caused deficiences of other B vitamins, producing abnormalities much more severe than the original complaint of fatigue.

Knowing the basic facts about vitamins and mineral supplements will help protect you against possibly dangerous excesses and will ensure that you are taking the right amount for *you* and *your own* unique needs. To make the best choice and cut down somewhat on the confusion, however, it's a good idea to consult someone who knows about both alcoholism and nutrition. Your treatment counselor or dietician may be able to guide you to a knowledgeable physician or nutritionist; or you can write to the International

College of Applied Nutrition (ICAN) and request a listing of physicians in your area who practice nutritional and preventive medicine (see page 81).

The following discussion of nutritional supplements and how to choose between them is not intended to be a substitute for the specific advice of a physician but, rather, to provide you with some basic understanding about those pills called supplements that you put in your mouth every day.

NATURAL OR SYNTHETIC?

Supplements can be made from either natural or synthetic ingredients. The natural vitamins found in food can be condensed from whole foods and concentrated into tablets or capsules. Synthetic vitamins are prepared in a chemist's laboratory. Chemically, synthetic and natural vitamins are the exact same molecule—but they do not necessarily act the same in the body. Synthetic vitamin C, for example, contains ascorbic acid (which is vitamin C) but nothing else, while natural vitamin C made from oranges or rose hips, for example, contains bioflavinoids and many other nutrients. (Rose hips are the berrylike seed pods that remain after the roses bloom and the petals have fallen; bioflavinoids are found in citrus fruits with vitamin C and are believed to aid in the vitamin's absorption and use in the body.)

Or look at vitamin E. Natural vitamin E consists of seven compounds called tocopherals. Alpha tocopheral is more active than the others, but it's speculated that the others have value, too. Tablets or capsules made from natural vitamin E contain all the tocopherals; synthetic tablets or capsules contain only the one or two considered to be the most active.

In other words, the supplements made from natural vitamins always contain a variety of vitamins and minerals, since nutrients never occur isolated in nature. Synthetic vitamins, however, are usually offered alone (i.e., niacin tablets or iron supplements), or they are combined by man—a combination that is undoubtedly incomplete and imperfect.

Some other advantages of taking natural vitamins:

• A jar or bottle containing natural vitamins will usually have a list of *all* the ingredients contained in the pills; many synthetic vitamins, however, will have "hidden" ingredients not listed. The natural vitamin supplement should be labeled: "a natural source from a whole food product."

• Synthetic vitamins often use coal-tar dyes in their coatings, which can cause allergic reactions. Natural vitamins shouldn't have anything artificial added. Again, read the labels carefully.

• Synthetic vitamins are often loaded with binders and fillers, many of which are "unnatural" or manmade. In certain chemically susceptible people, these can cause reactions, including hives, diarrhea, nausea, vomiting, or unpleasant upsets of the digestive system.

WHAT ABOUT TIME-RELEASE?

If you're taking 1,000 milligrams (1 gram) of vitamin C that aren't time-released, you're probably losing a lot of the vitamin in your urine. Vitamin C, like all water-soluble vitamins, is quickly absorbed into the blood stream and any excess is excreted in the urine within two to three hours. Time-release vitamins are absorbed over an eight- to twelve-hour period, minimizing loss by excretion and allowing stable blood levels of the vitamin throughout the day.

Which vitamins can you buy in time-release form? Vitamin C and some of the B-complex vitamins, including niacin, are usually available in time-release form. If these time-release vitamins are not available or are priced higher than your budget allows, you can take regular supplements in smaller doses spaced throughout the day. Rather than taking 1,000 milligrams of vitamin C in the morning, for example, you might take 500 milligrams with breakfast and 500 more with dinner, or you could take 250 milligrams four times a day.

TABLETS, CAPSULES, OR POWDERS?

Tablets and capsules are the most common forms of vitamins and minerals because they're convenient to carry, have a long shelf life, and are, for most people, easy to swallow. Most fat-soluble vitamins come in capsules, since they're in a liquid (oil) substance.

Powders, however, are more potent than either capsules or tablets. One teaspoon of vitamin C powder, for example, can provide up to 4,000 milligrams (4 grams), while a tablet or capsule containing that amount would look like a horse pill. Powders also have no fillers, binders, or additives and are thus preferred for people with allergies to those substances. Powders can be mixed with any liquid beverage and are particularly good for elderly people or others who may be unable to swallow capsules or tablets easily.

FILLERS, BINDERS, AND OTHER ADDITIVES

Most vitamin and mineral supplements are loaded up with all sorts of extras that enhance their marketability, appearance, shelf life, and flavor, and make them easy to swallow. Better brands contain more natural and, in some cases, more nutritious additives. Some of these are described below.

BINDERS. Cellulose, the major part of plant fiber, is often used as a binder in tablets or capsules to hold all the other ingredients together. Other "natural" binders include acacia (gum arabic), a vegetable gum; algin, a plant carbohydrate from seaweed; lecithin, a combination of fatty acid and phosphorus and a rich source of choline; and sorbitol, a sugar substitute.

FILLERS. Dicalcium phosphate, derived from purified

mineral rocks, is a source of both calcium and phosphorus and is used in better vitamin supplements to increase bulk. Sorbitol and cellulose (plant fiber) are occasionally used.

DISINTEGRATORS. Disintegrators are substances that allow the supplement to break up, or disintegrate, once ingested; natural disintegrators include gum arabic, algin, and alginate.

FLAVORS AND SWEETENERS. You can chew those chewable tablets without gagging because sugar and artificial flavoring have been added. If you must buy the chewable supplements, look for natural sweeteners, usually fructose (fruit sugar), malt dextrins, sorbitol or maltose. Supplements that list sucrose as an ingredient contain plain old refined sugar.

COATINGS. Zein, a natural substance derived from corn protein, and Brazil wax, a natural product from palm trees, are frequently used to coat vitamin and mineral supplements to protect them from moisture.

COLORS. Vitamins, like cars and lipstick, must be attractive if consumers are to buy them; look for colors derived from natural sources like chlorophyll.

CHELATED MINERALS

Chelated is a word that may or may not appear on labels. Chelated (pronounced *key*-lated) minerals are those that have been changed into digestible form. Chelation is a process of combining an inorganic, or non-living, substance (like a mineral) to an organic, or living, substance (like protein). This bonding—chelation—allows the minerals to be more easily digested, absorbed, and used by the body. Chelated supplements cost a little more, but the extra cost may be worth it since the body can more easily assimilate the chelated minerals. Of the non-chelated inorganic iron taken into the body, for example, only 2 to 10 percent is absorbed, and half of that small amount is eliminated.

Since chelated minerals are much more efficiently absorbed (80 to 90 percent), the mineral content of the supplement is much lower than in non-chelated forms, in which only 20 percent (at most) of the mineral will be absorbed. Strongly bonded chelates are usually labelled as chelated minerals. "Looser" chelate bonds are minerals combined with lactate or gluconate and have amino acid (protein) bonding.

WHERE TO STORE SUPPLEMENTS?

In a cool, dark place away from light, well-sealed vitamins and minerals should last for two to three years. Once opened, however, they won't retain their potency for much more than a year. Beware of storing your supplements in either the refrigerator, where temperature changes can moisten and soften them, or in your medicine cabinet, where steam from the hot water tap or shower will also present a moisture problem. A good place for storing supplements is with your spices in a cabinet some distance from the stove (again, tea kettles and boiling water will rob vitamins of their potency.)

Other storage hints: opaque containers will protect the supplement from sunlight, and a few grains of rice added to the container will protect against excess moisture, since rice is a natural absorbent.

WHEN TO TAKE?

Vitamins taken on an empty stomach are absorbed and excreted fairly quickly, so take your supplements with meals for best results. Besides, vitamins and minerals are needed when food is broken down and used by the body.

It's best to spread out your water-soluble vitamins (the B vitamins and vitamin C) throughout the day—with breakfast, lunch and dinner—to help keep the blood levels constant. If that's not possible, take your supplements after your biggest meal. Also, take vitamins and minerals together since the minerals are needed for proper absorption of the vitamins.

How to Choose a Good Supplement

The best way to choose a supplement is to have your physician choose it for you, basing the choice on knowledge of your history of alcoholism, other diseases or injuries, medications you're taking, and your specific nutritional needs and requirements.

Alcoholics looking for help in this area, however, will face two major hurdles: first, most physicians and alcoholism-treatment personnel mistakenly believe that alcoholism has only a minor and short-term effect on the body's nutritional status; second, the majority of physicians and alcoholism-treatment personnel have no training, knowledge, or interest in nutrition. Looking for help can be discouraging and disheartening when a physician responds to your questions about supplements with a frown and then avoids the subject or brushes it off with, "You don't need supplements; just eat three meals a day!"

Given the disdain and discomfort many physicians feel regarding nutrition and nutritional supplements, and the misleading advice sometimes offered to recovering alcoholics, the following guidelines for choosing a supplement are offered. These guidelines, of course, are not intended to replace the advice of a knowledgeable physician or nutritionist, but they will help you choose a supplement (or supplements) that will be optimal for your continuing good health.

• Make sure the strength of the vitamins and minerals in the supplement are at least equal to the RDA—recommended daily allowance (see Appendix 3). The RDA is used to determine how much of a certain nutrient is needed to maintain "good" health in an "average" person. The National Academy of Sciences–National Research Council acknowledges the incompleteness of scientific information available to establish these levels.

Supplement Potency

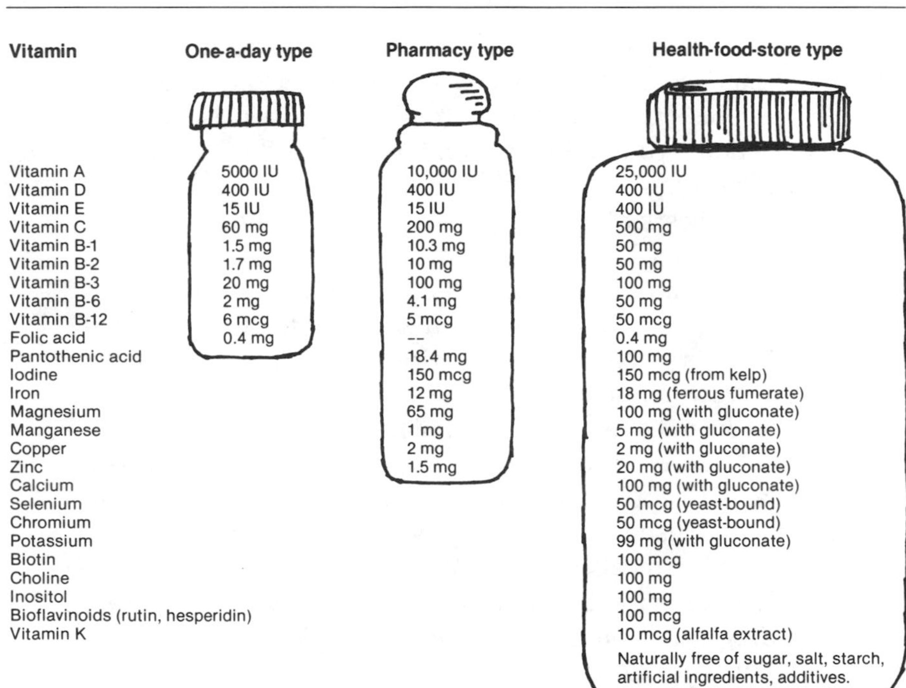

Vitamin	One-a-day type	Pharmacy type	Health-food-store type
Vitamin A	5000 IU	10,000 IU	25,000 IU
Vitamin D	400 IU	400 IU	400 IU
Vitamin E	15 IU	15 IU	400 IU
Vitamin C	60 mg	200 mg	500 mg
Vitamin B-1	1.5 mg	10.3 mg	50 mg
Vitamin B-2	1.7 mg	10 mg	50 mg
Vitamin B-3	20 mg	100 mg	100 mg
Vitamin B-6	2 mg	4.1 mg	50 mg
Vitamin B-12	6 mcg	5 mcg	50 mcg
Folic acid	0.4 mg	--	0.4 mg
Pantothenic acid		18.4 mg	100 mg
Iodine		150 mcg	150 mcg (from kelp)
Iron		12 mg	18 mg (ferrous fumerate)
Magnesium		65 mg	100 mg (with gluconate)
Manganese		1 mg	5 mg (with gluconate)
Copper		2 mg	2 mg (with gluconate)
Zinc		1.5 mg	20 mg (with gluconate)
Calcium			100 mg (with gluconate)
Selenium			50 mcg (yeast-bound)
Chromium			50 mcg (yeast-bound)
Potassium			99 mg (with gluconate)
Biotin			100 mcg
Choline			100 mg
Inositol			100 mg
Bioflavinoids (rutin, hesperidin)			100 mcg
Vitamin K			10 mcg (alfalfa extract)

Naturally free of sugar, salt, starch, artificial ingredients, additives. Coated with lecithin and protein.

Basically, RDAs describe the amount needed to *prevent* obvious vitamin-deficiency-induced illness. For example, the RDA of 60 milligrams of vitamin C will prevent scurvy in most people; the RDA of 10 milligrams of niacin will prevent pellagra in most people, and so on. But what about all the other health benefits of these vitamins if given in larger doses? The RDAs are not necessarily maximum amounts needed for optimum health, as many of us mistakenly believe, but amounts needed to prevent a given vitamin deficiency disease.

The RDA is also an average amount, and trying to find an average nutritional requirement, it's been said, is somewhat like trying to find an average fingerprint—no such "ideal" exists. Every one of us is unique and every one of us will vary in some way from the requirements satisfied by the standard RDA. That's why it's so important to be aware of your unique needs for specific vitamins and minerals and to remember that these needs change over time with illness, injury, increasing age, living conditions, and lifestyle.

• Since it's difficult to pack all the needed nutrients into a single tablet that can easily be swallowed, many "one-a-day" vitamins are actually made to be taken three or even six times a day. When comparing prices of one brand with another, be sure to read the label carefully to see how many tablets are required to supply the nutrients listed on the label.

• Now, some specifics. *For vitamins:*

Of the B vitamin series, the more complete, the better. If the supplement contains the lesser-known B vitamins like *pantothenic acid, inositol, choline, biotin,* and *PABA*, it's probably one of the more complete B vitamin supplements. These additional vitamins should be in milligram, not microgram, strengths.

Vitamin B-1 (thiamine) and *B-2* (riboflavin) are often included in adequate amounts in multivitamin and mineral supplements, but look also for *vitamin B-3* (niacin), which should be from five to ten times the strength of B-1 and B-2, and *folic acid*, which should be present in amounts greater than 100 micrograms (or 0.1 milligram).

Vitamin B-6, pyridoxine, should be included in a strength in milligrams (mg), *not* micrograms (mcg).

Vitamin B-12 and *folic acid,* on the other hand, are usually adequate in microgram strengths.

Vitamin C should be included in at least 100 to 200 milligram strength. If it's not, be sure to supplement daily with extra vitamin C. If you smoke or live in a heavily industrialized or polluted area, you'll need to take even more vitamin C. Amounts up to a gram (1,000 milligrams) can easily be tolerated by most people.

Vitamin E is often too low in many supplements, since most multipurpose vitamin supplements contain between 30 to 60 IU; 100 IU is a better amount. Again, it may be necessary to supplement separately.

The fat-soluble vitamins A, D, E, and *K* can be toxic if taken in large doses. Toxicity symptoms of each vitamin are described in the chapter on vitamins.

- *For minerals:*

  Calcium should be around 500 milligrams in strength; many standard supplements include calcium in amounts less than 100 milligrams.

  Magnesium should be present in an amount about half that of calcium.

  Iron should be between 10 to 20 milligrams.

  Zinc, iodine, chromium, copper, selenium, manganese, the less common minerals, as well as the array of other *trace minerals*, are also ones you should look for.

Some Cautions

When choosing or combining supplements, it's important to keep these basic principles in mind:

1. Prolonged use of vitamins in doses several times the RDA or in the megadose range should be supervised by a knowledgeable physician.

Drugs That Work Against Nutrients

	Primary Nutrients Depleted
Alcohol	B-complex vitamins Vitamin C Vitamin K Magnesium Calcium Potassium Zinc
Diuretics (water pills) and some high blood pressure pills	Folic acid Vitamin B-6 Magnesium Calcium Potassium Sodium Trace minerals (particularly zinc)
Tobacco	Vitamin C
Caffeine	Vitamin B-1 Pantothenic acid Inositol Potassium Iron
Birth-control pills	B vitamins, especially B-2, B-6, B-12, and folic acid Vitamin C
Aspirin	Vitamin C Folic acid Vitamin K
Antacids	Calcium-phosphorus balance Vitamin A B-complex vitamins
Anticonvulsants (Dilantin)	Vitamin C Folic acid Vitamin D (Dilantin interferes with metabolism of the vitamin)
Antituberculosis drugs	Folic acid Vitamin B-6 Vitamin B-12
Antidepressants (Doriden)	Vitamin D (antidepressants interfere with metabolism of the vitamin)
Antibiotics	
Sulfa	B-complex vitamins
Tetracycline	Iron (tetracycline decreases absorption of iron) Vitamin C
Broad spectrum	Vitamin K Vitamin B-12
Tranquilizers	Vitamin D (tranquilizers interfere with metabolism of the vitamin) Folic acid

2. Always take the B vitamins together, and don't regularly take one B vitamin in large doses while taking small doses of the others. The B vitamins work and function together, and large doses of one will throw off the activities of all the others.

3. Minerals are also interdependent with one another and with the vitamins, so be sure to take adequate amounts (including the trace minerals) with your vitamins. Once again, balance is the key for long-term supplementation.

4. When combining supplements, be careful not to duplicate (and thereby double or triple the dosage) of certain vitamins. Many multipurpose supplements, for example, contain the RDA for vitamins A and D, but do not include enough magnesium and calcium. Therefore, you may decide to add a calcium/magnesium supplement, but that may also contain vitamins A and D because of their association with calcium and magnesium metabolism. Since the fat-soluble vitamins (A, D, E, and K) can be toxic if taken in very large amounts, watch out for unnecessary duplication. Again, it's a matter of reading labels carefully.

5. Be aware that certain drugs and medications can disrupt the action of vitamins and minerals by stopping their absorption, interfering with the cells' ability to use the nutrients, or increasing the rate of excretion of nutrients.

6. Be aware also that certain vitamins can interfere with the action of drugs and medications.

Vitamin–Drug Interactions

Vitamin	Enemies	Primary Allies	Potential Adverse Vitamin-Drug Interaction	
			Drug	Result
Vitamin A	Mineral Oil Nitrates from nitrogen fertilizers	Protein Vitamin E Zinc	Oral anticoagulants ("blood thinners")	High doses of vitamin A (25,000 IU per day for a month) may increase blood thinning.
			Steroids (cortisone, creams, ointments)	Possible interference with skin's response to steroids.
B-1 (thiamine)	Heat (cooking) Excess sugar intake Antibiotics Stress Alcohol	Complete B complex Vitamin C Vitamin E		
B-2 (riboflavin)	Direct sunlight Heat (cooking) Antibiotics Alcohol Oral contraceptives	Complete B complex Vitamin C		
B-3 (niacin)	Excess sugar intake Heat (cooking) Antibiotics Alcohol Illness (reduces absorption)	Complete B complex Vitamin C		

Vitamin	Enemies	Primary Allies	Potential Adverse Vitamin-Drug Interaction	
			Drug	Result
B-6 (pyridoxine)	Steroid hormones (cortisone, estrogen) Aging (after 50, B-6 levels drop rapidly) Heat (cooking) Food processing High-protein diets Anti-tuberculosis drug (INH) Oral contraceptives	Complete B complex Magnesium Vitamin C	Phenobarbitol Dilantin	Reduced blood levels of the drug have been recorded in some cases.
Folic acid	Severe stress (surgery) Oral contraceptives Vitamin C deficiency Alcohol Aspirin Anticonvulsants (Dilantin)	Complete B complex Vitamin C	Dilantin (anticonvulsant)	Large doses of folic acid (10–15 mg) will decrease levels of Dilantin in the blood.
Vitamin B-12 (cobalamin)	Prolonged iron deficiency Oral contraceptives Stress (pregnancy) Strict vegetarian diet	Complete B complex Vitamin C Vitamin E		
Biotin	Heat (cooking) Avidin (found in raw egg whites) Antibiotics Sulfa drugs	Complete B complex Vitamin C		
Choline	Alcohol Excess sugar intake	Complete B complex Vitamin A		
Inositol	Antibiotics (because they destroy intestinal bacteria)	Complete B complex Vitamin E Vitamin C		

Pantothenic acid	Insecticides used on food	Complete B complex Calcium Vitamin C Biotin		
Vitamin C	Smoking Air pollutants Alcohol Anticonvulsant drugs Oral contraceptives Aspirin Heat, light, air Stress Diabetes	B-complex vitamins Bioflavinoids Vitamin E Selenium	Anticoagulants (oral) Phenothiazine (major tranquilizer) B-12	High doses of vitamin C may reduce response to blood-thinning drugs. Vitamin C deficiency may increase levels of the drug in the blood. High doses of Vitamin C may deplete B-12.
Vitamin D	Insufficient exposure to ultraviolet light Air pollution Laxatives Antacids Anticonvulsants	Calcium Vitamin A Vitamin C		
Vitamin E	Oral contraceptives Food processing Rancid fats and oils Mineral oil	Vitamin A Vitamin C B-complex vitamins Selenium Manganese	Anticoagulants (oral) Iron	Vitamin E increases blood-thinning response. Vitamin E may inhibit response to iron in iron-deficiency states.
Vitamin K	Antibiotics Anticoagulants Mineral oil Intestinal diseases (diarrhea, colitis, radiation)		Anticoagulants (oral)	Vitamin K inhibits blood-thinning response

Sources: Arthur G. Lipman, "Vitamins and Drugs: Various Interactions to Consider," *Modern Medicine,* May 1982; *The Complete Book of Vitamins,* compiled by Charles Gerras, Rodale Press, Emmaus, PA, 1977; Daphne A. Roe, M.D., *Drug-Induced Nutritional Deficiencies,* AVI Publishing Co., Westport, CT.

11

Recipes for Sobriety

THE recipes in this chapter will start you in the direction of more healthful eating. Most of these are less-meat or no-meat recipes since the vast majority of readers have less familiarity with that type of cooking. Our hope is that you will read through this section carefully and, over a period of several months, try out the recipes. You'll come up with some favorites, and you'll learn that whole-grain, unprocessed, and unrefined foods can be delightful to the eye as well as to the stomach. As teen-agers Amy and Heidi Mueller enthused after wolfing down a plateful of tacos made with homemade whole-wheat tortillas: "Mom, how did we ever eat that old cardboard stuff?"

Breakfast

> Food is fuel for your day's activity, so it makes no sense at all to eat your biggest meal at night when it's all behind you.
>
> *Laurel's Kitchen*

The two basic rules for breakfast should be: Eat, and eat well. Simple. But more people will have trouble following those two suggestions than any others offered in this chapter. Eating in the morning is a gagging thought to many people; eating a hearty breakfast may be unthinkable. Who but the most avid followers of Craig Claiborne or Julia Child can face an oven at 7:00 in the morning? And, later, a sink full of dirty dishes? Instead, most of us rush out the door, newspaper in hand, with barely enough time to give the dog a pat or the kids a goodbye kiss, and the only thing we can consider for breakfast is a cup of strong coffee and a doughnut. Sweet and stimulating such a breakfast may be, but it's no good for sustaining mental and physical energy. The temptation to munch down a few granola bars or a bowl of sugar-coated cereal defeats all of us at one time or another. Fight it—you can eat well, and it doesn't need to take you forever to prepare or eat a good, nutritious breakfast.

And eating a hearty, wholesome breakfast is crucially important, a fact that can't be emphasized enough. For those who have trouble even thinking about food in the morning, here are a few suggestions that may help you to get in the best frame of mind for thinking about breakfast as your most important and essential meal.

- Eat a light supper.
- Get up a little earlier so that you can develop an appetite. Do a few jumping jacks or stretching exercises; perhaps run or walk a mile or two.
- Even if you're a light eater, at least eat something nutritious—a piece of toast with natural peanut butter and a glass of milk, some hot oatmeal topped with raisins and nuts, or a high-protein milk shake (see recipe on page 301).

As a general rule, breakfast should supply a third of your daily requirements for protein and carbohydrates. A traditional, hearty breakfast that meets these requirements might include a fried egg, two strips of bacon, hash browns, half a grapefruit, a glass of orange juice, and a piece of toast with butter. But there are some problems with such a breakfast: it's too high in fat to eat every morning, it requires a hearty appetite, it's expensive, and it takes valuable time to prepare. Here's another, less traditional breakfast that also meets your breakfast needs, but is without the problems of the egg-and-bacon breakfast: a bowl of homemade granola, a glass of milk, a glass of orange juice, and a boiled egg. Such a breakfast is simple to prepare, low in fat, inexpensive, delicious, and nutritious!

In summary, it's important to find a breakfast that matches your body's "temperament" and metabolism, sustains you through the morning, helps meet your nutritional requirements for the day, and is pleasant, satisfying, and not too much trouble to put together. You can still have eggs and bacon—if you can't live without them—two or three times a week. But every other day or so, try to work into your breakfast some whole-grain cereals, breads, or pancakes, and some fruit and yogurt.

CEREALS

Whole-grain cereals make a great breakfast food that's nutritious, easy to prepare, and economical. Shredded Wheat, Grape Nuts, Puffed Wheat, and Puffed Rice are all commercial cereals that contain no refined sugar. "Cold" cereal, however, has been exposed to dry heat, a process that causes the loss of many vital nutrients, including protein—so, whenever possible, eat hot cereals, which are richer in nutrients and more sustaining in energy. Oatmeal, Cream of Wheat, and Cream of Rice are all available commercially and are good nutritional bargains. Buy the long-cooking type, however, not the "quick" or "instant" mix-with-hot-water types, which have been subjected to extra processing. And, for extra nutrition, serve your cereals with raisins, sliced banana, a sprinkling of wheat germ or sunflower seeds, or a spoonful of protein powder.

Homemade granola is far superior to the grocery-store

types, which are mostly oats with lots of honey and sugar. Following are two different granola recipes, both delicious and packed with nutritious ingredients.

Crunchy Granola

6 cups rolled oats
1 cup whole-wheat flour
2 cups grated unsweetened coconut
½ cup sesame seeds
1 cup almonds, peanuts, or walnuts
1 cup sunflower seeds
1 cup wheat germ
½ cup soy grits or cornmeal
1 cup honey
⅔ cup water
2 teaspoons salt
*2 teaspoons imitation vanilla**
raisins or other dried fruit

1. Preheat oven to 300°.
2. Stir first 8 ingredients together in a large bowl.
3. Mix honey, water, salt, and vanilla, and pour over cereal mixture. Mix well.
4. Spread the resulting mixture on a flat pan (a cookie sheet or broiler pan).
5. Roast for about 20 minutes, or until lightly browned, stirring every 5 to 10 minutes.
6. Cool and add raisins and/or other dried fruit.

Variations. Some people find this granola too dry. If you can afford the increased fat in your diet, try substituting ½ cup oil for the water.

To really liven up the granola, add ⅔ cup natural peanut butter instead of water or oil. Again, though, make sure you can afford the extra fat.

*Whenever a recipe calls for vanilla, make sure you use imitation vanilla—real vanilla has a potent alcohol content. Some imitation vanillas also contain alcohol, however, so read the labels carefully.

Granola

5 cups oats
½ cup water
½ cup oil
1 cup each: sesame seeds
sunflower seeds
dried coconut
1 cup each: powdered milk
wheat germ
soy flour
honey
peanuts
raisins

1. Preheat oven to 200°.
2. Mix together all ingredients except peanuts and raisins.
3. Spread mixture in a shallow pan and bake until light brown—about 50 minutes. Turn every 5 to 10 minutes.
4. Add the peanuts for the last 10 minutes of cooking.
5. Cool. Add raisins.

BREADS

Spread with peanut butter or served with slices of Monterey jack or Swiss cheese and broiled for one minute, whole-grain breads can be a breakfast mainstay. Or try toasted bagels with cottage cheese and tomato. But remember to watch your toasting: thinly sliced, darkly toasted bread may lose up to 30 percent of its thiamine content and 10 to 20 percent of the crucial amino acid, lysine. So toast lightly, or warm your bread in the oven, wrapped in foil, or in a loaf pan covered with a damp cloth.

Most supermarkets carry bread that's 100 percent whole grain, with no additives or preservatives. But be sure to read the labels carefully—the first ingredient on the label should read "whole-grain flour" and not "enriched flour." "Enriched" flour is simply flour in which the nutrients have been stripped away in processing and then added back again in selected amounts. Taking the germ and natural grains out of the flour gives the bread a longer shelf life, but enriched flour is simply not as nutritious as 100 percent whole grain.

If anyone in your household has an inclination to make bread, encourage that person as heartily as you would a budding musician or athlete. Homemade bread is delicious, nutritious, and so much more flavorful than the store-bought kind (even 100 percent whole-grain bread) that your bread-maker will inevitably glow with pride and praise. And don't keep the men or boys out of the kitchen. Bread-making can be a delightful Saturday project for the entire family and the menfolk might really take to bread-making and end up shooing the women outdoors to dirtier and less satisfying tasks like raking the leaves or cleaning the car. It's been known to happen.

The best way to learn to make yeast breads is to have a friend teach you. That way you can ask questions without embarrassment, pick up some handy tips from a veteran, enjoy a cup of tea or juice together while the bread is rising and baking, and congratulate each other on the magnificent result. Taking a class is another good way to learn the techniques necessary for making bread. Or you can consult any number of cookbooks that will lead you through the process step by step. *Recipes for a Small Planet* and *Laurel's Kitchen* contain lots of helpful hints for beginning bread-makers. The bread recipes in those cookbooks are unusual and delicious.

No-Rise Wheat-Oat Bread

This earthy bread is best when warmed or toasted. It takes only about an hour to make and needs no rising. Save leftovers to eat with soup at lunch or dinner.

1½ cups oatmeal
3 packages yeast
4 cups warm water
¼ cup plus 2 tablespoons honey
1 tablespoon salt
¼ cup oil
¼ cup wheat germ
1 cup soy grits
6 cups whole-wheat flour

1. Warm oatmeal in the oven.

2. In a large bowl dissolve yeast in warm water combined with 2 tablespoons honey, and let mixture stand 10 minutes in a warm place until foamy.

3. Add remaining honey, salt, and oil to yeast mixture, then add warm oatmeal and let stand a few minutes more.

4. Preheat oven to 275°.

5. Add in the wheat germ, soy grits, and 5 cups flour. Knead mixture well until elastic, adding the last cup of flour as you knead.

6. Place dough in 2 large loaf pans or 3 small ones. Bake for 15 minutes, raise heat to 350°, and bake for 30 to 40 minutes more.

7. Remove from bread pans and cool.

Quick Whole-Wheat Bread

This fairly sweet bread has the consistency of muffins. It's particularly good spread with unsweetened applesauce.

2 cups whole-wheat flour
1 teaspoon baking soda
2 teaspoons baking powder
½ teaspoon salt
½ cup soy flour
1 egg, beaten
¼ cup oil
1½ cups sour milk or 1½ cups milk with 2 teaspoons vinegar
3 tablespoons honey
*3 tablespoons artificial sweetener**
¼ cup wheat germ
¼ cup instant powdered milk

1. Preheat oven to 350°.

2. Sift the first 4 ingredients into a large bowl.

3. Add remaining ingredients.

4. Stir well, spoon into a greased 9-×-5-inch loaf pan, and let stand for 20 minutes. Bake for about 35 minutes or until nicely browned.

*In those recipes that call for sweeteners, we recommend the sugar substitute NutraSweet, which also appears under the brand name Equal. Although NutraSweet is more expensive than saccharines, there are no reports of potential ill effects with NutraSweet. The amounts listed in the recipes are sugar equivalents.

Corn Bread

Why not have corn bread for breakfast? This hearty bread is wonderful when served right out of the oven. Serve it with yogurt and fruit salad, or scrambled eggs and tomatoes.

1 cup cornmeal
1 cup whole-wheat flour
3 tablespoons soy grits
2 teaspoons baking powder
½ teaspoon baking soda
½ teaspoon salt
2 eggs, beaten
1 cup buttermilk or yogurt
¼ cup oil
2 tablespoons honey
2 tablespoons sweetener

1. Preheat oven to 350°.
2. In a large bowl, stir together all the dry ingredients.
3. In another bowl, stir together the liquid ingredients and the sweetener.
4. Add the liquid ingredients to the dry ingredients, mixing just enough to combine everything. The less mixing, the more tender the bread.
5. Pour batter into an oiled pan and bake for 40 to 50 minutes. The top will spring back when the bread is done.

English Muffins

These are much better than the store-bought kind and take only a little time and planning. To increase the protein, serve the muffins hot with melted cheese or poached eggs. Or layer ricotta cheese and tomato slices on top.

The ring from a Mason jar makes a good cutter, as does a 7-ounce tuna can with both ends removed.

1 cup milk, scalded
2 tablespoons honey
¼ cup oil
1 tablespoon salt
1 package dry yeast
1 cup lukewarm water
5 to 6 cups flour (whole wheat or a combination of unbleached white and whole wheat)
corn meal

1. Place hot milk in a large bowl and add honey, oil, and salt. Cool to lukewarm.

2. Dissolve yeast in the warm water and add to the cooled milk.

3. Add 3 cups of flour and beat until smooth.

4. Gradually add more flour, beating well after each addition until a soft dough is formed.

5. Knead on a lightly floured board until smooth and elastic, about 8 to 10 minutes, adding more flour as necessary.

6. Place in a greased bowl, cover, and let rise in a warm, draft-free place until doubled in bulk (about 1 hour).

7. Punch down and divide dough in half.

8. On a lightly floured board, roll out half the dough to a thickness of about ½ inch. Cut dough into circles about 3 inches in diameter.

9. Gently transfer the circles to a cookie sheet that has been heavily sprinkled with cornmeal. Sprinkle tops of the circles with cornmeal, too.

10. Push scraps together, roll out, and cut again. Repeat entire process for the second half of the dough.

11. Cover the muffins with a cloth and let rise until doubled.

12. Heat a griddle or electric frying pan to 300° (medium high) and grease lightly. Carefully transfer muffins with a large spatula to the griddle, fitting on as many as you can without letting them touch. Bake 10 to 15 minutes, or until bottoms are browned, and then turn and bake the other side.

Nutty Whole-Wheat Muffins

Serve these crunchy muffins hot. Leftovers can be toasted and spread with ricotta cheese or Better Butter (page 300) and served with yogurt and fruit or scrambled eggs. These muffins are also delicious with soups and salads.

1½ cups whole-wheat flour
¼ cup soy flour
1 tablespoon baking powder
½ teaspoon salt
¼ cup sesame seeds, toasted
⅓ cup sunflower seeds, toasted
¼ cup chopped peanuts, toasted
⅓ cup raisins
1 egg
1 cup milk
1 to 2 tablespoons oil
1 to 2 tablespoons honey

1. Preheat oven to 375° and thoroughly grease muffin tins.
2. Stir all dry ingredients together, including the seeds, nuts, and raisins.
3. In a separate bowl, beat the egg and add milk, oil, and honey and blend.
4. Make a well in the dry ingredients and add liquid mixture all at once. Stir with just a few strokes to moisten the dry ingredients.
5. Drop batter into muffin tins and bake for 15 to 20 minutes.

Oatmeal Muffins

1 cup whole-wheat flour
⅔ cup rolled oats
⅓ cup soy flour
1 teaspoon baking soda
½ teaspoon salt
½ cup instant powdered milk
1 egg, beaten
½ cup yogurt
½ cup water
2 tablespoons oil
2 tablespoons honey

1. Preheat oven to 350°.
2. Stir dry ingredients together in a small bowl.
3. Combine egg, yogurt, water, oil, and honey. Make a well in the dry mixture and pour in the liquid. Moisten with as few strokes as possible.
4. Drop batter into oiled muffin tins and bake until nicely browned—about 15 minutes.

Variations. Add ½ cup raisins, or ½ cup blueberries, or ½ cup sunflower seeds. Or substitute 1 cup buttermilk for the powdered milk, yogurt, and water.

Whole-Wheat Popovers

These are extra-special treats for a weekend morning, and they're simple to make. They won't puff up as high as all-white-flour popovers, but they have a wonderful texture and consistency. Because they have a low fat content, these popovers are superior to biscuits from the standpoint of nutritional value.

2 eggs
½ cup whole-wheat flour
½ cup unbleached white flour
½ teaspoon salt
1 cup milk
1 tablespoon oil

1. Preheat oven to 475°.
2. Combine everything but the oil, and beat for 1½ minutes with an electric beater.
3. Add oil and beat another half minute.
4. Thoroughly grease muffin tins and pour in batter until tins are two thirds full.
5. Bake muffins for 15 minutes, then reduce heat to 350° and bake for 25 to 30 minutes more—until nicely browned.

PANCAKES AND TOPPINGS

These pancakes are a far cry from the white-flour Aunt Jemima type, which are served with buckets of butter and maple syrup. "Pancakes made with whole wheat?" you ask. "No syrup or butter?" Set aside your doubts and try these. Recipes for toppings and sauces follow.

Quick Pancake Mix

6½ cups whole-wheat flour
1½ cups soy flour
1 tablespoon salt
3½ cups instant powdered milk
⅓ cup baking powder
2½ cups wheat germ

Combine and mix all ingredients and store in a tightly covered container in the refrigerator.

Pancakes

1 egg, beaten
1 cup water
3 tablespoons oil
2 teaspoons sweetener (optional)
1½ cups quick pancake mix (preceding recipe)

1. Combine first 4 ingredients.
2. Stir in the quick mix and, if necessary, a bit more water.
3. Fry batter on a hot griddle.

Makes 10 to 12 4-inch pancakes.

Oatmeal Pancakes

Moist, chewy, delicious.

¾ cup instant powdered milk
1½ cups water
1 cup plain yogurt
1½ cups rolled oats
1 cup whole-wheat flour
1 teaspoon soda
½ teaspoon salt
2 eggs, beaten
1 tablespoon sweetener (optional)

1. Combine first 4 ingredients and let soak for a few minutes.
2. Beat in remaining ingredients.
3. Fry on a hot griddle.

Makes about 18 to 24 4-inch pancakes.

Peanut-Butter Pancakes

These pancakes are light and slightly sweet, with just a subtle taste of peanut butter.

1 cup whole-wheat flour
⅔ cup instant powdered milk
½ teaspoon salt
2 teaspoons baking powder
2 eggs
2 tablespoons honey
2 tablespoons sweetener
½ teaspoon imitation vanilla
½ cup peanut butter
1¼ cups water

1. Stir together first 4 ingredients.

2. In a separate bowl, beat together the eggs, honey, sweetener, vanilla, and peanut butter. Mix in the water.

3. Combine liquid and dry ingredients and stir until smooth.

4. Fry on a hot griddle.

Makes 8 to 10 4-inch pancakes.

Fruit Topping

This topping is also a good alternative to jams and jellies for toast. Use fresh or frozen fruit whenever possible; however, canned fruit in natural juices is O.K., too.

3 to 4 cups fresh or frozen fruit
2 tablespoons cornstarch
2 tablespoons honey
pinch of salt

Combine ingredients, mash with dough blender until pulpy, and stir over medium heat until thickened. Serve hot or cold over pancakes.

Variation. Use applesauce in place of fruit.

Better Butter

Butter and margarine both have their problems (see page 175), so why not make your own butter-flavored margarine-like spread? Use cold-pressed oil whenever possible—since the fatty acids have not been oxidized into potentially harmful chemicals, and the natural vitamin E in the oil remains active.

1 cup softened butter
¾ to 1 cup safflower oil

Blend butter and oil (using less oil for a more solid spread), and refrigerate to solidify.

BREAKFAST QUICKIES

These recipes are for those who oversleep their alarm clocks, those who are just developing a taste for breakfast and want something quick and easy, or those who usually eat a sturdy midmorning snack and want something lighter for breakfast.

High-Protein Milk Shake

This delicious drink also makes a refreshing, filling snack.

½ cup fruit (fresh is best)
2 tablespoons honey (or sugar substitute to taste)
1 teaspoon imitation vanilla
1 cup yogurt
*2 tablespoons protein powder**

Mix ingredients in a blender. Keep blender on for a full minute to break up the protein powder and make a smoother drink.

Homemade Instant Breakfast

Regular-strength milk base:
1 cup milk
⅓ cup instant powdered milk

Double-strength milk base:
1 cup water
⅔ cup instant powdered milk

Blend the regular- or double-strength milk base in the blender with any of these combinations:

1. 1 tablespoon carob powder, ¼ teaspoon imitation vanilla, a dash of cinnamon, and ½ teaspoon honey;
2. ¼ teaspoon almond extract, ¼ to ½ teaspoon nutmeg, and honey to taste;
3. 1 tablespoon molasses;
4. ½ teaspoon imitation vanilla and 1 teaspoon honey;
5. 1 tablespoon sugar-free jam or preserves.

*Buy a powder without sugar—be sure to read the label carefully. Egg-based powder is less grainy and makes a smoother, creamier drink.

Egg Nog

This is wonderful either as a drink straight from the blender or as a topping for cereal.

2 cups regular- or double-strength milk base (preceding recipe)
1 egg
sugar substitute or honey to taste
½ teaspoon imitation vanilla

Blend all ingredients in blender.

Yogurt

Yogurt is a fermented milk product, high in protein and containing "friendly" bacteria that are necessary for healthy intestines and proper digestion of food. Buy low-fat yogurt and stay away from the store-bought fruited varieties, which are high in sugar. Instead, buy plain yogurt and flavor it with any of the following:

honey
molasses
carob powder mixed with honey for sweetening
cinnamon mixed with honey
rhubarb
sugar-free fruit preserves or jams
apple butter
home-canned fruits
fresh fruits or berries
frozen unsweetened fruits or berries
dried fruits
chopped nuts or toasted seeds
toasted coconut
wheat germ
Grape Nuts

Or make your own yogurt. Yogurt culture is available in health-food stores, and most packages contain instructions for making yogurt.

Enriched Peanut Butter

Two tablespoons of this spread on a piece of whole-grain toast gives you the protein equivalent of 2 eggs; add a glass of vegetable juice and some fruit and you've got a wholesome breakfast in a flash. Peanut butter is rich in fats and calories, however, so use sparingly.

1 cup peanut butter
½ cup instant powdered milk
2 teaspoons Better Butter (page 300) softened, or oil
3 tablespoons honey (optional)

1. Mix powdered milk with a few drops of water and stir into a paste.
2. Blend into peanut butter and Better Butter, and add honey if desired.

OLDIES BUT GOODIES

Eggs are a quick and easy source of protein and can be used 2 to 3 times a week for breakfast. If you scramble your eggs, watch the butter; and try to stay away from fried eggs, which soak up lots of fat.

Omelets

Simple but elegant, omelets are one of the truly wonderful things that can be done with eggs. You can make a really simple omelet by just mixing up some eggs with a little water or milk, or you can try this richer recipe, which makes 2 large omelets.

4 eggs
2 egg yolks
¼ cup cream or canned milk
½ teaspoon salt
pepper
2 tablespoons fresh chopped chives or parsley
3 tablespoons butter

1. Beat together all ingredients except butter.
2. Gently heat butter in a cast-iron skillet or omelet pan, watching the pan closely. When the butter gets frothy (but before it sizzles), pour in the egg mixture.
3. Let the eggs set for 1 minute. Give the pan a shake to make sure they're not sticking on the bottom.
4. Cover and cook 3 minutes.
5. Remove lid, tilt pan, fold omelet, and cook 1 minute more. Serve immediately.

Poached Eggs

Poached eggs are cooked in boiling water. Heat water to boiling in a wide-mouthed pan (like a Dutch oven). Break no more than 3 eggs into a bowl and slide them into the water, making sure they're widely separated. Fresh eggs should hold together in gently boiling water. Cook, uncovered, for 2 minutes. Spoon a little water over each yolk and cook 30 seconds more. Remove with a slotted spoon.

Lunch

> Breakfast like a king, lunch like a prince and dine like a pauper.
>
> Adelle Davis

Princely lunches can come in a wide variety of disguises —even in brown bags. But whether you're eating your lunch out, in, or in transit, be sure to eat and eat well. Nibbling on a candy bar at 11:00 in the morning, munching on a piece of cheese at noon, and gulping down a cup of instant chicken noodle soup at 2:00 won't do much good for either your insides or your outsides. Snackers tend to think they don't eat much and often complain about how their "low metabolism" contributes to their weight problem. But in six hours of nibbling, it's easy to put away 1,500 calories, which, in one sitting, would be a lot. If you sit down and eat a good meal, you'll probably feel more contentedly full while taking in a lot fewer calories, and your body will be able to put those calories to good use, saving what it doesn't need for later.

Sandwiches and salads can be the basis of hearty, wholesome lunches, but don't forget dinner leftovers. A piece of chicken, a cold cheese enchilada, or a mug of steaming split-pea soup can be the center of a wonderful, elegant lunch. Be sure to have a wide-mouth thermos and plastic Tupperware-type containers for soups, salads, and leftovers.

SANDWICHES AND SANDWICH SPREADS

Sandwiches can make a very satisfying and nutritious lunch, and they travel well to work or meetings or the park for a picnic. Have fresh fruit, fresh vegetables, raisins, nuts, or sunflower seeds as accompaniments.

What should you put in between those two slices of whole-grain bread? The following suggestions only scratch the surface of possible ways to liven up your sandwich fillings:

- For an especially tasty peanut-butter sandwich, mix some sesame seeds and honey with your peanut butter.
- For a salad sandwich, alternate greens, using romaine, red-leaf lettuce, fresh spinach, or sprouts.
- Add slices of boiled egg, tomato, mushrooms, and/or cheese to your sandwiches.
- Put chopped almonds in your chicken-salad sandwich —almonds are also good with egg salad, and we even have some friends who bury almonds in their hamburgers.
- For some extra protein with crunch for almost any sandwich, sprinkle on sunflower seeds.

• Try sliced avocado with cheese sandwiches or with tuna salad.

• Add fresh sliced tomato for color and zip.

• Remember that sliced pickles are wonderful with egg-salad, peanut-butter, or cheese sandwiches.

• Broil some cheese on whole-wheat, rye, or pumper-nickel bread. Hide a thin slice of tomato, onion, apple, or green or red pepper underneath. Add raisins, cashews, and/or walnuts if you feel exotic.

• Experiment with cream cheese mixed with fruit (a ripe banana, for example, or pineapple slices); add a squirt of lemon and some chopped nuts.

• Pack along an orange, an apple, some strawberries, or seedless grapes for dessert.

Blender Mayonnaise

There are at least three advantages to making your own mayonnaise: first, you can use unprocessed, cold-pressed oils; second, you won't be using any additives or preservatives; and third, when you make your own, you'll realize that mayonnaise is basically *fat,* and that realization should help you use it sparingly.

1 egg
1 tablespoon vinegar or lemon juice
½ teaspoon salt
½ teaspoon dry mustard
¾ cup oil

1. Put everything but the oil in the blender.
2. Add 2 tablespoons oil very slowly while blender is at its lowest speed. Pour in the remaining oil in a stream and continue blending for 1 or 2 minutes.

Makes about 1¼ cups.

Tahini with Lemon and Honey

Tahini is to soybeans what peanut butter is to peanuts. You can buy tahini in bulk at most health-food stores and co-ops.

1 cup tahini
½ stalk celery, minced
1 green onion, minced
½ green pepper, minced
½ cup lemon juice
¼ cup soy sauce
3 tablespoons water
1 teaspoon pepper

Mix together until well blended and refrigerate in a Tupper-ware-type container.

Bean Spread

This do-it-yourself spread also makes an excellent base for tacos made with whole-wheat tortillas (see dinner recipes).

1. Mash any leftover beans (pinto, kidney, or other) with a fork, potato masher or dough blender.
2. Salt and pepper to taste and, if desired, spice up with a little cayenne, chili powder, hot sauce, garlic powder, or cumin. And, if you like, add a bit of finely chopped onion and some grated cheese.

SALADS AND DRESSINGS

You can toss a lot of nutritional goodies into a salad. Be creative!

- Try tender dark spinach leaves as an accompaniment for various kinds of lettuce.
- Add chopped green or red cabbage for crunch and color.
- Throw some sesame seeds, sunflower seeds, chopped walnuts, or sliced almonds into your salads.

• Add alfalfa sprouts.

• Add chopped apples and mandarin orange slices to give color and sweetness.

A note on dressings. Most dressings, remember, are high in fat, and that includes most homemade dressings. Look for low-fat dressings in the supermarket. When making your own dressings, try substituting yogurt for half the mayonnaise.

Potato Salad

A refreshing salad for a summer day.

6 medium potatoes
3 eggs, hard-boiled
½ cup chopped onions
1 cup chopped celery

1. Scrub potatoes, boil in skins until tender, drain, and cool.
2. When potatoes are cool enough to handle, cut into small chunks.
3. Chop eggs. Add eggs, onions, and celery to potatoes.
4. Blend with Creamy Yogurt Dressing (following).

Creamy Yogurt Dressing

This dressing is much lower in fat than the usual mayonnaise-based dressings. And no wonder—it takes 3⅓ cups of low-fat yogurt to equal the fat content of 1 *tablespoon* of mayonnaise!

½ cup low-fat yogurt
½ cup instant powdered milk
1 tablespoon honey
2 tablespoons lemon juice
2 tablespoons vinegar
1 teaspoon celery seed
1 teaspoon salt
1 teaspoon prepared mustard

1. Make a smooth paste of yogurt and powdered milk.
2. Stir in remaining ingredients.
3. Pour over Potato Salad, mixing gently.

Yogurt Dressing

Here's another yogurt dressing. This one is delicious on green salads.

1 cup low-fat yogurt
1 teaspoon salt
¼ teaspoon pepper
½ teaspoon dry mustard
1 teaspoon salad herbs

Gently mix all ingredients and chill.

Makes about 1 cup.

Cole Slaw

red and green cabbage
raisins
sunflower seeds
grated carrots
pineapple bits (optional)

Grate cabbage and toss with other ingredients. Serve with Creamy Yogurt Dressing (preceding) to which 1 to 2 teaspoons additional sweetener have been added.

Variation. Add caraway and/or poppy seeds.

Broccoli, Tomato, and Cheese Salad

Great for picnics and potlucks.

1 pound fresh broccoli
2 to 3 tomatoes
6 ounces Cheddar or Monterey jack cheese

1. Steam broccoli until tender. Drain and cool.
2. Chop tomatoes and cheese into bite-size pieces.
3. Toss ingredients together with low-fat cucumber or ranch-style dressing. Yogurt mixed with lemon and honey is another delicious dressing for this salad.

Pineapple–Orange Gel

There's no added sugar in this molded gelatin salad.

1 envelope unflavored gelatin
1 cup orange juice
1 20-ounce can unsweetened pineapple chunks in juice

1. In a medium bowl, sprinkle gelatin over orange juice.
2. Drain the pineapple, saving the juice. Cut each chunk in half lengthwise.
3. Bring pineapple juice to the boiling point, pour over gelatin mixture, and stir until dissolved.
4. Add pineapple chunks. Chill until partly jelled, then stir to distribute chunks.
5. Turn into 6 ½-cup molds or 6 6-ounce custard cups. Chill to eat. Unmold before serving.

Makes about 6 servings.

Mexican Salad

½ cup cooked kidney beans
1 to 2 tablespoons mayonnaise (low-fat or homemade)
2 tablespoons chopped onions
¼ cup diced bell pepper (optional)
dash of chili powder, cumin, and salt to taste

1. Mix all ingredients.
2. Toss with leafy greens and bits of crisp, grilled tortillas (or use leftover homemade tortillas that have been baked until crunchy).
3. Top with grated cheese.

Dinner

". . . and dine like a pauper . . ."

The point isn't to starve, but to eat light. With a full belly you'll have a hard time moving around, planning the next day, dealing with troublesome children, or getting comfortable in bed. The ill effects of a too-large dinner can last into the night and the next day, with all the churning food and stomach acids giving you bad dreams and perhaps a bout of diarrhea or belching in the morning. After all that, who feels like sitting down to a big, steaming breakfast?

Light dinners can be simple, elegant, and colorful. Guests won't turn their noses up, children won't complain, and the cook won't get bored. It's been our experience that as you get used to lighter dinners, you'll begin to prefer them over the heavier, more-difficult-to-digest dinners. But even if you remain a solid meat-and-potatoes eater, you'll still be able to find something in the following recipes that will stretch your food horizons and introduce you to new and wonderful taste sensations.

SOUPS

If you were given the choice between canned and homemade soup, you'd choose the homemade every time. Yet most of us eat canned soups because they're so easy and fast to prepare. Still, soups aren't difficult to make, and you can double or triple a recipe and then freeze the leftovers for a week's worth of nutritious meals.

All the soup recipes included in this section are hearty enough to be a dinner's main course. Served with hot bread and perhaps a salad, soup's hard to beat on a cold winter night.

Turkey-Noodle Soup

6 cups turkey or chicken broth
1 cup whole-wheat noodles
1 cup leftover cooked turkey or chicken
¾ cup sliced mushrooms
2 teaspoons soy sauce

1. Make broth by cooking turkey or chicken bones in water over low heat for several hours. Or use 1 teaspoon chicken bouillon for each cup of water.
2. Bring broth to a boil (removing bones if broth is homemade), add noodles, and cook until tender—about 15 minutes.
3. Add chicken, mushrooms, and soy sauce and simmer for 2 to 5 minutes.

Serves 4 to 6.

Variation. Add any leftover vegetables to the pot for a turkey-based vegetable-noodle soup.

Potato-Clam Chowder

½ cup chopped onion
1 stalk celery, including leaves, finely chopped
oil for sautéeing
2 medium potatoes, scrubbed and diced
2½ cups water
1 can minced clams
1 cup instant powdered milk
1 to 2 teaspoons Better Butter (in Pancakes and Toppings) or margarine
1 teaspoon salt
pepper to taste

1. Sauté onion and celery with a little oil.
2. Add potatoes and 2 cups water. Simmer about 15 minutes, add clams, and continue simmering.
3. Whisk the powdered milk, ½ cup water, Better Butter, salt, and pepper into a thin paste and add slowly to the potato-clam mixture.
4. Heat through. Garnish with parsley, chives, or green onion.

Serves 4 to 5.

Lentil-Barley Soup

½ cup barley
1½ cups uncooked lentils
8 cups water or vegetable stock
½ onion, chopped
1 carrot, chopped
1 stalk celery, chopped
1 small potato, chopped
2 tablespoons oil
2 bay leaves
3 teaspoons salt
½ teaspoon pepper
2 teaspoons vinegar (optional)

Mix all ingredients except vinegar in a soup pot and cook until the lentils are very soft—about 1 hour. Add vinegar just before serving.

Makes about 8 cups.

Edie's Broccoli Bisque

This is a delicious, filling soup that takes less than a half-hour to make. Company will be impressed!

1½ pounds broccoli
1 onion, chopped
1 to 2 teaspoons curry
1 teaspoon salt
pepper to taste
2 13-ounce cans chicken broth
2 tablespoons lime
yogurt (optional)

1. Put all ingredients except last 2 together in a pot. Bring to a boil and simmer for 10 minutes.
2. Put soup in blender and blend until smooth.
3. Add lime just before serving and garnish with a dollop of yogurt.

Serves 4 to 6.

Hearty Split-Pea Soup

3 cups dry green split peas
5 cups water
1 bay leaf
2 teaspoons salt
1 cup minced onion
2 cloves crushed garlic
1 cup chopped celery
2 potatoes, chopped in small pieces
2 cups sliced carrots
2 tablespoons oil
¼ teaspoon dry mustard
¼ teaspoon thyme
parsley, chopped

1. Combine split peas, water, bay leaf, and salt in a soup pot and simmer for 3 to 4 hours. Remove bay leaf.
2. Sauté onion, garlic, celery, potatoes, and carrots in oil, adding a little water if necessary. When vegetables are tender, add to the soup.
3. Fifteen minutes before serving add dry mustard and thyme.
4. Garnish with parsley.

Makes 6 hearty servings.

Tomato Soup

4 cups fresh or canned tomatoes
1 cup chopped onion
1 carrot, grated
1 cup chopped celery
2 tablespoons oil
½ teaspoon oregano
1 teaspoon basil
3 cups hot vegetable stock
1½ teaspoons salt
pepper to taste

1. Cut the tomatoes into small pieces or, if you don't want the skins in the soup, rub the tomatoes over a grater to get the juice and the pulp. Or peel the tomatoes by putting them in boiling water until the skins split, which takes only a few seconds. The skin will slip off easily.
2. Sauté the onion in oil with the carrot and celery until onion is soft. Remove to a soup pot.

3. Add oregano, basil, and tomatoes to the vegetables and simmer gently for 15 minutes. At this point, you can purée the soup in a blender or food mill if you want a smoother, creamier texture.

4. Add the hot stock, bring the soup to a boil, and simmer over low heat for 5 minutes. Season with salt and pepper.

Makes 8 cups.

Creamy Tomato Soup

Follow the recipe above, but cut back on the herbs, using ¼ teaspoon oregano, ½ teaspoon basil, and 1 teaspoon salt.

Add 1 cup powdered skim milk to part of the stock or to the tomato–vegetable mixture. Mix well, add to the remaining ingredients, and heat thoroughly but do not boil.

LESS-MEAT MAIN DISHES

Mexican Rice

An easy-to-fix spicy rice-and-meat dish. Serve with cole slaw or a green salad.

½ to 1 pound lean ground beef
1 cup uncooked whole-grain rice
1 small onion, chopped fine
1 tablespoon oil
½ green pepper, chopped
1 teaspoon salt
1 to 2 teaspoons chili powder
1 16-ounce can tomatoes
2 cups water

1. Brown meat, rice, and onion in oil. Or omit oil and add enough water to keep the mixture from sticking.

2. Add remaining ingredients and mix well. Cover tightly and simmer until rice is done—about 1 to 1½ hours. Don't stir while mixture simmers or it will become sticky.

Serves 4 to 6.

Chicken and Vegetable Stir-Fry

This is a delicious variation of chicken chow mein and a good way to use up any overflow zucchini from your garden.

1 chicken breast
2 tablespoons cornstarch
5 tablespoons soy sauce
1/8 teaspoon garlic powder
2 tablespoons oil
2 stalks celery, sliced diagonally in ¼-inch pieces
1 medium zucchini, sliced
1 medium onion, chopped
½ to 1 pound mung bean sprouts
1 8-ounce can pineapple chunks

1. Cut chicken breast into strips.
2. Coat strips with 1 tablespoon cornstarch, 1 tablespoon soy sauce, and garlic powder.
3. Let strips sit for 10 to 15 minutes, then stir-fry 2 to 3 minutes in 1 tablespoon oil. (You can use less oil if you add just a little water.) Set aside.
4. Stir-fry celery, zucchini, onion, and bean sprouts in 1 tablespoon oil.
5. Drain juice from pineapple chunks into a small bowl. Add enough water to the juice to measure 1 cup. Mix with 1 tablespoon cornstarch and 4 tablespoons soy sauce.
6. Mix juice, vegetables, chicken, and pineapple and cook until thickened.
7. Serve over hot whole-grain rice or whole-wheat noodles.

Serves 4 to 5.

Chicken Casserole

The chicken, vegetables, grains, and nuts make this casserole a real "meal-in-a-bowl." Serve with a tossed green salad or raw vegetables, with a gelatin-fruit salad as a dessert.

1 cup diced cooked chicken or turkey
1 cup thinly sliced celery
2 teaspoons chopped onion
1½ cups cooked whole-grain rice (½ cup uncooked)
½ cup chopped walnuts
1 can cream of chicken soup
¼ teaspoon pepper
1 tablespoon lemon juice
3 tablespoons low-fat mayonnaise
¼ cup water
3 hard-boiled eggs, sliced

1. Preheat oven to 450°.
2. In a bowl, combine all but last 3 ingredients.
3. Mix mayonnaise with water and add to chicken mixture.
4. Gently stir in the sliced eggs.
5. Turn mixture into lightly greased casserole and bake for 15 minutes.

Variation. Top with 1 cup crushed whole-wheat crackers. Serves 4 to 6.

MEATLESS MAIN DISHES

Cheese Lasagna

Add a tossed salad and you've got a filling meal.

6 to 8 ounces whole-wheat lasagna, cooked until tender
1 large onion, chopped
¼ teaspoon garlic powder
2 cups tomato sauce or canned tomatoes
1 teaspoon oregano
½ teaspoon basil
¼ cup chopped fresh parsley or 1½ tablespoons dried
1½ teaspoons salt
½ pound sliced mushrooms, sautéed in oil or water
¾ cup small dried red beans, cooked until tender
½ pound mozzarella cheese, sliced thin
1 cup ricotta or cottage cheese
½ cup freshly grated Parmesan cheese

1. Rinse the cooked noodles in cold water so they won't stick together. Set aside.

2. Sauté the onion in 1 to 2 tablespoons of water until soft and transparent, but not browned. Stir in the garlic powder, tomato sauce, oregano, basil, parsley, and salt. Simmer this sauce about ½ hour, stirring often, until thickened. Stir in the sautéed mushrooms and cooked beans.

3. Preheat oven to 375°.

4. To assemble the lasagna: Place a layer of noodles on the bottom of a shallow baking dish or casserole, put ⅓ of the tomato sauce over the noodles, spread a layer of ricotta or cottage cheese over the sauce, and put on a layer of mozzarella. Sprinkle ⅓ of the Parmesan over all and repeat the layers twice more, ending with the remaining Parmesan.

5. Bake for 20 minutes. Let stand for 10 minutes before serving.

Serves 8.

Spanish Rice

Serve this colorful, crunchy rice dish with a green salad and hot bread. Or try it as an accompaniment to your favorite chicken dish.

1 cup uncooked brown rice
1 onion, minced
1 teaspoon oil
2 cups vegetable stock or water
1 cup finely diced celery
1 large green pepper, diced
3 medium tomatoes or 1 cup canned tomatoes, chopped
1 teaspoon salt
½ teaspoon oregano
½ teaspoon basil
dash of pepper
pinch of chili powder
¾ cup grated Cheddar or Monterey jack cheese

1. Bring rice, onion, oil, and stock to a boil and simmer, covered, over low heat for 25 minutes.

2. Add remaining ingredients except cheese. Simmer

another 20 minutes or until rice is well cooked.

3. Sprinkle cheese on top.

Makes 4 cups.

Cheesy Vegetable Enchiladas

1 dozen tortillas (following recipes)

Sauce:

3 to 4 cups tomato sauce
½ to 1 teaspoon cumin
½ teaspoon chili powder
3 tablespoons oil

Filling:

1 onion, minced
1 green pepper, chopped fine
1 cup finely chopped celery
1 cup chopped parsley
oil for sautéeing
2 cups coarsely chopped zucchini
2 cups green beans, chopped small
cornstarch
1 teaspoon salt
dash of cumin
dash of chili powder
dash of garlic
1 cup grated Cheddar and/or Monterey jack cheese

1. Combine sauce ingredients, bring to a boil, and simmer.

2. Sauté onion, pepper, celery, and parsley in oil. Add zucchini and beans and cook, covered, until tender. If mixture is very juicy, add cornstarch to thicken.

3. Add ¾ cup of the sauce, add seasonings, and set aside.

4. Preheat oven to 350°.

5. Fill each tortilla with a generous ⅓ cup of the vegetable mixture. Roll up the tortillas and place in a baking dish, seam side down, close together, and cover with remaining sauce. Top with cheese and bake until the sauce bubbles.

Variations. If you're partial to bean enchiladas, replace part or all of the zucchini with seasoned pinto, kidney, or other beans. Or substitute any vegetables you choose, as long as they are coarsely grated or chopped fine.

Serves 6.

Whole-Wheat Tortillas

2 cups whole-wheat flour
½ cup plus 1 tablespoon warm water
¼ teaspoon baking powder
1 teaspoon salt
2 tablespoons oil

1. Mix all ingredients together to make a very stiff dough.

2. Knead dough for 5 minutes, cover, and let stand for 10 to 15 minutes.

3. Shape dough into about 12 small balls and roll them out into thin 6-inch circles.

4. Fry on lightly greased griddle.

Makes 12 tortillas.

Corn Tortillas

1½ cups water
¼ cup oil
1 cup cornmeal
1¼ cups whole-wheat flour
1 teaspoon salt

1. Bring water to a boil, add half the oil, stir in cornmeal, cover, and cook slowly, over low heat, for 5 minutes. Remove from heat and stir in remaining oil.

2. Mix in flour and salt and adjust water (or flour) to make a soft dough.

3. Make 12 2-inch balls. Flatten them and roll into thin 6- or 7-inch circles.

4. Fry on ungreased griddle until lightly browned.

Makes 12 tortillas.

Tacos

lettuce, chopped
tomatoes, chopped
cheese, grated

Spread tortillas (preceding recipes) with Bean Spread (page 307), and sprinkle with tomatoes, lettuce, and cheese.

Variations. Add olives, peppers, refried beans, sautéed hamburger meat, even bean sprouts!

Spinach-Rice Casserole

This casserole, which is somewhat like a soufflé, makes a wonderful company dish. Serve with hot bran muffins or whole-wheat bread. When cooking the rice, you might want to prepare more than just the amount required here—rice freezes well, so you can have enough in the freezer for the next time you make a rice-based casserole.

2 cups cooked brown rice (about ¾ cup uncooked)
½ to ¾ cup grated Cheddar cheese
2 eggs, beaten
1 tablespoon chopped parsley
½ teaspoon salt
¼ teaspoon pepper
1 pound fresh spinach, chopped
2 tablespoons wheat germ
1 tablespoon melted butter

1. Cook the rice.
2. Preheat the oven to 350°.
3. Combine the cooked rice and cheese.
4. In another bowl, combine eggs, parsley, salt, and pepper.
5. Stir the 2 mixtures together, add spinach, and pour into an oiled casserole.
6. Mix wheat germ with melted butter and sprinkle over the top of the casserole.
7. Bake for 35 minutes.

Serves 4.

Barley Casserole

This dish is a tasty introduction to a delicious and nutritious grain: barley.

2 cups chicken broth
1 cup uncooked whole-grain rice
1 cup barley or lentils
1 cup grated Cheddar or Monterey jack cheese
½ cup chopped onion
1 teaspoon oregano
½ teaspoon salt
½ teaspoon basil
pepper to taste

1. Preheat oven to 350°.

2. Mix all ingredients together, put into casserole, and bake, covered, for 50 to 60 minutes.

Serves 5 to 6.

Pizza

Pizza isn't hard to make, and it's fun to experiment with different topping combinations.

Dough:
2 packages dry yeast
1 cup warm water (110 to 115°)
1 teaspoon honey
1 teaspoon salt
1½ cups flour (half whole-wheat, half unbleached white)
2 tablespoons oil

Sauce:
1 15-ounce can tomato sauce
½ onion, chopped
dash of garlic powder
1 teaspoon oregano
½ teaspoon basil
¼ teaspoon salt

Toppings:
grated cheese
tomatoes
olives
peppers
mushrooms
onions
pineapple chunks

1. You'll be making the dough first. Soften and dissolve yeast in water; add honey and salt and let sit for 5 minutes.

2. Add flour and stir only until blended. Coat with oil, place in a covered bowl, and allow to rise in a warm place for 20 minutes.

3. Simmer sauce ingredients together while dough is rising.

To assemble pizza:

1. Preheat oven to 375°.

2. Divide dough in half and roll out into 2 large pizza pans (or divide into 4 sections and spread out in pie pans).

3. Top with sauce and your favorite toppings.

4. Bake for about 15 minutes. Use the lower shelf of your oven so the crust will brown before the cheese melts.

Eggplant Parmesan

Most recipes for eggplant Parmesan are extremely high in calories. This one isn't, yet it's still rich and delicious. Use fresh Parmesan for best results.

½ cup whole-wheat flour
1 teaspoon salt
2 eggs, slightly beaten
¼ cup milk
2½ cups whole-wheat bread crumbs or crushed whole-wheat crackers
dash of pepper
¼ teaspoon oregano
1 medium eggplant
1½ cups tomato sauce
½ cup grated Parmesan cheese
1 cup grated mozzarella cheese

1. Preheat oven to 350°.
2. In 3 bowls, into which eggplant slices will be dipped, combine:
   whole-wheat flour with ½ teaspoon salt;
   eggs with milk;
   bread crumbs or crushed crackers with ½ teaspoon salt, pepper, and oregano.
3. Cut eggplant into ¼-inch slices. (It's not necessary to peel the eggplant.) Dip slices into each mixture in turn, coating them completely.
4. Layer the eggplant slices in a 9-×-13-inch baking dish. Slices can overlap, but don't cover them up completely.
5. Sprinkle each layer with tomato sauce and Parmesan, reserving a bit of the Parmesan for topping.
6. Cover tightly and bake for 30 to 45 minutes, or until eggplant is tender.
7. Top with mozzarella and remaining Parmesan. Return uncovered to the oven and bake just until cheese melts.

Serves 4 to 6.

DESSERTS

Desserts can be nutritious, healthy, and almost sugar-free. Homemade fruit-gelatin molds, fruited yogurt, puddings, custards, and various fruits and melons are examples. The dessert recipes we've included in this section were chosen because of their scaled-down sweet and fat content and for their nutritious additives like whole-grain flours, nuts, seeds, and wheat germ.

Carrot-Raisin Cake

A moist, rich, and spicy cake that is always a big hit with the kids.

1 cup grated carrots
1 cup raisins
¼ cup honey
¼ cup artificial sweetener
2 teaspoons cinnamon
2 teaspoons allspice
½ teaspoon nutmeg
¼ teaspoon cloves
1 teaspoon salt
2 tablespoons margarine
1½ cups water
1½ cups whole-wheat flour
1 teaspoon baking soda
½ cup wheat germ
½ cup chopped walnuts
2 egg yolks, beaten
2 egg whites, beaten stiff

1. Preheat oven to 300°.
2. Cook carrots, raisins, honey, sweetener, spices, salt, and margarine in the water for 10 minutes. Cool.
3. Mix together the flour, baking soda, wheat germ, and walnuts, and combine with carrot mixture. Add egg yolks, then fold in egg whites.
4. Pour into 2 small well-greased loaf pans.
5. Bake for 45 minutes.

Makes 2 small loaves.

Apple Crisp

Filling:

5 apples (tart green apples are best)
1 teaspoon grated lemon rind or
1 teaspoon lemon juice
2 tablespoons whole-wheat flour
¼ cup raisins
water or apple juice

Topping:

1½ cups rolled oats
½ cup toasted wheat germ
½ teaspoon salt
2 teaspoons cinnamon
¼ cup honey
3 tablespoons oil

1. Preheat oven to 375°.
2. Slice but do not peel apples, and mix them with lemon rind or juice, cinnamon, flour, and raisins.
3. Place apple mixture in a greased 9-×-13-inch baking dish, adding enough water or apple juice to cover the bottom.
4. Mix topping ingredients in a bowl and press on top of apples. Bake for 25 minutes, or until apples are soft.

Serves 6.

Banana Pudding

A simple, wholesome dessert that is delicious as is, or when served with fresh berries or orange slices.

2 tablespoons honey
2 tablespoons flour
pinch of salt
2 eggs, well beaten
2 cups milk
1 teaspoon imitation vanilla
3 bananas
½ cup chopped nuts (optional)

1. In a saucepan, mix honey, flour, salt, and eggs, beating well.
2. Add milk and cook over medium-high heat, stirring constantly, until mixture thickens.
3. Remove from heat, add vanilla, and set aside to cool.
4. Add sliced bananas and, if desired, chopped nuts.

Baked Custard

This light, creamy custard is a wonderful dessert after a heavy meal. It also makes a delicious between-meal snack, or you can add it to your breakfast cereal.

1 cup 2 percent milk
1 cup water
⅔ cup instant milk powder
2 to 3 tablespoons honey
1 teaspoon imitation vanilla
2 eggs

1. Preheat oven to 325°.
2. Blend or beat all ingredients together until well mixed, and pour into a lightly greased casserole or baking dish.
3. Place casserole in a pan filled half-way up with hot water.
4. Bake for about 50 minutes, cool, and refrigerate to set until solid.

Variations. Substitute any of the following for the vanilla: 1 tablespoon carob powder, ½ cup unsweetened carob chips, or ½ cup lightly toasted unsweetened coconut.

Fresh Strawberry Yogurt

Another simple dessert that can double as a between-meal snack or breakfast food.

1 box strawberries, washed and sliced
2 cups homemade yogurt
½ cup unsweetened apple juice

Purée half the strawberries, 1 cup yogurt, and apple juice in blender. Stir in remaining strawberries and serve over, or mixed with, the rest of the yogurt.

Makes about 5 cups.

Frozen Yogurt

Commercial ice cream can have some really horrendous ingredients in it, including diethyl glucol (a chemical used in antifreeze and paint remover), piperonal (a chemical substitute for vanilla that is also used to kill lice), and, in nut-flavored ice creams, butraldehyde (which is one of the common ingredients in rubber cement). And that's only a partial listing.

Try this easy and delicious recipe for frozen yogurt and take comfort in the knowledge that when you make your own ice cream or yogurt, you know exactly what goes into it.

1 cup (8 ounces) plain yogurt
½ cup milk or light cream
1 cup fruit or berries
2 tablespoons honey
1 to 2 tablespoons sweetener (optional)

1. Place all ingredients in a blender and mix for a few seconds until smooth.
2. Pour mixture into a 10-×-6-×-2-inch dish. Place in freezer and stir briskly several times during freezing. The yogurt will be ready to serve after about 2 hours.

Makes 4 servings.

Pumpkin Cookies

Pumpkin cookies may sound strange, but are they ever good! This recipe calls for a lot of spices—the pumpkin and whole-wheat flour need them, so don't skimp. Save these cookies, though, for special occasions, since they contain a lot of fat in the margarine.

½ cup margarine
¼ to ⅓ cup honey
¼ to ⅓ cup sweetener
2 eggs
1 cup canned pumpkin
2 teaspoons imitation vanilla
2 teaspoons grated orange rind
½ cup unsweetened applesauce or 1 apple, grated
1½ cups whole-wheat flour
½ cup wheat germ
2 teaspoons baking powder
1 teaspoon baking soda
½ teaspoon salt
2 teaspoons nutmeg
3 teaspoons cinnamon
3 teaspoons allspice
½ cup chopped walnuts
1 cup carob chips

1. Preheat oven to 350°.
2. Cream together margarine, honey, and sweetener. Beat in eggs, pumpkin, vanilla, orange rind, and applesauce.
3. Mix dry ingredients and add to creamed mixture, stirring well.
4. Add walnuts and carob pieces. Mix thoroughly.
5. Drop dough by teaspoons onto well-greased cookie sheets. Bake 12 to 15 minutes or until lightly browned. Remove from cookie sheets while still warm and cool on racks. After they're cool, these cookies can be bagged and frozen—they're delicious right out of the freezer.

Makes about 4 dozen cookies.

Crunchy Oatmeal Cookies

These cookies are so chock-full of good things that, for people who don't need to worry about the fat in the margarine, they can double as a between-meal snack. They tend to be somewhat crumbly, though, so try adding a little extra water, or eat them straight from the freezer.

½ cup margarine
¼ cup honey
¼ cup sweetener
1 egg, slightly beaten
3 teaspoons imitation vanilla
½ teaspoon salt
½ cup whole-wheat flour
¾ teaspoon baking powder
1 cup wheat germ
1½ cups rolled oats
¾ cups raisins
¾ cup toasted sunflower seeds or chopped walnuts
¼ cup water

1. Preheat oven to 375°.
2. Cream together the margarine, honey, and sweetener. Add the egg, vanilla, and salt and beat well.
3. In a separate bowl, stir flour, baking powder, wheat germ, and rolled oats together. Blend well with creamed mixture, and stir in raisins and nuts, adding ¼ cup water to hold the mixture together. Let sit for 5 to 10 minutes before baking.
4. Place by tablespoonfuls on greased cookie sheets. Flatten slightly and bake for 10 to 12 minutes.

Makes about 3 dozen cookies.

SNACKS

Nutritious snacks are an essential part of the diet for sobriety. Positioned between major meals (in mid-morning, in the afternoon, and after dinner), they help sustain energy and motivation. The ideal snack contains a small portion of protein, fruit, and vegetable.

Snacks don't have to be complicated. Whole-wheat or sesame crackers with peanut butter and an apple make a delicious, nutritious snack, as does celery stuffed with peanut butter, tunafish, or cream cheese. Or try leftover popovers stuffed with cheese or tuna. Leftovers, in fact, can make terrific snacks: Try a slice of pizza, a cup of split-pea soup, or a whole-wheat tortilla spread with Bean Spread (page 307). The high-protein milkshake in the breakfast section (page 301) also makes an easy, nutritious snack.

Don't underestimate the following high-energy snack recipes. It will take only a handful of trail snack or one or two peanut-butter balls with a glass of vegetable or fruit juice to provide enough "go" to last until your next meal.

Peanut-Butter Balls

Be sure to use the "natural" peanut butter rather than the lard-hardened commercial brands.

½ cup peanut butter
1 to 2 tablespoons honey
¼ cup raisins, chopped fine
¼ cup dates, chopped fine
¼ cup instant powdered milk
carob powder or shredded coconut

1. Blend together peanut butter, honey, raisins, and dates.
2. Stir in powdered milk.
3. Shape mixture into small balls and roll in carob powder or coconut.
4. Store in an air-tight container in refrigerator.

Variation. Add 1 cup Crunchy Granola (page 291).

Makes 2 dozen balls.

Trail Snack

1 cup each: nuts (almonds, walnuts, peanuts, or others)
seeds (sesame, sunflower, pumpkin, or others)
raisins and other dried fruit
coconut
carob chips, unsweetened

Mix together and refrigerate.

Carob Drink

4 cups 2 percent milk
2 to 3 tablespoons carob powder
½ teaspoon vanilla
½ teaspoon cinnamon
2 tablespoons honey

Blend all ingredients in a blender until frothy. Drink cold, or heat up as a substitute for hot chocolate.

Variation. Substitute a ripe banana for the honey.

Serves 4.

APPENDIX 1

Drugs That "Wake Up" the Alcoholic's Addiction

PART 1: DRUGS THAT AFFECT THE CENTRAL NERVOUS SYSTEM

Analgesics (pain medication)

- Codeine
- Codeine compounds
  - Aspirin with codeine
    - Empirin with codeine
    - Fiorinal with codeine
    - Percogesic with codeine
    - Tylenol with codeine
    - Tylox
- Darvon and Darvon compounds
- Darvocet
- Fiorinal
- Midrin
- Narcotics: opiate derivatives and synthetics
  - Codeine and codeine compounds (above)
  - Demerol
  - Dilaudid
  - Methadone
  - Mepergan
  - Meperidine
  - Morphine
  - Talwin
- Percocet
- Percodan

Anesthetics

- All general anesthetics
- *Local* anesthetics are safe if not otherwise contraindicated

*Anticonvulsants**

- Clonopine
- Mebaral
- Mysoline
- Tegretol
- Valium

Antidepressants

- Adapin
- Amitriptyline
- Asendin
- Aventyl
- Deprol
- Elavil
- Etrafon
- Limbitrol
- Ludiomil
- Marplan
- Meprobamate
- Nardil
- Norpramin
- Parnate
- Pertofrane
- Sinequan
- Tofranil
- Triavil
- Vivactil

Antidiarrhea medications

- Donnagel-PG
- Lomotil
- Paregoric
- Other opiate-derivative or opioid types

Antihistamines (decongestants)

- Many over-the-counter and prescription varieties (because of their secondary effect of drowsiness, antihistamine preparations are suspected of having a low-level effect on the central nervous system)

DRUGS THAT AFFECT THE CENTRAL NERVOUS SYSTEM (continued)

Decongestants *preferred* for alcoholics include
- Pseudoepinephrine agents
- Sudafed

Antinauseants

- Atarax
- Compazine
- Phenergan
- Vesprin
- Vistaril
- Others with antihistamine properties (same caution as above)
  - Antivert
  - Dramamine
  - Merezine
  - Tigan

Antispasmodics

- Belladenal
- Bellergal
- Combid
- Donnatal
- Librax
- Pathibamate
- Valpin PB
- Others with antihistamine properties (came caution as above)
  - Bentyl

Bronchial dilators

- Alcohol-based inhalators
- Bronchial dilators in liquid (elixir) form
- Bronchial dilators with phenobarbital or other sedative combinations
  - Marax
  - Mudrane
  - Quadrinal
  - Tedral
  - Theofedral
  - Valpin

Cough and cold medicines

- All alcohol-based expectorants, cough and cold preparations
- All antihistamine decongestants: use same caution as under antihistamines
- Cough suppressants with narcotic compounds
  - A.P.C. with codeine
  - Actifed-C
  - Hydocan
  - Tussionex tablets
- Cough suppressants with non-narcotic compounds but with C.N.S. effects:
  - Dextromethorphan (DM)
  - Formula 44 cough discs
  - CoTylenol tablets and capsules
- Expectorants and cough medicines recommended as *safe*
  - Glycotuss tablets
  - SSKI (Potassium Iodide Drops)
  - Tessalon

Muscle relaxants

- Dantrium
- Flexeril
- Norflex
- Norgesic
- Robaxin
- Soma
- Valium

Sedatives/sleeping pills

- All barbiturate medication
  - Amytal
  - Butisol
  - Nembutal
  - Pentobarbital
  - Pentothal
  - Secobarbital
  - Seconal
  - Tuinal

- Non-barbiturate sedatives
  - Ativan
  - Dalmane
  - Equanil
  - Hydroxyzine
  - Mepergan
  - Noludar
  - Phenergan

Stimulants

- Amphetamines
  - Desoxyn
  - Dexedrine
- Non-amphetamine diet pills
- Parnate
- Pertofrane
- Ritalin
- Tofranil

Tonics

- All alcohol-based elixirs

Tranquilizers

- Benzodiazepines
  - Ativan
  - Librium
  - Limbitrol
  - Serax
  - Tranxene
  - Valium
- Hydroxyzines
  - Atarax
  - Hydroxyzine
  - Vistaril
- Meprobamate and combinations
  - Deprol
  - Equanil
  - Milpath
  - Miltown
- Phenothiazines
  - Chlorpromzine
  - Etrafon
  - Mellaril
  - Prolixin
  - Serentil
  - Stelazine
  - Thorazine
  - Triavil
  - Vesprin
- Others
  - Haldol
  - Navane
  - Taractan
  - Loxitane
  - Moban

Note: This is not a complete listing of drugs that affect the central nervous system, but includes common drugs in major categories for which alcoholics need to exercise discretion and caution. In all over-the-counter drugs, read labels carefully, and for medicines prescribed by your doctor ask for information regarding contents.

*Consult with your doctor and/or alcoholism specialist before changing anticonvulsant medications.

PART 2: MEDICATIONS CONTAINING ALCOHOL COMMONLY STOCKED IN HOSPITALS AND PHARMACIES

Drug	Percentage of Alcohol
Actol Expectorant Syrup	12.5
Alertonic	0.45
Alurate Elixir	20.0
Ambenyl Expectorant	5.0
Anahist	0.5
Anaspaz—Pb Liquid	15.0
Aromatic Elixir	22.0
Asbron Elixir	15.0
Atarax Syrup	0.5
Bactrim Suspension	0.3
Belladonna Tr.	67.0
Benadryl Elixir	14.0
Bentyl—Pb Syrup	19.0
Benylin Expectorant	5.0
Brondecon Elixir	20.0
Bronkelixir	19.0
Butibel Elixir	7.0
Calcidrine Syrup	6.0
Carbrital Elixir	18.0
Cas Evac	18.0
Cascara Sagroda (Aromatic)	18.0
Cerose & Cerose DM Expectorant	2.5
Cheracol & Cheracol D	3.0
Chlor-Trimeton Syrup	7.0
Choledyl Elixir	20.00
Citra Forte Syrup	2.0
Coldene Cough Syrup	15.0
Cologel Liquid	5.0
Conar Expectorant	5.0
Copavin Cmpd Elixir	7.0
Coryban D	7.5
Cosanyl DM & Cosanyl Syrup	6.0
Darvon—N Suspension	1.0
Decadron Elixir	5.0
Demazin Syrup	7.5
Dexedrine Elixir	10.0
Dilaudid Cough Syrup	5.0
Dimacol Liquid	4.75
Dimetane Elixir	3.0
Dimetane Expectorant	3.5
Dimetane Expectorant—D.C.	3.5
Dimetapp Elixir	2.3
Donnagel Suspension	3.8
Donnagel PG Suspension	5.0
Donnatal Elixir	23.0
Doxinate Liquid	5.0
Dramamine Liquid	5.0
Elixir Theophylline	20.0
Elixophy	20.0
Elixophylline—K1	10.0
Ephedrine Sulfate Syrup U.S.P.	3.0
Ephedrine Sulfate Syrup—Note U.S.P.	12.0
Feosol Elixir	5.0
Fer-In-Sol Syrup	5.0
Fer-In-Sol Drops	0.2
Geriplex—FS	18.0
Gevrabon Liquid	18.0
Hycotuss Expectorant & Syrup	10.0

Drug	*Percentage of Alcohol*
Hydryllin Comp	5.0
Iberet Liquid	1.0
Ipecac Syrup	2.0
Isuprel Comp. Elixir	19.0
Kaochlor	3.8
Kaon Elixir	5.0
Kay-Ciel Elixir	4.0
Lanoxin Elixir Pediatric	10.0
Lomotil (liquid)	15.0
Luffylin—GG Elixir	17.0
Marax Syrup	5.0
Mediatric Liquid	15.0
Mellaril Concentrate	3.0
Mesopin Elixir	12.5
Minocin Syrup	5.0
Modane Liquid	5.0
Mol Iron Liquid	4.75
Nembutal Elixir	18.0
Nico—Metrazol Elixir	15.0
Nicol Elixir	10.0
Novahistine Elixir	5.00
Novahistine Expectorant	5.0
Novahistine DH	5.0
Novahistine DMX	10.0
Nyquil Cough Syrup	25.0
Organidin Elixir	23.75
Ornacol Liquid	8.0
Paregoric Tincture	45.0
Parapectolin	0.69
Parelixir	18.0
P.B.Z. Expectorant with Codeine and Ephedrine	6.0
P.B.Z. Expectorant with Ephedrine	6.0
Periactin Syrup	5.0
Pertussin 8 Hour Syrup	9.5
Phenergan Expectorant, Plain	7.0
Phenergan Expectorant with Codeine	7.0
Phenergan Expectorant V.C., Plain	7.0
Phenergan Expectorant V.C., with Codeine	7.0
Phenergan Expectorant, Pediatric	7.0
Phenergan Syrup Fortis (25 mg)	1.5
Phenobarbital Elixir	14.0
Polarmine Expectorant	7.2
Potassium Chloride Sol. Standard (a no-alcohol solution can be requested)	10.0
Propadrine Elixir HC1	16.0
Quibron Elixir	15.0
Robitussin Syrup	3.5
Robitussin A.C. Syrup	3.5
Robitussin PE	1.4
Robitussin D.M. and Robitussin C.F.	1.4
Roniacol Elixir	8.6
Rondec D.M.Syrup and Drops	0.6
Serpasil Elixir	12.0
Tedral Elixir	15.0
Temaril Syrup	5.7
Terpin Hydrate Elixir	42.0
Terpin Hydrate Elixir with Codeine	42.0
Theo Organidin Elixir	15.0
Theolixir (Elixir Theophylline)	20.0
Triaminic Expectorant	5.0
Triaminic Expectorant D.H.	5.0
Tuss-Ornade Syrup	7.5
Tussar S.F. Syrup	12.0
Tussar-2 Syrup	5.0
Tussend Liquid	5.0

Drug	Percentage of Alcohol
Tussi-Organidin Expectorant	15.0
Tylenol Drops	7.0
Tylenol with Codeine Elixir	7.0
Tylenol Elixir	7.0
Ulo—Syrupp	6.65
Valadol Liquid	9.0
Valpin—PB Elixir & Valpin	5.3
Vicks Formula 44	10.0
Vita Metrazol Elixir	15.0

NOTES:

1. Mouthwashes—Scope, Listerine, Cepacol, Colgate 100, Micrin—all have approximately 15–25% alcohol.
2. All elixirs contain some alcohol.
3. Liquids that do not contain alcohol:

Chloraseptic mouthwash/gargle	Kaopectate and Parget, etc.
Liquiprin (acetaminophen)	Sudafed Syrup
Dilantin Suspension	Actified Syrup
Alupent Syrup	Triaminic Syrup
	Naldecon Syrup
	Nydrazid Syrup

Courtesy of
Milam Recovery Centers, Inc.
1421 Minor Ave.
Seattle, WA 98101

APPENDIX 2

Taking Drugs in Crises

Many recovering alcoholics have needlessly relapsed and started drinking again after taking central nervous system (CNS) drugs in unavoidable situations like accidents, injuries, or surgery. The following steps will help recovering alcoholics prepare themselves and protect their sobriety when exposed to CNS medication.

1. First, it's essential that the alcoholic fully understand why major pain medications and general anesthetics are dangerous to sobriety.* See pages 43 to 44.

2. If you are scheduled for surgery in which CNS drugs will be used and are unavoidable, plan a course of restabilization. It's important to do this before you are exposed to the drug(s), since you won't be thinking very clearly once you're under the influence of the medication.

The best and safest plan is to return to your in-patient alcoholism treatment facility after you've been released from the hospital where you were treated for the illness, accident, or surgery. A two- to three-day stay, under the care and protection of staff who understand alcoholism and the consequences of using CNS medication, will help your body readjust and stabilize itself.

For many alcoholics, however, this may not be feasible, and here are some suggestions for such cases.

(a) Don't take prescription CNS drugs home from the hospital, if at all possible. Extend your stay in the hospital if your doctor feels that you need to continue on major pain medications, sedatives, or sleeping pills.

(b) Once released from the hospital, have someone stay with you in the first week of home recovery. This will help protect you from the power of the addiction (reawakened by exposure to the CNS drugs), which could manipulate you into getting more drugs (or alcohol) in this unstable phase.

(c) Increase your vitamin C to 2 to 4 grams a day for four or five days if there are no medical contraindications. Vitamin C will help detoxify your system naturally.

(d) Follow a good, balanced diet (see Chapter 7) and don't give in to cravings for such common offending foods as sugar, caffeine, and junk foods.

3. Alert your family or a close friend to the above plan in case unexpected tragedy should occur, exposing you to CNS drugs. Then, they can take the steps necessary to protect you and your sobriety.

*_Local_ anesthetics that simply numb the skin are safe for the alcoholic.

APPENDIX 3

Recommended Daily Dietary Allowances (1980)

Food and Nutrition Board
National Research Council
National Academy of Sciences

				Fat-Soluble Vitamins			Water-Soluble Vitamins							Minerals					
Age	Weight (pounds)	Height (inches)	Protein (grams)	Vitamin A (mcg in retinol equivalents)*	Vitamin D (mcg)*	Vitamin E (mg in alpha-tocopherol equivalents)*	Vitamin C (mg)	Thiamine (mg)	Riboflavin (mg)	Niacin (mg in niacin equivalents)*	Vitamin B-6 (mg)	Folacin (mcg)	Vitamin B-12 (mcg)	Calcium (mg)	Phosphorus (mg)	Magnesium (mg)	Iron (mg)	Zinc (mg)	Iodine (mcg)
Males																			
11–14	99	62	45	1000	10	8	50	1.4	1.6	18	1.8	400	3.0	1200	1200	350	18	15	150
15–18	145	69	56	1000	10	10	60	1.4	1.7	18	2.0	400	3.0	1200	1200	400	18	15	150
19–22	154	70	56	1000	7.5	10	60	1.5	1.7	19	2.2	400	3.0	800	800	350	10	15	150
23–50	154	70	56	1000	5	10	60	1.4	1.6	18	2.2	400	3.0	800	800	350	10	15	150
51 +	154	70	56	1000	5	10	60	1.2	1.4	16	2.2	400	3.0	800	800	350	10	15	150

Females																				
11–14	101	62	46	800	10	8	50	1.1	1.3	15	1.8	400	3.0	1200	1200	300	18	15	150
15–18	120	64	46	800	10	8	60	1.1	1.3	14	2.0	400	3.0	1200	1200	300	18	15	150
19–22	120	64	44	800	7.5	8	60	1.1	1.3	14	2.0	400	3.0	800	800	300	18	15	150
23–50	120	64	44	800	5	8	60	1.0	1.2	13	2.0	400	3.0	800	800	300	18	15	150
51+	120	64	44	800	5	8	60	1.0	1.2	13	2.0	400	3.0	800	800	300	10	15	150

*This is the new unit of measurement for this vitamin in the 1980 update of RDA's.

Professionals will want to know that the measurement for

Vitamin A, 1 retinol equivalent = 1 mcg retinol or 6 mcg beta carotene;
Vitamin D (as cholecalciferol), 10 mcg cholecalciferol = 400 IU of vitamin D;
Niacin, 1 niacin equivalent = 1 mg of niacin or 60 mg of dietary tryptophan.

APPENDIX 4

Vitamin Dosages for Alcoholics

PART 1
RECOMMENDED DOSAGES FOR EARLY STAGES OF RECOVERY

Vitamin	*Daily Doses*
A	10,000–25,000 IU
E	300–600 IU
K	1–10 mg
C	2–10 gm
B-1	100 mg
B-2	10–50 mg
B-3	1–3 gm
B-6	10–50 mg
Folacin	1–4 mg
Pantothenic acid	50–250 mg

These are treatment dosages to be given in the first weeks or months of recovery. They should be administered only under medical supervision.

PART 2
RECOMMENDED SAFE MAINTENANCE DOSAGES

Vitamin	*Dosages for Alcoholics*	*U.S. RDA*
A	5000–10,000 IU*	3000 IU
D	400 IU	200 IU
E	100 IU	12–16 IU
K	500 mcg	300–500 mcg
C	500 mg–2 gm	60 mg
B-1 (thiamine)	2–5 mg	1.0–1.4 mg
B-2 (riboflavin)	2–5 mg	1.2–1.6 mg
B-3 (niacin)	100–200 mg	13–18 mg
B-6 (pyridoxine)	2–5 mg	2.0–2.2 mg
B-12 (cobalamin)	3.0 mcg	3.0 mcg
Folacin	400 mcg	400 mcg
Pantothenic acid	20–50 mg	4–7 mg
Biotin	100–200 mcg	100–200 mcg**

*Alcoholics with chronic liver disease will require medical supervision for vitamin A supplements.

**No RDA has been established, but this is considered a safe and adequate dosage.

The U.S. RDAs were updated in 1980 by the Food and Nutrition Board. In some cases the units of measure used in this chart have been changed to correspond with those most commonly used in supplements. However, the dosage is the same as the 1980 RDAs. No RDA has been established for vitamin K, biotin, or pantothenic acid; the dosages given here are considered "safe and adequate amounts" by the Food and Nutrition Board.

APPENDIX 5

ALCOHOL'S PRIMARY TARGETS IN THE HUMAN BODY

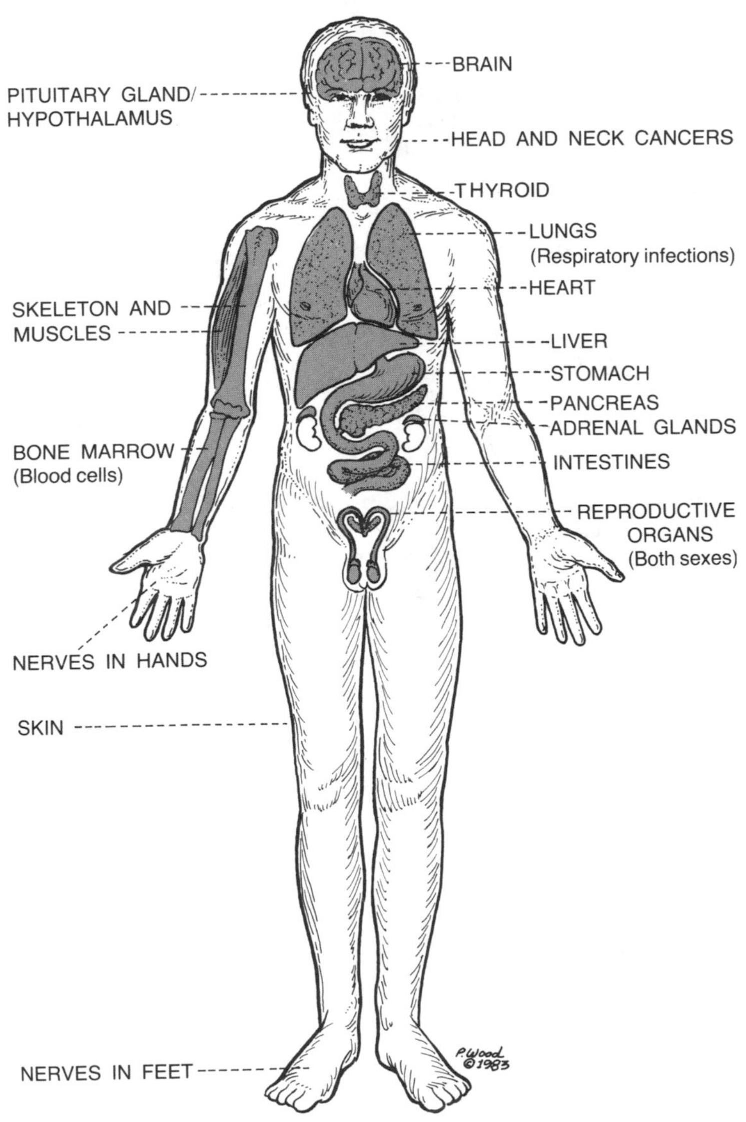

References

Alvarez, W.C., *The neuroses,* Philadelphia, W.B. Saunders, 1952.

Barnes, M., Detection and incidence of B and C vitamin deficiency in alcohol-related illness, *Annals of Clinical Biochemistry,* 15(6), November 1978, pp. 307–312.

Bennion, Marion, *Clinical nutrition,* New York, Harper and Row, 1979.

Bland, Jeffrey, *Your health under siege: using nutrition to fight back,* Brattleboro, VT, Stephen Greene Press, 1981.

Bogden, J.D., and R.A. Troiano, Plasma calcium, copper, magnesium, zinc concentrations in patients in alcohol withdrawal, *Clinical Chemistry,* 24(9), 1978, pp. 1553–1556.

Brin, M., Dilemma of marginal vitamin deficiency, Procedings of Ninth International Congress of Nutrition, Mexico, Vol. 4, 1972, pp. 102–115. (Published in Basel, Switzerland, Kargei, 1975).

______ Red cell transketolase as an indicator of nutritional deficiency, *American Journal of Clinical Nutrition,* 33, 1980, p. 169.

Buehler, M.S., Relative hypoglycemia: a clinical review of 350 cases, *Lancet,* July, 1962, pp. 289–292.

Burton, B.T., *Human nutrition,* third edition, New York, McGraw-Hill, 1976.

______ The significance of serum B-1 and magnesium in D.T.'s and alcoholism, *Journal of Clinical Psychiatry,* 40, 1979, pp. 476–479.

Cheraskin, E. and W. M. Ringsdorf, *Predictive medicine,* Mountain View, CA, Pacific Press Publishing Association, 1973.

______ *Psychodietetics,* New York, Bantam Books, 1974.

Cheraskin, E., W. M. Ringsdorf, and J.W. Clark, *Diet and disease,* New Canaan, CT, Keats Publishing, 1968.

Cohen, G. and M.A. Collins, Alkaloids from catecholamines in adrenal tissue: possible role in alcoholism, *Science,* 167, 1970, pp. 1749–1751.

Davis, V. E. and M.J. Walsh, Alcohol, amines, alkaloids: a possible biochemical basis for alcohol addiction, *Science,* 167, 1970, pp. 1005–1007.

de Lint, J. and W. Schmidt, *Biological basis of alcoholism,* New York, John Wiley & Sons, 1971.

Emrick, C.D., A review of psychologically oriented treatment of alcoholism, *Quarterly Journal of Studies on Alcohol* 36, 1975, pp. 88–108.

Gerras, C., compiler, *Complete book of vitamins,* Emmaus, PA, Rodale Press, 1977.

Goodhart, R.S., The role of nutritional factors in the cause, prevention, and cure of alcoholism and associated affirmities, *American Journal of Clinical Nutrition,* 5, 1957, p. 612.

Goodhart, R.S., Bacon Y. Chow, and Samuel D. Yeh, Marginal deficiencies of vitamins: (1) in animals, (2) observations on man, *Journal of New Drugs,* Vol. 1, no. 1, January–February 1961.

Goodwin, D.W., *Chronic effects of alcohol and other psychoactive drugs on cerebral function,* Toronto, Addiction Research Foundation, 1975.

______ *Is alcoholism hereditary?* New York, Oxford University Press, 1976.

______ Genetic aspects of alcoholism, *Drug Therapy,* October 1982.

Grant, M. and P. Guinner, *Alcoholism in perspective,* Baltimore, University Park Press, 1979.

Hoes, M.J.A.J.M., The significance of B-1 and magnesium in D.T.'s and alcoholism, *Journal of Clinical Psychiatry,* 40, 1979, pp. 476–479.

Hudspeth, W.J., et al., Neurobiology of the hypoglycemia syndrome, *Journal of Holistic Medicine,* 3(1), 1981, p. 60.

Jellinek, E.M., *The disease concept of alcoholism,* New Haven, College and University Press, in association with Hillhouse Press, New Brunswick, NJ, 1960.

Kalbfleisch, J.M. et al., Effects of ethanol administration on urinary excretion of magnesium and other electrolytes in alcoholic and normal subjects, *Journal of Clinical Investigation,* 42, 1963, p. 1471.

Kissin, B. and H. Begleiter, eds., *The biology of alcoholism* (five volumes), New York, Plenum Press, 1971–1976.

Korsten, M.A., and C.S. Lieber, Nutrition in the alcoholic, *Medical Clinics of North America,* 63, 1979, pp. 963–972.

Lieber, C.S., The metabolism of alcohol, *Scientific American,* Vol. 234, No. 3, March 1976, p. 29.

______, ed., *Metabolic aspects of alcoholism,* Baltimore, University Park Press, 1976.

______ Alcoholism and nutrition: a seminar, *Alcoholism Clinical & Experimental Research,* 3, 1979, p. 125.

______ *Medical disorders of alcoholism: pathogenesis and treatment,* Philadelphia, W.B. Saunders, 1982.

______ Symposium: interactions of alcohol and nutrition, in *Alcoholism Clinical & Experimental Research,* 7(1), winter, 1983.

Lieber, C.S., et al., The effect of chronic ethanol consumption on acetaldehyde metabolism, in the role of acetaldehyde in the actions of ethanol, K.O. Lindros and C.J.P. Ericksson, eds., Helsinki, Finnish Foundation for Alcohol Studies, vol. 23, 1975.

Lipman, A.G., Vitamins and drugs: various interactions to consider, *Modern Medicine,* 1982.

Marks, V., Alcohol and carbohydrate metabolism, *Clinics in Endocrinology,* 7, 1978, pp. 333–349.

Marks, V. and J.W. Wright, Endocrinological and metabolic effects of alcohol, *Proceedings of the Royal Society of Medicine,* 70, 1977, pp. 337–344.

Meyer, J.G. and K. Urban, Electrolyte changes and acid base balance after alcohol withdrawal, with special reference to rum fits and magnesium depletion, *Journal of Neurology,* 215(2), May 13, 1977, pp. 135–140.

Milam, J.R., *The emergent comprehensive concept of alcoholism,* Kirkland, WA, ACA Press, 1974.

Milam, J.R. and K. Ketcham, *Under the influence: a guide to the myths and realities of alcoholism,* Seattle, Madrona Publishers, 1981.

Newbold, H.L., Mega-nutrients for your nerves, New York, Peter H. Wyden, 1975.

Pfeiffer, C.C., *Mental and elemental nutrients,* New Canaan, CT, Keats Publishing, 1975.

Philpott, W.H., Allergy and alcohol addiction, *Texas Key Newsletter,* February 1975.

Philpott, W.H. and D.K. Kalita, *Brain allergies: the psychonutrient connection,* New Canaan, CT, Keats Publishing, 1980.

Register, U.D. et al., Influence of nutrients on intake of alcohol, *Journal of the American Dietetic Association,* 61(2), 1972, p. 159.

Rodgers, J.E., Brain triggers: biochemistry and behavior, *Science Digest,* January 1983.

Roe, D.A., Drug-induced nutritional deficiencies, Westport, CT, AVI Publishing, 1976.

______ Alcohol and the diet, Westport, CT, AVI Publishing, 1979.

Saville, P.D., Changes in bone mass with age and alcoholism, *Journal of Bone and Joint Surgery,* 47a, 1965, p. 492.

Schroeder, H.A., *The trace elements and man,* Old Greenwich, CT, Devin-Adair Publishing Co., 1973.

Schuckit, M. Alcoholism and genetics: possible biological mediators, *Biological Psychiatry,* 15(3), 1980, pp. 437–447.

Schuckit, M.A., D.W. Goodwin, and G. Winokur, A study of alcoholism in half siblings, *American Journal of Psychiatry,* 128, 1972, pp. 122–126.

Schuckit, M.A. and V. Rayses, Ethanol ingestion: differences in blood acetaldehyde concentrations in relatives of alcoholics and controls, *Science,* 203, 1979, p. 54.

Scientific American issue on the brain, September 1979.

Sereny, G., L. Endrenzi, and P. Devenyi, Glucose intolerance in alcoholism, *Journal of Studies on Alcohol,* 36, 1975, p. 359.

Smith, R. F., A five-year field trial of massive nicotinic acid therapy of alcoholics in Michigan, *Journal of Orthomolecular Psychology,* 1974, p. 327.

Snyder, S., *Biological aspects of mental disorder,* New York, Oxford University Press, 1980.

Stone, I., *The healing factor: vitamin C against disease,* New York, Grosset & Dunlap, 1972.

Thompson, A.D., Alcohol and nutrition, *Clinics in Endocrinology and Metabolism* 7(2), July 1978, pp. 405–428.

Tintera, J.W., Stabilizing homeostasis in the recovered alcoholic through endocrine therapy: evaluation of the hypoglycemia factor, *Journal of the American Geriatric Society,* 14, 1966, p. 126.

Vaillant, G., *The natural history of alcoholism: causes, patterns and paths to recovery,* Cambridge, Harvard University Press, 1983.

Wallgren, H. and H. Barry, *Actions of alcohol* (2 vols.), New York, Elsevier Publishing, 1970.

Williams, R.J., Alcoholism as a nutrition problem, *Journal of Clinical Nutrition,* 1, 1952–53, p. 32.

______ *Alcoholism: the nutritional approach,* Austin, University of Texas Press, 1959.

______ *You are extraordinary,* New York, Pyramid Books, 1967.

______ *Nutrition against disease,* New York, Pittman, 1971.

______ *Physician's handbook on nutritional science,* Springfield, IL, Charles Thomas, 1975.

______ *The wonderful world within you: your inner nutritional environment,* New York, Bantam Books, 1977.

______ *The prevention of alcoholism through nutrition,* New York, Bantam Books, 1981.

Williams, R.J. and D.K. Kalita, *A physician's handbook on orthomolecular medicine,* New Canaan, CT., Keats Publishing, 1979.

Wolff, P.H., Ethnic differences in alcohol sensitivity, *Science* 175, 1972, pp. 449–450.

Worden, M. and G. Rosellini, Applying nutritional concepts in alcohol and drug counseling, *Journal of Psychedelic Drugs,* Vol. 11 (3), July–September 1979.

______ Role of diet in people work: use of nutrition in therapy with substance abusers, *Journal of Orthomolecular Psychiatry,* Vol. 7, No. 4, 1978, pp. 249–257.

Wright, J., Endocrine effects of alcoholism, *Clinics in Endocrinology,* 7, 1978, pp. 351–367.

Suggested Reading List

ALCOHOLISM: NONFICTION

Alcohol Problems and Alcoholism: A Comprehensive Survey. James E. Royce, New York, Free Press, 1980.

This excellent college textbook thoroughly surveys the alcoholism literature.

Alcoholics Anonymous. A.A. World Services, Inc., New York, 1955.

The Bible of A.A. literature, this book outlines the basic A.A. program and includes numerous personal histories. A.A. literature is not available through bookstores, but can be purchased through local A.A. offices or ordered from the General Services Board of A.A., 468 Park Avenue South, New York, N.Y. 10016.

Alcoholism: The Nutritional Approach. Roger J. Williams, Austin, University of Texas Press, 1959.

In this short, easy-to-read book, a pioneer in the field of alcoholism and nutrition presents his "genetotrophic" concept that alcoholism develops from a genetically determined nutritional disorder.

Bill W. Robert Thomsen, New York, Popular Library, 1979.

A biography of Bill Wilson, cofounder of Alcoholics Anonymous.

The Disease Concept of Alcoholism. E.M. Jellinek, Center City, MN, Hazelden Foundation.

A classic work by one of the great pioneers in alcoholism theory and treatment, this book catapulted into public awareness the theory that alcoholism is a disease.

The Emergent Comprehensive Concept of Alcoholism. James R. Milam, Kirkland, WA, ACA Press, 1974.

Another classic, this scholarly work presents the concept that alcoholism is a physiological disease and that all psychological symptoms are caused by alcohol's effect on the body and brain.

Getting Them Sober. Toby Rice Drews, South Plainfield, NJ, Bridge Publishing, 1980.

A practical guide for the families of alcoholics, with chapters like "Stop Arguing With Him (It Works!)," "Confront Him," and "Use Tough Love."

I'll Quit Tomorrow. Vernon E. Johnson, New York, Harper and Row, 1973.

The best parts of this informative and readable book are the chapters detailing the symptoms of alcoholism, particularly rationalization and denial, and the chapters on intervention strategies.

Is Alcoholism Hereditary? Donald Goodwin, M.D., New York, Oxford University Press, 1978.

The author, a journalist, physician, and researcher, writes with clarity about the role of heredity in determining alcoholism. The discussion about his adoption studies conducted in Denmark is particularly informative.

Marty Mann Answers Your Questions About Drinking and Alcoholism. Marty Mann, New York, Holt, Rinehart and Winston, 1981 (revised ed.)

One of the first women members of Alcoholics Anonymous and also the founder of the National Council on Alcoholism answers the most frequently asked questions about alcoholism.

The Natural History of Alcoholism: Causes, Patterns, and Paths to Recovery. George Vaillant, Cambridge, Harvard University Press, 1983.

Written by a Harvard psychiatrist and researcher in adult development, this landmark study followed 200 Harvard graduates and 400 inner-city working-class men from Boston and Cambridge for about forty years. Vaillant makes some fascinating conclusions from his long-term study: (1) people are not predisposed by personality to become alcoholics; (2) once a person becomes an alcoholic, a return to social drinking is virtually impossible; (3) psychological approaches are useless in treating alcoholics.

The Neutral Spirit: A Portrait of Alcohol. Berton Roueche, Boston, Little, Brown and Co., 1960.

A lively, illuminating review of alcohol and its use and abuse from ancient to modern man.

The Prevention of Alcoholism Through Nutrition. R.J. Williams, New York, Bantam Books, 1981.

A seven-step program for maintaining good health and protecting yourself against alcoholism.

New Primer on Alcoholism. Marty Mann, New York, Holt, Rinehart and Winston, 1963.

An overview for both the alcoholic and the nonalcoholic of how people drink, how to recognize alcoholics, and what to do about getting help.

Under the Influence: A Guide to the Myths and Realities of Alcoholism. James R. Milam and Katherine Ketcham, Seattle, Madrona Publishers, 1981.

Lively and readable, this book—recommended by numerous recovery centers throughout the U.S.—makes the case that physiology, not psychology, determines whether one drinker will become an alcoholic while another will not. Included among the physiological factors that make some people vulnerable to alcohol are heredity, prenatal influences, ethnic susceptibilities, and abnormal metabolism.

Understanding Alcoholism. Compiled and edited by the Christopher D. Smithers Foundation, New York, Scribner Book Companies, Inc., 1968.

Although somewhat dated, this book touches on just about every facet of alcoholism: history of research efforts, causes, treatment, the controlled-drinking controversy, the family, legal issues, alcohol in industry, and alcohol education. Extensive appendices, vocabulary, and reading list.

ALCOHOLISM: DRAMA AND FICTION

Long Day's Journey Into Night. Eugene O'Neill, New Haven, Yale University Press, 1956.

". . . there's no strength of the spirit left in her to fight against her curse," one of the characters in this somber, autobiographical play remarks about his alcoholic mother. "Only I wish she hadn't led me to hope this time. By God, I never will again!" A fascinating look at the effects of alcoholism on the family.

The Lost Weekend. Charles Jackson, Cambridge, Robert Bentley, 1979.

Charles Jackson was an alcoholic himself and died by suicide. In this book, he stunningly portrays the alcoholic lifestyle.

COOKBOOKS

Deaf Smith Country Cookbook. J. Ford et al., New York, Macmillan, 1973.

A natural food cookbook, with emphasis on maximizing the nutritional value of these foods.

Diet for a Small Planet. F.M. Lappé, New York, Ballantine, 1975.

The "grandma" of vegetarian cookbooks. Lappé was the first to present the complementary protein concept, and her book helped make *vegetarian* a household word. Thousands of meat eaters were persuaded by Lappé's examination of the way meat is produced in this country to cut back or do without.

Laurel's Kitchen. L. Robertson, C. Flinders, and B. Godfrey, Petaluma, CA, Nilgiri Press, 1976 (paperback edition: New York, Bantam Books, 1978).

In the last 150 pages of this delightful vegetarian cookbook, you'll learn more about the basic principles of nutrition than you would in a ten-week course—and it's so well written, you'll enjoy the lesson. The recipes are, for the most part, unusual and delicious. Career women, however, may take offense at the introduction, which extols the virtues of home and kitchen.

The Low Blood Sugar Cookbook. Francyne Davis, New York, Bantam Books, 1974.

Helpful suggestions and practical recipes for cooking without sugar.

The Moosewood Cookbook. Mollie Katzen, Berkeley, Ten Speed Press, 1977.

A collection of vegetarian recipes from the Moosewood Restaurant in Ithaca, New York. Beautifully illustrated, with preparation times included.

Recipes for a Small Planet. Ellen Buchman Ewald, New York, Ballantine Books, 1973.

More recipes based on the concept of protein complementarity.

DOCTOR-PATIENT RELATIONSHIPS

The Clay Pedestal. Thomas Preston, M.D., Seattle, Madrona Publishers, 1981.

A physician looks at the doctor-patient relationship and finds it wanting. The patient, he insists, is too often the victim of medical treatment. Knock your physician off his pedestal, he counsels patients, and learn how to participate in your own treatment.

Anatomy of an Illness. Norman Cousins, New York, W.W. Norton and Co., 1979.

"It all began," Normal Cousins writes in this astonishing chronicle of his recovery from a supposedly irreversible disease, "when I decided that some experts don't really know enough to make a pronouncement of doom on a human being. And I said I hoped they would be careful about what they said to others; they might be believed and that could be the beginning of the end."

DRUGS

The Times of My Life. Betty Ford with Chris Chase, New York, Ballantine Books, 1979.

Chapters 38 and 39 of this special edition of the former first lady's biography tell of her addiction to alcohol and pills, her family's intervention, her recovery, and her commitment to live "this beautiful new life of mine to the fullest."

The Tranquilizing of America. Richard Hughes and Robert Brewin, New York, Warner Books, 1979.

A hard-hitting, illuminating, and highly readable look at prescription drug use in the U.S.

HYPOGLYCEMIA

Body, Mind and Sugar. E.M. Abahamson, M.D. and A. Pezet, New York, Avon Books, 1977. *Low Blood Sugar and You.* Carlton Fredericks, Ph.D., and Herman Goodman, M.D., New York, Berkley Publishing Group, 1979.

Laymen's primers on hypoglycemia by early pioneers in the field.

Hypoglycemia: A Better Approach. Paavo Airola, Ph.D., Health Plus Publishers, P.O. Box 22001, Phoenix, Arizona 85028, 1977.

A look at the causes, symptoms and treatment of hypoglycemia, written for the layperson. Airola is a nutritionist whose theories are often at odds with the medical establishment.

Nutrigenetics: New Concepts for Relieving Hypoglycemia. Dr. R.O. Brennan with William C. Mulligan, New York, New American Library, 1975.

Malnutrition and genetic weakness combine to cause hypoglycemia, Dr. Brennan claims, and hypoglycemia can affect mental and physical health, making people more susceptible to other diseases. Brennan counsels prevention through fast and accurate diagnosis and dietary control.

NUTRITION

Basics of Food Allergy. J.C. Breneman, Springfield, IL, Charles C. Thomas, 1978. *Dr. Mandell's 5-Day Allergy Relief System.* M. Mandell and L.W. Scanlon, New York, Pocket Books, 1979.

Two books that take a new look at how allergies affect health and sanity, with suggestions on managing troublesome foods and other allergies.

The Complete Book of Vitamins. Charles Gerras, ed., Emmaus, PA, Rodale Press, 1977.

An 800-page volume of vitamins and other nutrients, written in clear and simple language to help the layperson understand how vitamins maintain health and act as natural "medication."

Earl Mindell's Vitamin Bible. Earl Mindell, New York, Rawson Associates, 1979.

Mindell is a nutritionist and pharmacist, and he crams a lot of information into this thoroughly readable and entertaining book. If you have bad breath, acne, or a bee sting, he's got a vitamin or mineral for you.

Eater's Guide: Nutrition Basics for Busy People. Candy Cumming and Vicky Newman, Englewood Cliffs, NJ, Prentice Hall, 1981.

A zippy, energetic book designed to help busy people make better eating choices. Extensive recipe section.

Jane Brody's Nutrition Book. Jane Brody, New York, Bantam Books, 1981.

A complete home reference on nutrition, covering everything from "Feeding Your One-Year-Old" to "Why We Overeat" to "Do Vegetarians Live Longer?" Brody's advice on vitamin and mineral supplementation is somewhat conservative, but otherwise this is an excellent and thorough review of what we eat, what we should eat, and how to tell the difference.

Know Your Nutrition, revised edition. Linda Clark, New Canaan, CT, Keats Publishing, 1981.

A well-researched examination of vitamins and minerals: why we need them, how much we need, and what they can do for us.

Let's Eat Right to Keep Fit, revised edition. Adelle Davis, New York, Harcourt Brace Jovanovich, 1970. *Let's Have Healthy Children.* Adelle Davis, revised by Marshall Mendel, New York, New American Library, 1981. *Let's Get Well.* Adelle Davis, New York, New American Library, 1972.

Adelle Davis, a pioneer in the field of nutrition, paved the way for the general public's understanding of the importance of nutrition and putting that knowledge into practice.

Nutrition Almanac, revised edition. Nutrition Search, Inc. New York, McGraw-Hill, 1979.

Probably the best quick-information guide on vitamins and minerals now on the bookshelves. Includes a detailed section on "ailments and other stressful conditions" and lists nutrients that may be beneficial for treatment of these conditions.

Nutrition in a Nutshell. Roger J. Williams, New York, Doubleday.

A concise handbook of nutrients written by a pioneer in the field of nutrition.

The Supermarket Handbook. Nikki Goldbeck and David Goldbeck, New York, Harper and Row, 1973.

Everthing you wanted to know about the foods you buy in the grocery store is contained in this interesting book. An excellent guide to determining the nutrient content of common foods in the supermarket and picking out the best nutritional values.

PERSONAL ACCOUNTS

A Sensitive, Passionate Man. Barbara Mahoney, New York, David McKay, 1974.

The slow, agonizing destruction of a life and a family by alcoholism has never been more graphically described than in this true-to-life account.

Prodigal Shepherd. Father Ralph Pfau and Al Hirshberg, New York, Popular Library, 1958.

A priest's account of his addiction to alcohol and the courage he ultimately found to help himself and others.

Off the Sauce. Lewis Meyer, Center City, MN, Hazelden Foundation, 1967.

An anecdotal account by a man who finally made it "off the sauce" with the help of A.A.

Index